Love and the Politics of Intimacy

Love and the Politics of Intimacy

Bodies, Boundaries, Liberation

Edited by
Stanislava Dikova,
Wendy McMahon and
Jordan Savage

BLOOMSBURY ACADEMIC
NEW YORK • LONDON • OXFORD • NEW DELHI • SYDNEY

BLOOMSBURY ACADEMIC
Bloomsbury Publishing Inc
1385 Broadway, New York, NY 10018, USA
50 Bedford Square, London, WC1B 3DP, UK
29 Earlsfort Terrace, Dublin 2, Ireland

BLOOMSBURY, BLOOMSBURY ACADEMIC and the Diana logo are trademarks of
Bloomsbury Publishing Plc

First published in the United States of America 2023
Paperback edition published 2024

Cover design: Eleanor Rose
Cover Image © Getty Images

Library of Congress Cataloging-in-Publication Data
Names: Dikova, Stanislava, editor. | McMahon, Wendy, editor. | Savage, Jordan, editor.
Title: Love and the politics of intimacy : bodies, boundaries, liberation / edited by
Stanislava Dikova, Wendy McMahon and Jordan Savage.
Description: New York, NY : Bloomsbury Academic, 2022. |
Includes bibliographical references and index. | Summary: "Interdisciplinary
studies on the position of love in contemporary global thought and literature that reflect on
experiences of intimate, romantic, and sexual love, and the role of individual
identity"– Provided by publisher.
Identifiers: LCCN 2022028608 (print) | LCCN 2022028609 (ebook) |
ISBN 9781501387371 (hardback) | ISBN 9781501387418 (paperback) |
ISBN 9781501387388 (epub) | ISBN 9781501387395 (pdf) |
ISBN 9781501387401 (ebook other)
Subjects: LCSH: Love–Social aspects. | Intimacy (Psychology) | Emotions–Political aspects.
Classification: LCC HM1151 .L69 2022 (print) | LCC HM1151 (ebook) |
DDC 306.7–dc23/eng/20220901
LC record available at https://lccn.loc.gov/2022028608
LC ebook record available at https://lccn.loc.gov/2022028609

ISBN: HB: 978-1-5013-8737-1
PB: 978-1-5013-8741-8
ePDF: 978-1-5013-8739-5
eBook: 978-1-5013-8738-8

Typeset by Newgen KnowledgeWorks Pvt. Ltd., Chennai, India

To find out more about our authors and books visit www.bloomsbury.com
and sign up for our newsletters.

For Amy May

CONTENTS

Part 2 Intimate bodies

Part 3 Love's boundaries

FIGURES

CONTRIBUTORS

Crisia Constantine is a cultural studies scholar, writer and curator, educator, art facilitator and practitioner. As a doctoral researcher at Queensland College of Art, Griffith University, Constantine surveys the relation between 'seeing' and 'knowing' in the field of visual arts and literary studies. Also, her work explores nomadism, childhood and women's trauma and community memory.

Gemma Curto is a PhD candidate in English literature at the University of Sheffield. Her research lies in interdisciplinary approaches to the relationship between literature, scientific methodologies and ecology. Gemma has published an article in *Green Letters* on floods in biocentric graphic novels (2020).

Ian Davidson is Professor of Poetry at University College Dublin. He is a poet and critic and teaches literature and creative writing. He has written extensively on modern and contemporary poetry and most recently on Diane di Prima, Bill Griffiths and Tom Pickard. Recent poetry publications are *From a Council House in Connacht* (2021) and *By Tiny Twisting Ways* (2021).

Stanislava Dikova is a postdoctoral researcher and a visiting fellow in the Department of Literature, Film, and Theatre Studies at the University of Essex, UK. Her research interests revolve around twentieth-century literature and thought, writing by women, histories of knowledge and feminist social theory. Stanislava's writing has appeared in Modernist Review, the LSE Review of Books and Feminist Modernist Studies. She is currently working on her first monograph.

Lauren Edwards, JD, is a PhD candidate in philosophy and a neuroscience graduate diploma candidate at York University (Toronto). Lauren's PhD dissertation centres on the philosophy of love, philosophy of emotion, cognitive science and feminist ethics. In particular, the dissertation argues that love can exist without a beloved despite all contemporary philosophical and scientific theories of love to the contrary.

Gary Kelly is Distinguished University Professor at the University of Alberta and teaches English and comparative literature. He has written numerous books and essays on long eighteenth-century literature in Britain, Ireland and America, especially the novel, women's writing and popular print culture. Current projects include a history of cheap romanticism and a political history of fun.

Hannah Loret is a PhD researcher at Nottingham Trent University and works as an NHS clinical support worker. Her research focuses on cross-national perceptions of vulvovaginal sexual pain. She is particularly interested in studying how women experience intimate life within complex systems of care, currently in England and France.

Adelina Mbinjama is a lecturer in the Department of Media Studies at the Cape Peninsula University of Technology in Cape Town, South Africa. Her teaching and research interests are in social media communications, cyber-ethics, black feminism and representation of women in the media. She holds a doctoral degree in media studies from the Nelson Mandela University.

Wendy McMahon is Associate Professor in American Studies at the University of East Anglia, UK. Her research interests centre around contemporary literatures of the American hemisphere and their intersections with disaster studies, human rights, law, capitalism and globalization, conflict and security, migration and exile, place, belonging and citizenship. Wendy has a particular interest in the relationship between Caribbean and US topographies, colonialism, and decolonial emancipatory art, activism and writing. Wendy has published on Cuban exile writing, Caribbean literature and masculinity, African American literature and human rights, as well as the relationship between landscape and history in literature.

Deya Mukherjee is a lover of radical bookshops who has worked in movements for worker's rights, justice for migrants, anti-racism and housing justice. She has contributed articles to *The Bristol Cable* and her poetry has been published in *Verse Kraken, Atlas + Alice* and *Tears in the Fence*. She is currently working on a novel about tired, brown women making mistakes and befriending ghosts.

Daniele Nunziata is Lecturer in English Literature at the University of Oxford. He specializes in postcolonial and world literatures. His first published book is *Colonial and Postcolonial Cyprus: Transportal Literatures of Empire, Nationalism, and Sectarianism* (2020). He has published widely on postcolonial subjects in various peer-reviewed journals (including in *PMLA* and the *Journal of Postcolonial Writing*), and he contributes to both *Great Writers Inspire* and *Writers Make Worlds*. He primarily teaches literary studies at St Anne's College and for the Oxford Prospects and Global Development Institute. His poetry has received several accolades.

Vicky Panossian is an early career scholar of sociology and social anthropology from the Central European University in Vienna, Austria. She is currently serving as editor-in-chief of *Afkar: The Undergraduate Journal of Middle East Studies*. Vicky's research interests range from cultural identity studies to contemporary Middle East studies.

Daniel O'Brien is a lecturer in film and digital media at the University of Essex. His interests and areas of research span across film, interactive media art and computer game studies. He has published work in all these subjects. Recent publications include *The Pervasive and the Digital: Immersive Worlds in Four Interactive Artworks* (2020), *Extant's Flatland: Disability and Postphenomenological Narrative* (2020) and *Hap-Tech Narration and the Postphenomenological Film* (2019).

Francesca Pierini is an adjunct lecturer in the English Department of the University of Basel. A former postdoctoral fellow at the Institute of European and American Studies (Academia Sinica, Taiwan) and an international scholar at KU Leuven (Belgium), Francesca's academic interests include cultural studies, anglophone literary representations of Italian culture, E. M. Forster, and the modern and contemporary anglophone romance novel.

Lawrence Quill is a professor in the Department of Political Science at San Jose State University, CA. His research interests focus on the contribution of political theory to understanding the impact of technology on self, society and politics.

Jordan Savage is Lecturer in US Literature. Her research centres on literary and cinematic constructions of US nationalism and national identity. She is interested in the iconography of dirt in the Western poetry, especially Native poetry, offering counter-narratives to US nationalism; and the myth structure of American exceptionalism. Jordan has published on contemporary poetry from Britain and the United States, modern poetics and Western generic studies.

Salma Yassine is an early career scholar of gender studies at the Central European University in Vienna, Austria. Her academic interests mainly tackle gender and sexuality in Arab contexts of culture, literature and media.

PREFACE

This collection of essays, and its companion volume *Love and the Politics of Care*, presents an interdisciplinary, global study of love, drawing on sociology, philosophy, social care work, literary studies, film, the performing arts, the digital and medical humanities and creative writing practice. The case studies discussed in each chapter are situated in various locations across Europe, Africa, Asia and the Americas and provide a comprehensive coverage of love, both conceptually and practically, as an essential aspect of personal and public life. The temporal reach spans from the Enlightenment period, when most current forms of political, monetary and institutional organization were elaborated, to the present day.

Every essay or creative piece included in this collection has something to say about love and the difficulties encountered while trying to lead a loving life. The locations of love explored through these studies range from the deeply intimate space of a sexual encounter to the transnational arena of the global care work industry. This broad landscape demonstrates the foundational role love plays in the very fabric of our individual and social lives. The body, the family, the workplace, the home, the digital, the institutional and the global are all enclosures in which love meets with restrictions, which condition the lives of those who experience it. From racial and class barriers to physical borders between nations, love's boundaries are drawn by discourses of power, institutional and systemic practices of control and the forces of the marketplace. The intended consequences of this ritualistic demarcation reach far into the lives of those individuals who love and wish to be loved intimately, deeply, protectively and freely. All contributions to this collection work with these ideas and ask the following questions: Who is allowed to love, and in what ways? What discourses of love do we feel obliged to participate in or be excluded from? How do national and international superstructures alter or instrumentalize love, and what is the effect of this? Questions of gender and sexuality, race, nation, faith and disability are all addressed. The guiding aim in this approach has been to provide a conceptual and genealogical overview of the existing tension between love and the lived conditions within which it is practised. In doing so, these volumes present an alternative history of love that, though not exhaustive, goes beyond its traditionally discussed theological and moral manifestations, focusing instead on its presence in everyday life.

Talking about love across the disciplinary divide provides a further impetus for renewed investigation of a set of ideas that is all too often confined within the history of Western thought. Our two collections also look at the present and future moments in search of an inspiration for transforming and recharting the pathways of love in such a way as to lead us to a more diverse and emancipatory model of social life. The present volume, *Love and the Politics of Intimacy*, engages with the construction of love as intimacy as a practice that occurs *between, through, within* and, increasingly, *beyond* bodies, asking questions about the norms and contexts in which they operate. Its companion volume, *Love and the Politics of Care*, addresses the politicization of love through practices of care that stretch from the familial to the institutional and looks at practices of regulation directed both by the state and the market and the interconnections between the two within the neoliberal ideological framework.

The emergence of this project was rooted in our experiences of the contemporary university in the UK, where ideas of love and care are often weaponized by government and management against staff in order to extract additional work and further erode working conditions.[1] This rhetoric is also commonly used to diminish resolve for industrial action and weaken union power within the UK higher education sector. We wondered whether this power dynamic was in operation in other sectors of the economy and, by extension, in the homes and personal lives of those who labour in them, particularly in situations where there is an expectation of care. Our call for submissions generated a strong response, which convinced us that scholars and practitioners from many disciplines are interested in asking similar questions, and that our collection could contribute to the burgeoning field of 'Love Studies' identified by Anna G. Jónasdóttir and Ann Ferguson as an emerging 'historically specific field of knowledge interests' that is both 'heterogeneous' and 'conflicted'.[2] The two volumes were conceived together, and we hope they will continue their joined existence by being read together, but this is by no means a requirement for productive engagement with either.

Notes

1   See Amelia Horgan, *Lost in Work: Escaping Capitalism* (London: Pluto Press, 2021), 58, 132–4. According to data provided by the University and College Union (UCU), 46 per cent of universities use precarious labour in the form of zero-hours contracts to deliver their teaching, and 68 per cent of research staff are on fixed-term contracts. Source: UCU, 'Stamp Out Casual Contracts', https://www.ucu.org.uk/stampout (accessed 11 January 2022).

2   Anna G. Jónasdóttir and Ann Ferguson, eds, *Love: A Question for Feminism in the Twenty-First Century* (London: Routledge, 2014), 2.

Bibliography

Horgan, Amelia. *Lost in Work: Escaping Capitalism*. London: Pluto Press, 2021.

Jónasdóttir, Anna G., and Ann Ferguson, eds, *Love: A Question for Feminism in the Twenty-First Century*. London: Routledge, 2014.

ACKNOWLEDGEMENTS

We, the editors, would like to convey our immense gratitude and appreciation to all contributors to the volume for sharing their work with us at the most turbulent of times. This project began to take shape in the spring of 2019, before any of us knew that a global pandemic was about to alter the course of our professional and personal lives. Despite this, our contributors persisted with their searching inquiries and presented us with a selection of chapters, which we are honoured to present in this collection. We also wish to extend our gratitude to our commissioning editor at Bloomsbury, Amy Martin, whose faith in the project kept us on track throughout the process, and to the three anonymous readers, who gave us their time and generously provided thoughtful feedback. A very special thanks is due to Matias Vienener at the Kathy Acker Literary Trust for permission to reproduce images from Kathy Acker's novel, *Blood and Guts in High School* (New York: Grove Press, 1978). A further thanks is also due to all the anonymous participants who have taken part in the research interviews and questionnaires that have informed the research insights developed in some of the chapters. We would also like to acknowledge the support of our colleagues at the University of Essex, the University of East Anglia and Keele University. We're also grateful for the support and loving inspiration of our families, especially Ian, Russel and Andy.

Introduction

Stanislava Dikova, Wendy McMahon and Jordan Savage

In a collection titled *Love and the Politics of Intimacy*, we are inevitably asking about the relationship between the intimate – which is so often conceived of as private, personal, even secret or hermetic – and the social and public. To be intimate, from the Latin *intimus*, inner or inmost, is to be private – to be intimate with another, to share that privacy and to share the 'inner-self'. But, as Lauren Berlant tells us in the opening of their 1998 special issue on intimacy, 'the inwardness of the intimate is met by a corresponding publicness':[1] part of the frisson of romantic intimacy, for example, might derive from what is hidden, what is shared and what is at risk of discovery or exposure. Berlant's special issue set some significant parameters for rethinking intimacy, calling:

> Not only for a redescription but for transformative analyses of the rhetorical and material conditions that enable hegemonic fantasies to thrive in the minds and the bodies of subjects while, at the same time, attachments are developing that might redirect the different routes taken by history and biography. To rethink intimacy is to appraise how we have been and how we live and how we might imagine lives that make more sense than the ones so many are living.[2]

This collection of essays takes up the challenge of this rethinking in its broad appraisal of how intimacy is conceived and experienced in the context of twenty-first-century neoliberalism. As Eileen Boris and Rhacel Salazar Parreñas state, 'one of the most striking features of contemporary global capitalism is the heightened commodification of intimacy that pervades social life'.[3] Furthermore, in agreement with Berlant, they tell us that 'intimacy occurs in a social context; it is accordingly shaped by, even as it shapes, relations of race, class, gender, and sexuality'.[4] We have in mind, too, Sara Ahmed's insistence that we must resist conceptualizations of emotions as merely internally experienced, but rather think of them as 'social and cultural practices'.[5] While the neoclassical taxonomy of love (eros, agape, philia, aphroditē) is useful and references to it emerge throughout the essays here in a variety of ways, our understanding of love and, subsequently, intimacy in relation to love chimes with Jónasdóttir's in that love is a 'human activity' that results from 'the relational flows of forces and processes in sociosexual relationships' that is 'comparable with but *not reducible to* work and human labor', and that it is an 'alienable *and* exploitable human social force'.[6] This is not to say that our view on love is that it cannot be transformative; on the contrary, we agree with Jónasdóttir's thought that it can be a 'specific creative/productive power [that] can bring about changes and "make history"'.[7] We understand love and intimacy to be socially, culturally and economically constructed[8] and, as our contributors show, confined by heteronormative, patriarchal and racialized boundaries. Until those borders are breached entirely, love's potential for emancipatory social transformation cannot be realized. This is why the work of intimacy within these conditions of constraint requires clarification and reconsideration from a broadly interdisciplinary and transcultural perspective. In doing so, we are not seeking to present the reader with a definition or a singular theory of love, but, following Ahmed's work on emotions, our collection instead traces the multiple interconnected ways in which love circulates 'between bodies'[9] – individual, collective and cultural. It also examines the epistemological norms that have led to the historical inclusion or marginalization of loving subjects and objects of love under a dominant politics of heteronormative desire. As integral as this analysis of limitation is in the context of a contemporary crisis of precarity, the majority of our contributors also direct their attention to thinking through this crisis and imagining new forms of embodiment, subjectivity and togetherness. As such, all of the essays in this volume are concerned in various ways with the relationship between love and intimacy, experiences of intimate love, whether romantic or otherwise, and the intersections of intimate forms of knowledge with the cultural, social, historical and political conditions of their practice. It is through this articulation that we approach the unifying principle of this volume: the love ethic.

In *All about Love*, bell hooks writes that 'a love ethic presupposes that everyone has the right to be free, to live fully and well'.[10] hooks goes on to offer the small town or the (outer) New York borough as examples of spaces where communities work together to manifest a love ethic: the love ethic is the social expression of a personal or intimate desire to love and to be loved. Berlant's work helps us to put hooks's love ethic on an intimate footing. They tell us, 'the story that love is invulnerable to the instabilities of narrative or history, and is a beautifully shaped web of lyrical mutuality, is at the ideological core of modern heterosexuality. It enables heterosexuality to be construed as a relation of desire that expresses people's true feelings. It says nothing of the institutions and ideologies that police it.'[11] Berlant's identification of compulsory heterosexuality as existing within a 'policed' power matrix chimes with hooks's chilling observation that 'male fantasy is seen as something that can create reality, whereas female fantasy is regarded as pure escape'.[12] In order to enact a love ethic, hooks insists that we must 'utilize all the dimensions of love – "care, commitment, trust, responsibility, respect, and knowledge" – in our everyday lives'. This appeal to a plurality of loving practices must also, implicitly, be coupled with a destabilizing of the binaries – of gender, orientation or ethnicity – that create a monolithic cultural construction of intimate love.

For Ahmed, in order for us to fully understand the ways that politics and emotions intersect to create such boundaries and binaries, we must move away from the psychological model towards the sociological whereby the individual is not the originator of feeling and where emotions are not individual self-expression but rather a social form.[13] However, for Ahmed, this is not simply a case of reversing the direction of emotion from a psychological inside to outside to one from outside to inside. Instead, she informs us that

> emotions create the very effect of the surfaces and boundaries that allow us to distinguish an inside and an outside in the first place. So emotions are not simply something 'I' or 'we' have. Rather, it is through emotions, or how we respond to objects and others, that surfaces or boundaries are made: the 'I' and the 'we' are shaped by, and even take the shape of, contact with others … emotions are not 'in' either the individual or the social, but produce the very surfaces and boundaries that allow the individual and the social to be delineated as if they were objects.[14]

In this formulation, the objects of our devotions and emotions, our love and intimacy, 'take shape as effects of circulation' with those objects becoming 'sticky, or saturated with affect, as sites of personal and social tension'.[15] This stickiness of the object of love is also the trickiness of love as a politics in and of itself. Thinking with Ahmed is important for us across this collection where there is a strong feeling that 'a politics of love is necessary in that how one loves matters',[16] but an understanding of the difficulties that a politics of love presents when it is abundantly clear that challenging power relations requires more than a love that is exclusive to some bodies at the expense of others.

* * *

Like its sister volume, *Love and the Politics of Care*, this collection is divided into three parts, namely, 'Love and communities', 'Intimate bodies' and 'Love's boundaries'. Each deals with contemporary concerns about the politics of intimacy through case studies drawn from global locations. Part 1, 'Love and communities', addresses our collective concerns about the liberatory potential of intimacy and love through spaces that challenge a heteronormative, patriarchal, racially unequal and capitalist world. Daniele Nunziata's essay, '"Love is a battle, love is war": James Baldwin's use of love to represent race, gender and sexuality in segregated America', heads up our exploration of intimate love and sexuality in the context of struggles for liberation and art. Here, Nunziata reads Baldwin's 1956 novel *Giovanni's Room* and a selection of his personal and polemic essays to understand the power of queer love as an identity-shaping practice and a resistance strategy in the context of segregated America. Significantly, the liberatory potential of love is intimately entwined with artistic practice, specifically writing and music, and Nunziata shows us that, for Baldwin, fighting for individual and collective freedom within a deeply racist and homophobic society requires a resistance mobilized by this combination of loving, writing and music.

Vicky Panossian and Salma Yassine move the conversation on queer love to nineteenth-century England in Chapter 2 'Liberating the Victorian politics of love through Jack the Lass and Anne Lister', where they trace the various challenges Lister poses to the normative shapes of Victorian womanhood, including in the familial, legal and economic spheres. The essay pays tribute to Lister's ground-breaking life and relationship with Ann Walker, drawing both on her *Diaries* and their recent BBC adaptation, *Gentleman Jack* (2019), without shying away from the complexities of their choices, concluding with a discursive parallel between the forms of patriarchal oppression faced by Lister in their time and the contemporary experiences of Arab women.

In 'The lover and the tribe', Ian Davidson is working within the sphere of literary history considering the significance of thinking about love in a feminized context, specifically in the work of three women Beat Generation poets: Kay Johnson, Lenore Kandel and Diane di Prima. Intimacy, as we have seen, is often conceptualized as being a private and personal feeling quite separate from the social realm, but Davidson suggests that through poetry and art, the atomized individual, too, can be brought into the intimate space, transforming intimate love into a mobilizing social force. For Davidson, the potential of this love of community or communities is a radical transformation of society and, in the case of the poets in question, mid-twentieth-century America.

The final contribution to this section cautions us about the limitations of love's liberatory potentiality in a racialized and racist society and reminds us that institutions of all kinds, including those involved in radical work, can be complicit with oppressive social and political forces. In this personal essay, climate activist and anti-fascist organizer, Deya Mukherjee, explores some of the racial dynamics of inclusion on the British left. Triangulating between bell hooks, Sara Ahmed and Audre Lorde, Mukherjee uses her own experiences and those of her friends to explore the racialized limitations of two specific forms of love and intimacy: solidarity and the 'safe' activist social space. This work resonates with Eleanor Wilkinson's critique of Hardt and Negri's insistence that a vital part of the common political struggle against neoliberalism is love, with the common assumed to result in solidarity across difference, a solidarity that Mukherjee shows us as unrealized.[17]

* * *

In Part 2, 'Intimate bodies', our attention turns towards other forms of intimacy and intimate love that trouble western social spaces and epistemologies. Chapter 5 sharpens our focus and directs us to think about intimacy in terms of the relationship between sexual embodiment and the articulation of the self. It also comments on the separation of women's sexual experience and sexual health as in some ways *too* intimate or personal to be readily and properly treated by mainstream medical services. Researcher and NHS clinical support worker Hannah Loret's study explores the stories of women who experience vaginal pain during sexual intercourse through their interaction with healthcare services in England and France and gives careful consideration to the ways in which their intimate lives are subjected to particular forms of power dynamics and politicization, which leads to increased pain, stigma, conflict and vulnerability for patients.

Gemma Curto's analysis of Kathy Acker's *Blood and Guts in High School* (1978) explores the proliferation of intimacies through the mechanics of the written word. Curto's essay explores the ways in which this anti-realist text interrogates the limiting effects caused by the joint operations of Oedipal family structures and capitalist exploitation of desiring bodies that can only be liberated through a radical and disruptive engagement with desire. Her reading of Kathy Acker's original "Dream Maps", informed by the work of Deleuze and Guattari, enables a new understanding of the imaginative processes of a single, desiring, individual. A new map for understanding desiring production is offered, rejecting a dominant, patriarchal discourse in post-structuralist terms. Curto's essay also speaks to the intimacy of reading itself, with the novel encouraging the reader to map their own way through the text and to resist an authoritative voice. Instead, it insists on a marriage of aesthetics and liberatory forms of expression with the potential to emancipate us politically and socially.

The next two essays move the conversation towards a consideration of the impact of technologies on practices of intimacy and love and their relationship to the body in its individual and collective forms. As Michelle

Janning reminds us, 'whether people believe digital communication to be problematic or helpful within intimate relationships, the fact of the matter is that it is increasingly a part of intimacy', and 'new research about romantic relationships' must consider the ways in which human relationships are increasingly mediated by technology.[18] The integration of digital technologies, in particular, raises questions about where love and intimacy are located – in person, in private, online or in public – and how subjects come to know and experience such connections with others.

In Chapter 7, Daniel O'Brien considers some of the ways in which contemporary concerns about the intersections of love and technology are being explored in cultural texts (film, in this case). His essay, 'Digital love: Love through the screen/of the screen', analyses two forms of digital love on screen – love mediated *through* the screen (Pierre-Paul Renders's *Thomas est Amoureux*, 2000) and love *of* a technological device itself (Spike Jones's *Her*, 2013). These cultural readings are juxtaposed with a wider consideration of the increased permeation of technologies within our intimate lives through a discussion of LifeNaut and Bina48, a digital platform that stores personal 'mind-files' and digital selves for loved ones and a prototype cyborg with the same aims, respectively.

Chapter 8 brings us to the very moment of writing and thinking about love within the context of a global pandemic. Media studies scholar Adelina Mbinjama brings her specialisms in social media and cyber ethics to bear on the use of dating sites in South Africa by Black internet users seeking love during the (still current at the time of writing) Covid-19 pandemic. As Mbinjama asserts, little is known about this particular demographic of users in the South African context. The chapter addresses this gap through a thematic narrative analysis of interviews conducted in 2021 about people's experience of dating sites. What becomes clear is that the philosophy of Ubuntu is at the heart of the interviewees' desire for connection in digital spaces as much as in real life, and Mbinjama's contribution examines the cyber-ethical implications of digital platforms in a neoliberal marketplace which, conversely, denies or fails to recognize the common humanity so central to Ubuntu thinking and practice. As Devi Dee Mucina highlights in his work on Ubuntu and masculinity in a world dominated by white supremacy and capitalist modes of being, 'to centre Ubuntu is to be critical of how our realities are political in an interconnected and interdependent world' with love being the 'expression of relational care for our interconnectedness'.[19]

Part 3, 'Love's boundaries', interrogates traditional conceptualizations of intimate love as located at the intersection between the loving subject and loved object through textual relations with the reader as well as wider networks of knowledge production and ethics. Our contributors explore intimate, romantic love through literary history, poetics, psychoanalysis and philosophy and show that the most intimate of human relations is always already public and that there is liberatory potential in addressing the historical and contemporary policing of the intimate in the social, particularly as it relates to the demand for female emancipation, the freeing of female desire and the liberation of love from traditional philosophical and ethical restraints.

The section opens with two chapters that engage with questions of gender and textuality exploring genres and modes of writing that challenge the traditional allocation of love as a personal and internal phenomenon by showing its specifically social and political role. In Chapter 9, 'Imploding fireworks: Love and self-knowledge in the contemporary Italian sentimental novel', Francesca Pierini transposes the construction of gender and femininity as an important concern in the contemporary Italian setting through a poetically voiced engagement with two contemporary novels, written by women and largely unknown in the English-speaking world – Susanna Tamaro's *Follow Your Heart* (1995) and Margaret Mazzantini's *Il catino di zinco* ['The Zinc Basin'] (1994). Pierini discusses intergenerational relationships between women who struggle to form an autonomous practice of being in the context of extended familial trauma, through the prism of a critical exploration of the 'romanzo sentimentale' (sentimental novel) as a processing space for long-carried feelings of guilt and ineptitude. Central to Gary Kelly's contribution in Chapter 10 is the concept of 'lovespeak' as it develops through the love novel across the eighteenth century. Throughout this chapter, there is an accretive sense of the developing subversive power of the female reader and the love novel as a semi-permeable arena in which women's desire, volition and history are given new space. Kelly shares, for example, the powerful example of Sophia Lee's *The Recess* (1883–5) as a text in which the overlooked role of women in the formation of national history is brought to the fore, addressing gaps in archival research. The case here is that the minimizing of loving social roles has been part and parcel of the minimization of women's political and social history, with the novel providing something approaching a space of self-organization to redress that oversight.

The next two essays of this section focus our attention on questions about the ways in which intimacy and love are understood and experienced: how we come to know love, and what we understand to be love and to be loved. Chapter 11, 'Love as theoretical object in Marguerite Duras's writings' by Crisia Constantine, asks us to consider the intersubjective ways of knowing through a reading of three novels by Duras (*La maladie de la mort*, *Moderato Cantible* and *Hiroshima mon amour*), which Constantine analyses by way of Lacanian conceptualizations of the 'gaze' and the 'subject supposed to know' as love narratives that interrogate the conditions for knowing through seeing. As such, Constantine demonstrates that even in intimate private spaces, love can never be fulfilled since it is a continuous act of expanding the boundaries of knowledge, reducing it – or elevating it – to an abstraction and theoretical object. Lauren Edwards's chapter launches a challenge to the philosophical assumption that love must have an object. Edwards's argument in 'Love without object' is informed by a richly constructed conceptual tapestry, which draws on various philosophical traditions, from ancient ethics to phenomenology, and contemporary analytical approaches to relationality and the emotions. In doing so, it provides an intriguing provocation to our definitional understanding of love as a directional practice articulated by a subject towards a specifically identifiable object and expands our understanding of the self and its capacity to construct loving practices.

The volume closes with a careful consideration of the impacts of technology on the self and society in a literary analysis by political scientist Lawrence Quill of Jeanette Winterson's 2019 novel *Frankissstein: A Love Story*. Quill engages with discourses of trans-humanism to illuminate the ways in which Winterson's novel interrogates technology-fuelled capitalism's insistence that love is a problem to be solved and interrogates whether *Frankinsstein* is offering an alternative to neoliberal heteronormative narratives, or whether the novel itself is bound by neoliberalism's own insistence on the transition of boundaries through capitalist-driven technology with its opposition to the 'irrationality' of love.

Throughout this volume, we see explorations of the liberatory and emancipatory potentials of intimacy and love, and we see, too, caution in the face of this. Articulating a social ethics of intimacy is perhaps always bound to be marked by oscillation as any approach that aims to categorize a definitive trajectory towards a fully practical liberatory politics would inevitably have to concretize a new normative order and preside over a new model of exclusion. Hesitancy in the face of the often claustrophobic certainties offered by current regimes of desire brings attentiveness to difference as well as the kindness and curiosity to live with others in, to borrow Ahmed's term, 'the intimate "withness" of social relations', without seeking to confine them.[20]

The intention behind *Love and the Politics of Intimacy*, and its accompanying volume *Love and the Politics of Care*, is simple. It is an interdisciplinary survey of the field that reveals where love is useful, where love is difficult, what stands in the way of love and where we might hope that the fuelling and developing of loving practices will take us. We hope it helps to bring loving practices more readily to hand for all of our readers.

Notes

1 Lauren Berlant, 'Intimacy: A Special Issue', *Critical Inquiry* 24 (Winter 1998): 281.

2 Ibid., 296.

3 Eileen Boris and Rhacel Salazar Parreñas, eds, *Intimate Labors: Cultures, Technologies, and the Politics of Care* (Stanford, CA: Stanford University Press, 2010), 1.

4 Ibid., 1.

5 Sarah Ahmed, *The Cultural Politics of Emotion*, 2nd edn. (Edinburgh: Edinburgh University Press, 2014), 9.

6 Anna G. Jónasdóttir, 'Love Studies: A (Re) New (ed) Field of Knowledge Interests', in *Love: A Question for Feminism in the Twenty-First Century* (London: Routledge: 2014), 13, original emphasis.

7 Ibid., 14.

8 For a thorough examination of the relationship between love and capitalism, see Eva Illouz, *Consuming the Romantic Utopia: Love and the Cultural Contradictions of Capitalism* (Berkeley: University of California Press, 1997).

9 Ahmed, *The Cultural Politics of Emotion*, 4.

10 bell hooks, *All about Love* (New York: HarperCollins, 2000), 87.

11 Lauren Berlant, *Desire/Love* (Brooklyn, NY: Punctum Books, 2012), 92.

12 bell hooks, *All about Love*, xxiii.

13 Ahmed, *The Cultural Politics of Emotion*, 9.

14 Ibid., 10.

15 Ibid., 10–11.

16 Ibid., 140.

17 Eleanor Wilkinson, 'Love in the Multitude: A Feminist Critique of Love as Political Concept', in *Love: A Question for Feminism in the Twenty-First Century*, ed. Anna G. Jónasdóttir and Ann Ferguson (London: Routledge, 2014), 237–49.

18 Michelle Janning, *Love Letters: Saving Romance in the Digital Age* (London: Routledge, 2018), 18.

19 Devi Dee Mucina, *Ubuntu Relational Love: Decolonizing Black Masculinities* (Winnipeg: University of Manitoba Press, 2019), 2.

20 Ahmed, *The Cultural Politics of Emotion*, 141.

Bibliography

Ahmed, Sara. *The Cultural Politics of Emotion*. 2nd edn. Edinburgh: Edinburgh University Press, 2014.

Berlant, Lauren. *Desire/Love*. Brooklyn, NY: Punctum Books, 2012.

Berlant, Lauren. 'Intimacy: A Special Issue'. *Critical Inquiry* 24 (Winter 1998).

Boris, Eileen, and Rhacel Salazar Parreñas, eds. *Intimate Labors: Cultures, Technologies, and the Politics of Care*. Stanford, CA: Stanford University Press, 2010.

hooks, bell. *All about Love: New Visions*. New York: Harper Perennial, 2000.

Horgan, Amelia. *Lost in Work: Escaping Capitalism*. London: Pluto Press, 2021.

Illouz, Eva. *Consuming the Romantic Utopia: Love and the Cultural Contradictions of Capitalism*. Berkeley: University of California Press, 1997.

Janning, Michelle. *Love Letters: Saving Romance in the Digital Age*. London: Routledge, 2018.

Jónasdóttir, Anna G. 'Love Studies: A (Re) New (ed) Field of Knowledge Interests'. In *Love: A Question for Feminism in the Twenty-First Century*, edited by Anna G. Jónasdóttir and Ann Ferguson, 12–30. London: Routledge, 2014.

Jónasdóttir, Anna G., and Ann Ferguson, eds. *Love: A Question for Feminism in the Twenty-First Century*. London: Routledge, 2014.

Lauer, Christopher. *Intimacy: A Dialectical Study*. New York: Bloomsbury, 2016.

May, Simon. *Love: A History*. New Haven, CT: Yale University Press, 2010.

Mucina, Devi Dee. *Ubuntu Relational Love: Decolonizing Black Masculinities*. Winnipeg: University of Manitoba Press, 2019.

Wilkinson, Eleanor. 'Love in the Multitude: A Feminist Critique of Love as Political Concept'. In *Love: A Question for Feminism in the Twenty-First Century*, edited by Anna G. Jónasdóttir and Ann Ferguson, 237–49. London: Routledge, 2014.

PART 1

Love and communities

1

'Love is a battle, love is a war': James Baldwin's use of love to represent race, gender and sexuality in segregated America

Daniele Nunziata

Introduction

James Baldwin was born in Harlem, New York, in 1924 and raised by his mother, Emma Berdis Jones, and stepfather, David Baldwin, a Pentecostal preacher. As a queer African American born into a poor family, Baldwin experienced multiple and intersecting forms of societal oppression, which inspired his future literary works to investigate the possibilities and strategies of achieving freedom in heteronormative and racially segregated America. At the centre of his work was the importance and possibilities of love – a concept often tied to, and facilitating, the pursuit of individual and social freedoms. Writing during the civil rights movement, Baldwin's texts utilize his own experiences to comment on wider social and political issues. Composed in the same year as the March on Washington for Jobs and Freedom, 'My Dungeon Shook' (1963) exemplifies this process.[1] Published as an open letter, it functions as both a confessional text for his nephew and a public social commentary on racism across America. In his earlier essay collection, *Nobody Knows My Name* (1961), he argues that 'freedom is not something that anybody can be given; freedom is something people take, and people are as free as they want to be', demonstrating how he positions 'freedom' as an active pursuit which can only be reached through agency and self-mobilization.[2] Across his writing, Baldwin asserts that freedom depends on love as a means of first liberating the internal, psychic prisons of the individual mind, before it can then be used to reconstruct the broken external society of contemporary America. Consequently, he imagines freedom as involving the existential formation of an (American) identity beyond the categories of race and sexuality constructed by privileged white and straight Americans. He suggests that – through music, writing and *loving* – individuals can autonomously resist the violence inflicted by those with power.

Baldwin's works express the oppression experienced by Americans based on constructs of race and sexual orientation while emphasising the intersections between these experiences. He employed motifs of love – romantic, familial and social – to understand how humans are able to inflict its opposite expression (hatred) on others and how, in turn, love might offer the basis for an antidote to existing inequality and discrimination. His first-person novel, *Giovanni's Room* (1956), describes the romantic love between two men, one American and another European (composed after Baldwin's own travels across the latter continent), while *Go Tell It on the Mountain* (1953) explores the complex layers of love within the religious African American family of its Harlem-born protagonist, John Grimes. Both have different autobiographical traces, which reveal how Baldwin brings his own lived experiences to bear on his writing and how the love he feels for others (relatives, friends and partners) informs his sense of identity. Just as importantly, his extensive collection of meticulous essays and articles frequently meditates on the nature of loving, in ways which uniquely merge the personal with the academic to create a comprehensive creative-intellectual voice. He often expresses his love of music – a powerful tool for societal emancipation – reflecting how impassioned forms of cultural production can be a means of improving a divided and loveless contemporary society. This is never an easy process, and his assessment that 'Love is a battle' demonstrates the polemic nature of the very act of choosing love over hatred.[3] It is a philosophy which carries vitally important consequences today.

The essay from which the above quotation emerges, 'In Search of a Majority', first took shape as a paper delivered at Kalamazoo College in 1960, before being published in *Nobody Knows My Name* the following year. The paper examines the construction of 'majority' and 'minority' communities in segregated America. It is also one of Baldwin's pieces of writing in which he clearly defines his understanding of love. Drawing on his surroundings, he begins by indicating the places in which love cannot be found: 'segregated schools or [in] mobs'.[4] Love is the antithesis of the white racist violence which manifests in the construction of institutionalized segregation (in schools, universities and other public spaces) and in bloodshed Baldwin saw on the streets of Harlem. Explaining what love can be, Baldwin stresses that 'to be with God is really to be involved with some enormous, overwhelming desire' and that he specifically 'conceive[s] of God ... as a means of liberation and not a means to control others ... Love is a battle, love is a war; love is a growing up.'[5] The purpose of this love, and this battle, is 'to create a country in which there are no minorities – for the first time in the history of the world'.[6] To love, then, is to participate in an active and assertive mode of resistance against all forms of prejudice, including that which is used to create binary divisions between 'majority' and 'minority' communities through violent marginalization of American Americans and LGBT+ Americans during and after Baldwin's lifetime. Love is indelibly linked to 'liberation', and it can be achieved, according to Baldwin, through a spiritual focus – but only in a form of worship beyond the institutional 'control [of] others' enacted by the powerful white-owned churches of the 1960s. In addition, the assertion that 'love is a growing up' engages with one of the writer's key terms – innocence – which he uses as a negative byword for the kinds of ignorance that directly lead to either hatred of the Other or self-hatred (in the case of internalized racism or homophobia). If love is phrased as a kind of personal development, then innocence is equivalent to hatred.

Baldwin expands on some of these concepts in a televised interview with Colin MacInnes and James Mossman, which aired in 1965 for the BBC programme *Encounters*. He explains that, while he attempted to work as a preacher for three years as a teenager (a few years older than the age of his protagonist in *Go Tell It on the Mountain*), he left his church because he was 'not a believer in any sense which would make sense to any church, and any church would obviously throw me out [but] I believe – what do I believe? ... I believe in love ... I believe we can save each other.'[7] He goes on to present love as a force of positive and potent revolution, 'something active, something more like a fire, like the wind, something which can change you. I mean energy [which can] change the world'.[8] Honing in one example of this vision of love as radical 'energy', he briefly discusses music by drawing on the potential intersections between the categories of 'singers' and of 'lovers', including moments when singers successfully produce love with their music and moments when they totally fail.[9] Overall, love is equated with personal and social salvation. It is again linked to God, but only in ways which circumvent the failed and hypocritical practices of unaccepting churches. The reference to churches which 'would obviously throw [him] out' tacitly alludes to Baldwin's queerness or, to use a phrase he employs later, his being a member of 'the sexual minorities' of America. As well as thinking about love as a way to enact change, Baldwin explores how this might be *expressed* – namely through the production of music. In many ways, he is concerned with the performativity of love, including performances of music (and other cultural forms), the false performances of love in unwelcoming religious spaces and the ways in which innocence is a kind of performance which prevents personal development and civil freedom. This chapter will take Baldwin's theories of love forward and demonstrate the nuanced ways in which they play out across his writing. It will begin by analysing Baldwin's depictions of music as an expression of love and freedom (especially in 'Sonny's Blues'), then explore the concept of love as the opposite of heteronormative 'innocence' (including that of the closet in *Giovanni's Room* preventing its protagonist from loving freely or loving himself) and conclude with a discussion of the links between love, religion and spirituality (as are depicted in his essay collection *The Fire Next Time* and in *Go Tell It on the Mountain*).

Love and music

Throughout his oeuvre, Baldwin represents the intimate relationship between love, social and psychological freedoms and the production and consumption of music. In many ways, music was significantly bound up in the civil rights movement, with Eyerman and Jamison suggesting that 'the civil rights movement made it possible for black music to bring a new kind of truth into American society … even emancipatory truth'.[10] Moreover, according to Saadi Simawe, the 'purportedly absolute freedom that music promises seems to have fascinated Baldwin, and with [an] almost … religious passion, he embraced the music of his ancestors'.[11] Indeed, contemporary spirituals, gospel, blues and jazz permeate many of Baldwin's texts, especially through intertextual allusions in *Go Tell It on the Mountain*, where the narrator describes a congregation and how 'the song might be: *Down at the cross where my Saviour died!* … They sang with all the strength that was in them … Something happened to their faces and their voices, the rhythm of their bodies … it was as though … the Holy Ghost were riding on the air.'[12] Despite Baldwin's ambivalent relationship with the Pentecostal Church – having previously disavowed organized religion – his portrayal of singing and dancing within a church as transcendent experiences altering and elevating participants' 'faces', 'voices' and 'bodies' to a spiritual status demonstrates how music, which depends on the 'strength' and agency of the individual, results in psychological escapism from the limitations of quotidian life in Harlem.

This association between music and community, both religious and secular, is extended in 'Down at the Cross' (one of the two essays contained in *The Fire Next Time*), the title of which uses the name of the very same hymn from within *Go Tell It on the Mountain*. In the essay, Baldwin recalls 'church suppers and outings, and … waistline parties where rage and sorrow sat in the darkness … and we … danced and forgot all about "the man".

We had ... the music, and each other ... This is the freedom that one hears in some gospel songs ... in jazz ... and especially in the blues.'[13] Baldwin explicitly associates 'music' with 'freedom'. He suggests that the former is a vital element in the creation of communal solidarity, stating (with the plural first-person pronoun) that 'we had ... the music, and each other', emphasizing the relationship between music and social identity formation. Simultaneously, he demonstrates how music suppresses the psychological haunting of social oppression, allowing one to 'forg[e]t all about "the man"', rather than affirm or internalize the hatred espoused by white supremacists. These depictions of freedom correlate with Ralph Ellison's contemporaneous assessment that 'art – the blues, the spirituals, the dance – was what we had in place of freedom', revealing the cultural and social importance of all art forms, but especially music, in inspiring emancipation and equality during Baldwin's lifetime.[14]

Fred Moten has described 'the freedom drive that animates black performances' and the 'venerable phonic propulsion' that culture can exert over oppression, within his analysis of the intersections between jazz and Black political resistance.[15] In comparable ways, Baldwin's fictional short story 'Sonny's Blues' explores, as its central theme, the importance of jazz and blues both to the personal freedom of the story's protagonist and as integral parts of the wider African American civil rights movement. Narrated by Sonny's brother, the latter admits that he 'sensed ... that Sonny was at that piano playing for his life', stressing how the creation of music was a means of survival for marginalized individuals who are struggling with addiction in similar ways to the eponymous character.[16] Moreover, Sonny later equates 'singing' with heroin use by suggesting that 'it makes you feel – in control', before arguing that 'there's no way not to suffer. But you try all kinds of ways to keep from *drowning* in it.'[17] The narrator later repeats these idioms when observing Sonny perform; he notes that 'I was in Sonny's world ... his kingdom' and that the other musicians were 'having a dialogue with Sonny. [They] wanted Sonny to leave the shoreline [and] witness that deep water and *drowning* were not the same thing ... Sonny was part of the family again.'[18] The narrator presents music as a means of achieving autonomy, power and esteem while also demonstrating its importance in creating 'a dialogue' and communication between individuals, providing a solidarity which challenges the metaphorical 'drowning' of racial oppression. Music is directly framed as a facilitator of 'family' in three senses: the traditional (or biological) familial connection between the narrator and his brother, the metaphorical sense of family between Sonny as his fellow musicians in Harlem and the more abstract sense of an African American community as an imagined family structure. All three are dependent on expressions of interpersonal and creative love. As Baldwin states in 'Down at the Cross', 'to be born, in a white ... antisexual country, black' makes one 'give up all hope of communion. Black people ... do not look at each other.'[19] This reveals how white supremacy has corrupted all possible expressions of love across American society, denying the existence of familial, communal and sexual love. 'Sonny's Blues', therefore, demonstrates the potency of music in reviving not only a 'hope of communion' but also explicit dialogue and love between people in defiance of both racial and familial segregation.

Similarly, in his essay 'Many Thousands Gone' in *Notes of a Native Son*, Baldwin suggests that 'it is only in his music' that an African American individual 'has been able to tell his story ... a story which otherwise has yet to be told and which no American is prepared to hear'.[20] Here, he directly identifies the power of music in enabling an independent self-articulation which affords individual freedom of expression while resisting the systematic silencing and epistemic repression of African Americans because of racial segregation. Returning to 'Down at the Cross', Baldwin repeats how 'for the horrors of the [African American] life there has been almost no language ... the power of the white world is threatened whenever a black man refuses to accept the white world's definitions'.[21] Baldwin, therefore, isolates the necessity of expressing one's lived experiences through the creative medium of 'language' – both musical and, in his case, literary – in order to expose the first-hand suffering and injustice within contemporary America. This provides the individual the liberty of self-representation beyond the violent dominant discourses of 'the white world's definitions', using a counter-canonical mode of life-writing to directly resist the hegemony 'of the white world' itself. As Martin Luther King (n.d.) similarly suggests in his 'Letter from Birmingham Jail', 'normal and healthy discontent can be channelled into the creative outlet of nonviolent direct action', articulating a related theorizing of the importance of 'non-violent' creativity as a means of cultural, social and political resistance.[22]

Love and innocence

If music represents the resistant power of love, then 'innocence' operates antithetically as a symbol of loveless inaction and regression. The freedom Baldwin associates with individual self-expression outside the limitations of American society relates to the importance he ascribes to disavowing 'innocence' across his writing – a moral category akin to ignorance and aligned to privilege – particularly the white, heteronormative 'innocence' which imprisons Americans. According to Lawrie Balfour, Baldwin 'spends a great deal more energy identifying what freedom is not than he does elaborating on what it is ... The rarity or even absence of freedom is illustrated ... in the racial innocence of so many white Americans. By contrast, Baldwin contends that freedom requires the exercise of moral agency.'[23] Indeed, in *Nobody Knows My Name*, Baldwin suggests that 'human freedom is a complex, difficult – and private – thing ... freedom is the fire which burns away illusion ... The recovery of th[e] standard [of human freedom] demands of everyone who loves this country a hard look at himself.'[24] The imagery Baldwin employs to represent 'freedom' as involving the destruction of 'illusion' demonstrates how the achievement of personal liberty fundamentally necessitates the rejection of ignorant white privilege and the false visions of society it engenders. In his essay 'My Dungeon Shook', Baldwin assesses the violent legacies of colonial history to conclude that 'innocent people [are] still trapped in a history which they do not understand; and until they understand it, they cannot be released from it. They [white Americans] have had to believe ... that black men are inferior to white men' to sustain their colonialist worldview of binary oppositions between self and Other.[25] Baldwin, therefore, identifies how freedom is inhibited by ignorance. He demonstrates how this 'innocence' results in racist white Americans being 'trapped' by their own false images of the past, which are then used to violently oppress other members of society. Baldwin's category of 'innocence' is a denial of empathy, a foreclosing of fraternity and the antithesis of love. As Clarence E. Hardy observes, 'Baldwin describes the false ... innocence that characterizes whiteness with its adult pretensions to a childlike purity. In making a show of innocence, those who cling to this white social identity fail to communicate true purity; they manage only to verify their guilt and reveal the stench as the center of white identity.'[26]

Furthermore, Baldwin implicitly associates the ignorance of racism with the so-called innocence of heteronormativity in both his novel *Giovanni's Room* and his later article 'Here Be Dragons' (1985). The former recounts the ill-fated love between two men, Giovanni and David, a closeted, white American. Out of fear of his burgeoning sexuality, David confines himself to the eponymous room set in France; it is a symbol of his self-imposed repression and his internalized anxieties towards his queerness and his love for Giovanni. David describes it as 'frightening ... when one began searching for the key to this disorder one realized that it was not to be found ... For this was ... a matter of punishment and grief'.[27] Composed after Baldwin's brief incarceration in Paris in 1949 and set in the same city, the novel presents the room as a metaphorical prison created by suppressive heteronormative social conventions, a process in which its prisoners are ironically complicit due to the self-willed 'punishment' and concealment of same-gender desires and queer identities.

Approaching the end of the novel, David finds a momentary sense of freedom when he indirectly confesses his love for Giovanni to his effective girlfriend, Hella. He tells her that he is 'very fond of Giovanni', before laughing. Feeling 'protected by the tone of my voice, I found great relief in adding: "I love him, in a way. I really do"' (118–19). David gains a fleeting escape from the confinement of the preceding sections of the text through his verbalized expression of his queer 'love' for Giovanni. It is a scene which covertly marks his coming out, not only in generalized way but to the woman with whom he had been performing a sham heteronormative relationship. Either Hella does not understand the significance of David's confession, or David wilfully obfuscates his intended meaning. In both cases, there is an obstructive misunderstanding of the two men's relationship as one of platonic friendship. Indeed, David's ability to hide behind his laughter – figured as the protection of his 'tone of voice' – indicates the way in which this constitutes a half-reveal and one shrouded by a performance, not unlike his recurring performative displays of heteronormativity (including his relationship with Hella). Binaries of public and private play out here, and elsewhere in the novel, to showcase the false 'protect[ion]' of David's linguistic performances, (half) silences and self-confinement in the eponymous room. Baldwin presents a glimmer of hopeful 'great relief' from David's self-imposed chastisement. It is one which can only be achieved through an open admission of 'love'. Love is freedom, but only if it is recognized, confessed and practised. Indeed, the 'relief' in this scene is short-lived as David immediately returns to his heteronormative masquerade and returns to the 'miserable closet of a room' (126), with Baldwin obviously playing with the doubleness of the term 'closet'.

After only a few sentences, Hella makes an offhand reference to 'our love' which, not unlike David's quasi coming out, is framed in laughter. In response, David glibly observes that 'we're not the first people who thought that' before the two 'lay silent and still' (119). After a short argument about their future, 'there was a long silence' (120). This section of the novel is structured mostly through lines of dialogue which adds to the theatre-like performativity of their relationship. The echoes of nervous laughter which cloaks both characters' accounts of love indicate how Hella, at least unconsciously, cannot bring herself to discuss their love without some buffer – in the same way that David cannot speak truthfully unless hiding behind a comedic façade. The repeated moments of 'silence' punctuate the episode, emphasizing how the aphasias in their relationship – and David's withholding of both his affair with Giovanni and his queerness – is a symptom of their lack of freedom. The power of love as an emancipatory tool dies through quietness and repression.

David's presentation of heterosexuality resonates with Judith Butler's seminal theories on the performativity of gender identities and sexuality. In Butler's words, the character's recurring 'acts, gestures, enactments, generally construed, are *performative* in the sense that the essence of identity that they otherwise purport to express are *fabrications* manufactured and sustained through corporeal signs and other discursive means'.[28] Baldwin's writing reveals how this gender performativity also extends to the ostensible *absence* of these socially constructed signs and discourse. In the construction of David's fabricated and socially permissible identity, what remains unsaid is as powerful as what he chooses to say. Through silence, the character adheres to what Butler calls 'the law of heterosexual coherence', creating

·an inaudible yet obedient performance of masculinity and heterosexuality within which he is barricaded and through which love cannot enter.[29]

When David returns to Giovanni the next evening, he attempts to justify ending their relationship (to live with Hella instead) by claiming 'I *do* love her'. Enraged by David's self-delusion, Giovanni passionately retorts: 'You do not ... love anyone! You never have loved anyone! I am sure you never will! You love your purity, you love your mirror ... you walk around ... as though you had some precious metal, gold, silver, rubies, maybe *diamonds* down there between your legs! ... You want to be *clean* ... and you do not want to *stink*' (125). At the core of Giovanni's diatribe is his insistence that David lacks the ability to openly manifest emotional, interpersonal love towards others. The repeated allusions to expensive metals and gemstones indicate how David reifies himself and others, choosing to favour a materialistic performance based around the directives of white, heteronormative American capitalism. Similarly, the adjective 'clean' signals a purging of authentic identity in order to reproduce a sanitized and easily consumable version of his selfhood. David is fixated on adhering to what Butler describes as 'the regulatory ideal' of compulsory heterosexuality which is 'a fiction that disguises itself as a developmental law'.[30] These decisions, Giovanni argues, are symptomatic of an auto-dehumanization which prevents David from experiencing or expressing love – and, thus, inhibiting any possible freedom from the queerphobia which hangs over their existence. The love of a commodifying performance of normalcy constrains any romantic love which could have flourished between the two men. Dwight McBride's convincing interpretation states that David 'represents the pitfalls and suffering of a life lived in observance of the rules about what we should be, how we should love, indeed, what we should feel'.[31] This desire to comply with contemporary American conventions strips David of his humanity and produces an existence devoid of happiness or vitality. In this case, *love is a battle* with the self.

Matt Brim's important critical readings of the novel reveal the 'trans- and homophobia-induced gender dysphoria' experienced by David and how he '*feels* dirty as a gay man, and that feeling renders him not only unable to accept his homosexuality but, crucially, unable to *feel* the gay body overlaid with figurative-but-felt dirt'.[32] David's self-hatred emanates from internalized homophobia and misogyny which manifests as his disgust for his own corporeal externality and its apparent lack of cleanliness – in both the hygienic and moralistic connotations of the word. For Baldwin's self-hating protagonist, to be 'clean' is to be – or to appear – heterosexual; to 'stink' is to be perceptively queer and Other. Both words are italicized (and therefore verbally emphasized by Giovanni) to give emphasis to what they truly signify, two words David cannot express aloud: straight and gay. This equation of queerness with dirtiness illustrates David's anxieties surrounding same-sex desire. Viewing queerness as impure and pathogenic, David twists (queer) love into (homophobic) panic. Importantly, it is his physical body · which becomes the target of his hatred. As Christopher Schmidt asserts in his analysis of 'the poetics of waste' across modernist literature, 'the rules separating dirty from clean ... are patriarchal in nature'. In *Giovanni's Room*, David clings to this very binary as a way of dividing his inner self from an ostensibly transgressive and contaminated outside world. He uses the categories of clean and dirty to conceptualize the duality between straight and gay through reference to the outermost layer of his body, the protective buffer of the visible skin. He attempts to expunge queerness from himself, as one might remove dirt from the outer dermis. His aim is to associate his observable selfhood with a heteronormative and patriarchal vision of cleanliness which can be performed in order to denounce and disguise his queerness. This is an act of existential cleansing, a way of literally removing dirt and figuratively removing queerness from the sanitized social identity he chooses to perform. It hides his queerness and makes conspicuous his display of 'clean' heterosexual masculinity. It is a heteronormative cleansing ritual which prevents David's potential love for himself – and Giovanni's love for David – from penetrating the surface of his visiblized social 'purity'. As Baldwin shows his readers, David's purification rituals (which begin with David looking in the mirror in the novel's opening sentences) symbolize and foreshadow his self-hatred and self-destruction.

Many of these ideas are echoed in 'Here Be Dragons', in which Baldwin describes queer men who 'so far from ... resembling faggots, looked and sounded like the vigilantes who banded together on weekends to beat faggots up', before revealing that 'these men looked like cops, football players, soldiers, sailors ... they had wives, mistresses, and children'.[33] Here, Baldwin demonstrates the way ignorance causes individuals to fear and repress the complex reality of their identities and to become trapped, like David, in the performance of heteronormative appearances and relationships. These public performances conform to the 'ideal of masculinity' disseminated by contemporary American society, especially Hollywood cinema, to the extent that the performers hate themselves and commit acts of violence against others who remind them of their repressed selfhood. As emphasized in 'My Dungeon Shook', 'it is the innocence which constitutes the crime ... these innocent ... people ... have caused [African Americans] to be born under [inhumane] conditions ... in a ghetto'.[34] Baldwin stresses the undeniable culpability of straight white Americans in creating the conditions of segregation, imprisonment and marginalization experienced by Black and queer Americans. He suggests that the violence of racism and homophobia in contemporary America emerges from the internal insecurities of white and straight Americans being externalized and then weaponized against communities dehumanized as being Other. Baldwin concludes his confessional essay by stressing that 'we cannot be free until they are free'.[35] The opposing pronouns appear to be consciously confusing. Freedom for one community (for the self) is dependent on freedom of another (the Other), and vice versa. If the first-person 'we' specifically includes African Americans (of all gender identities and sexualities) and queers Americans (of all races and ethnicities), then it indicates how freedom in a divided America might only be realized when its straight, white citizens undergo a radical transformation and expunge themselves of the hatred of their racist, colonialist and heteronormative ideologies.

Baldwin proposes that what is needed to overcome 'innocence' is self-acceptance and the acceptance of others through love. Not only does he attempt to challenge existing expectations of 'love' by associating it with unconventional martial and unromantic connotations, but his suggestion that 'love is growing up', noted earlier, symbolizes how love is a means through which an individual matures away from destructive 'innocence' and 'naïveté' and ultimately approaches 'liberation'.[36] As Carlyle Stewart argues in his reading of Baldwin, 'love remains the centering force of African American life ... To love and be loved is an expression of freedom in a society that promulgates and promotes human hatred as a way of life and self-actualization.'[37] Indeed, in 'Down at the Cross', Baldwin reveals that 'I am very much concerned that [African Americans] achieve their freedom ... But I am also concerned for their dignity, for the health of their souls, and must oppose any attempt that [African Americans] may make to do to others what has been done to them ... *Whoever debases others is debasing himself.*'[38] In his assessment of the separatist teachings of Malcolm X and the Nation of Islam, Baldwin explicitly concludes that 'freedom' cannot be realized through reactionary violence and that an internalization of racial hatred reproduces the hostility of contemporary American society, resulting in the hatred of both others and the self and a degradation of one's own 'soul'. Even his allusion to Malcolm X and George Lincoln Rockwell – 'the chief of the American Nazi party' – as 'racially speaking ... in complete agreement' identifies separatism and Nazism as analogous in their dissemination of racist ideology.[39] Instead, Baldwin advocates integration by claiming that 'if the word integration means anything, ... it means: that we, with love, shall force our brothers to see themselves as they are, to cease fleeing from reality and begin to change it. For this is your home'.[40] Through his emphasis on America as his 'home' and the use of the first-person plural pronoun to refer to white Americans as 'our brothers', Baldwin imagines a united American society in which 'love' is instrumentalized to overcome the ignorance of white citizens who attempt to 'flee ... from reality' and, thus, disavow the destruction of racial violence and discrimination.[41]

Later in the same essay, alongside the need for African Americans to 'accept them [white Americans] with love', Baldwin stresses the importance of self-acceptance, claiming that his stepfather, David Baldwin, 'was defeated long before he died because ... he really believed what white people said about him'.[42] In 'Notes of a Native Son', Baldwin similarly evokes his family background to disclose that David

> had been ill a long time – in the mind ... the disease of the mind allowed the disease of the body to destroy him ... locked up in his terrors ... Hatred, which destroyed so much, never failed to destroy the man who hated ... The [solution] was acceptance ... of life as it is ... This fight begins ... in the heart ... to keep my own heart free of hatred and despair.[43]

In both texts, Baldwin draws on autobiographical narratives to demonstrate how David's psychological imprisonment (or the state of being metaphorically 'locked up in his terrors') was a result of him internalizing the 'hatred' subjected towards him, including 'what white people said about him'. This signals, therefore, that psychic freedom – which acts a precursor to social freedom – involves a cathartic rejection of all 'hatred' in order to prevent one 'destroy[ing]' oneself and to avoid the inheritance of 'hatred' across generations. Baldwin expresses how social freedom can be achieved through the love which confronts and challenges the ignorance and hatred of white racists while simultaneously revealing that internal, psychological liberty is similarly attained by the love of self-'acceptance' – and the subsequent 'acceptance', rather than 'hatred', of others.

Love and spirituality

In related ways, Baldwin isolates the specific culpability of organized, social institutions in repressing individual freedoms, asserting that 'there was no love in the church. It was a mask for hatred and self-hatred and despair ... we, for white people, were the descendants of Ham, and ... white people were, for us, the descendants of Cain ... we feared and distrusted and ... hated almost all strangers ... and despised ourselves.'[44] Baldwin, in his assessment of the relationship between Western Christianity and colonialism, repeats many of the idioms he employs earlier in the essay to incriminate the church as reproducing 'hatred' within a community – rather than the Christian virtue of love – demonstrating that such a process results in a dual defamation of both the receiver and the disseminator of hate speech. This echo chamber of hatred maintains racial segregation in America. He subsequently concludes that

> people always seem to band together in accordance to a principle that has nothing to do with love, a principle that releases them from personal responsibility ... the whole root of our trouble, the human trouble, is that we will sacrifice all the beauty of our lives, will imprison ourselves in totems, taboos, crosses ... steeples, mosques, races, armies, flags, nations,

in order to deny the fact of death, which is the only fact we have ... One clings then to chimeras ... and the entire hope – the entire possibility – of freedom disappears.[45]

Baldwin identifies how institutional groups – both nationalist, as represented by 'armies, flags, nations', and religious, signified by 'crosses', 'steeples, mosques' – are the fundamental cause of social 'imprison[ment]'. These are (in Benedict Anderson's terms) 'imagined communities' which compel individuals to disavow 'personal responsibility' through the very adoration of figurative political and religious symbols, at the expense of expressing 'love' for themselves or for others within a shared society.[46] These centralized organizations, therefore, decrease and suppress an individual's ability to act autonomously. As a consequence, such nationalist and religious worship diverts followers from recognizing the reality of 'the fact of death' and, thus, affirms a state of innocence. This summary, therefore, amalgamates Baldwin's notions of both innocence and love, as well as his ambivalence towards the church, relating them in his theorizing of freedom's circumscription in contemporary America. This reveals how a simultaneous disavowal of hatred, innocence and organized religion will increase an individual's independence and self-determination. As Balfour argues, 'from this ... existential innocence grows ... the evasion of responsibility for participation in an avowedly democratic society ... the realization of freedom at any level involves accepting the radical un-freedom of human life without being defeated by it'.[47]

Baldwin's ambivalence towards the church may also relate to the alienation he personally experienced which was directed by anti-LGBT+ religious organizations. While his quasi-autobiographical novel, *Go Tell It on the Mountain*, seldom represents homosexuality directly, it does illustrate the author-narrator's lifelong difficulties with finding acceptance in religious spaces, including his family household. In the text, John's mother, Elizabeth, maintains a conventional and pious Christian lifestyle, much like Baldwin's own mother. There are moments, however, when Elizabeth is presented as a figure who recognizes the problematically selective love offered by hegemonic Christian institutions. In one scene, Elizabeth reflects on how 'love' might be a 'kind of imprisonment', but it 'was also, mysteriously, a freedom for the soul and spirit, was water in the dry place, and had nothing to do with the prisons, churches, laws, rewards, and punishments, that so positively cluttered the landscape of her [austere, conventionalist] aunt's mind'.[48] Echoing Baldwin's first-person commentaries on love throughout his essays, the fictional Elizabeth's realization dramatizes Baldwin's own coming to terms with how to define love. Much like his second novel, a restrictive (mis)understanding of love can become a source of psychological repression with the metaphor of 'imprisonment' foreshadowing both David's self-confinement in *Giovanni's Room* and Baldwin's theories of 'innocence'.

However, a truer form of love is also recognized as its antithesis. It is a form of spiritual and interpersonal expression which is anathema to the moral (and moralizing) codes of 'churches, [national] laws, ... and punishments', and it is a means through which an individual can achieve internal and emotional 'freedom'. Only pages later, Elizabeth plots her escape from her zealot aunt: 'She now went into battle with her aunt for her freedom. And she won it' (186). There are obvious reverberations of the quotation being used as the title of this very chapter: love and freedom are figured as battles and wars. While Elizabeth's hard-'won' freedom is not entirely permanent, her characterization demonstrates how Baldwin affords Elizabeth a perspective which (at the start of his literary career) begins to articulate many of his enduring axioms. Love, when uncoupled from institutions, power and privilege, can be a source of personal or social freedom, but this process is one defined by struggle and sacrifice. The results of this process are not always happy ones (as is the case of Giovanni's death). Nonetheless, it is the only option available as non-violent resistance to a hate-riddled America.

Conclusion

In his meditations on the possibility of freedom for contemporary Americans – Black, white, heterosexual and queer – Baldwin demonstrates that his understanding of 'innocence' – a wilful ignorance held by Americans with privilege and power and incubated systemically by organized political and religious organizations – is responsible for the repression of Black and queer Americans according to spurious and reductive views on both race and sexual identity. Baldwin vehemently suggests, across his writings, that love is capable of combating this state of innocence and engendering both social and psychic liberty through the acceptance of others and, more importantly, the acceptance of one's autonomous selfhood. This is far from the superficial or selective love of hypocritical institutions, but one closer to the familial, intercommunal and creative love which is expressed in 'Sonny's Blues'. Through this short story in particular, Baldwin isolates music and life-writing as instrumental in providing escapism and emancipation, especially as discursive representations of suffering are able to counter the ignorance and hatred of those who disavow the realities of racism, violence and death which circumscribe racially segregated, heteronormative America.

Notes

1   The March on Washington for Jobs and Freedom was organized by A. Philip Randolph and Bayard Rustin and held on 28 August 1963. Its aim was to campaign for civil rights for African Americans, and its closing section was

the famous 'I Have a Dream' speech by Dr Martin Luther King Jr. The march helped pave the way for the introduction of the Civil Rights Act of 1964. Baldwin attended the march but was asked not to speak.

2   James Baldwin, *Nobody Knows My Name* (London: Penguin, 1991), 127.

3   Ibid., 114–15.

4   Ibid., 114.

5   Ibid., 114–15.

6   Ibid., 115.

7   James Baldwin, *Conversations with James Baldwin* (Oxford: University of Mississippi Press, 1989), 48.

8   Ibid.

9   Ibid., 49.

10   Ron Eyerman and Andrew Jamison, *Music and Social Movements* (Cambridge: Cambridge University Press, 1998), 44.

11   Saadi Simawe, 'What Is in a Sound?', in *Re-Viewing James Baldwin: Things Not Seen*, ed. Daniel Quentin Miller (Philadelphia, PA: Temple University Press, 2000), 19.

12   James Baldwin, *Go Tell It on the Mountain* (London: Penguin, 2001), 15–16.

13   James Baldwin, *The Fire Next Time* (London: Penguin, 1964), 42.

14   Ralph Ellison, *Shadow and Act* (New York: Random House, 1966), 247.

15   Fred Moten, *In the Break: The Aesthetics of the Black Radical Tradition* (Minneapolis: University of Minnesota Press), 12.

16   James Baldwin, 'Sonny's Blues', in *The Jazz Fiction Anthology*, ed. Sascha Feinstein and David Rife (Bloomington: Indiana University Press, 2009), 35.

17   Ibid., 40–1, emphasis added.

18   Ibid., 44, 46, emphasis added.

19   Baldwin, *The Fire Next Time*, 33.

20   James Baldwin, *Notes of a Native Son* (New York: Bantam, 1955), 18.

21   Baldwin, *The Fire Next Time*, 62.

22   Martin Luther King, 'Letter from Birmingham Jail', University of Pennsylvania. http://www.africa.upenn.edu/Articles_Gen/Letter_Birmingham.html. Accessed 3 January 2021.

23   Lawrie Balfour, 'Finding the Words', in *James Baldwin Now*, ed. Dwight A. McBride (London: New York University Press, 1999), 91.

24   Baldwin, *Nobody Knows My Name*, 100.

25   Baldwin, *The Fire Next Time*, 16–17.

26   Clarence E. Hardy, *James Baldwin's God: Sex, Hope, and Crisis in Black Holiness Culture* (Knoxville: University of Tennessee Press, 2003), 89.

27   James Baldwin, *Giovanni's Room* (London: Penguin, 2007), 78. All subsequent references will be provided in text.

28   Judith Butler, *Gender Trouble: Feminism and the Supervision of Identity* (New York: Routledge, 1990), 136.

29   Ibid., 137.

30   Ibid., 136.

31   Dwight McBride, *Why I Hate Abercrombie & Fitch: Essays on Race and Sexuality* (New York: New York University Press, 2005), 53.

32   Matt Brim, *James Baldwin and the Queer Imagination* (Ann Arbor: University of Michigan Press, 2014), 89, original emphasis.

33   James Baldwin, 'Here Be Dragons', in *The Price of the Ticket: Collected Nonfiction 1948–1985* (New York: St Martin's Press, 1985), 683.

34   Baldwin, *The Fire Next Time*, 14–15.

35   Ibid., 18.

36   Baldwin, *Nobody Knows My Name*, 114–15.

37   Carlyle Fielding Stewart, *Soul Survivors: An African American Spirituality* (Louisville, KY: Westminster John Knox Press, 1997), 44.

38   Baldwin, *The Fire Next Time*, 73, original emphasis.

39   Ibid., 72.

40   Ibid., 17.

41   Ibid.

42   Ibid., 16, 13.

43   Baldwin, *Notes of a Native Son*, 74, 75, 95.

44   Baldwin, *The Fire Next Time*, 40–1.

45   Ibid., 79.

46   Benedict Anderson, *Imagines Communities* (London: Verso, 1983), 6.

47   Balfour, 'Finding the Words', 92.

48   Baldwin, *Go Tell It on the Mountain*, 180–1.

Bibliography

Anderson, Benedict. *Imagined Communities*. London: Verso, 1983.
Baldwin, James. *Notes of a Native Son*. New York: Bantam, 1955.
Baldwin, James. *The Fire Next Time*. London: Penguin, 1964.
Baldwin, James. 'Here Be Dragons'. In *The Price of the Ticket: Collected Nonfiction 1948–1985*, 677–90. New York: St Martin's Press, 1985.
Baldwin, James. *Conversations with James Baldwin*. Oxford: University of Mississippi Press, 1989.
Baldwin, James. *Nobody Knows My Name*. London: Penguin, 1991.
Baldwin, James. *Go Tell It on the Mountain*. London: Penguin, 2001.
Baldwin, James. *Giovanni's Room*. London: Penguin, 2007.

Baldwin, James. 'Sonny's Blues'. In *The Jazz Fiction Anthology*, edited by Sascha Feinstein and David Rife, 17–48. Bloomington: Indiana University Press, 2009.

Balfour, Lawrie. 'Finding the Words'. In *James Baldwin Now*, edited by Dwight A. McBride, 75–99. London: New York University Press, 1999.

Brim, Matt. *James Baldwin and the Queer Imagination*. Ann Arbor: University of Michigan Press, 2014.

Butler, Judith. *Gender Trouble: Feminism and the Supervision of Identity*. New York: Routledge, 1990.

Ellison, Ralph. *Shadow and Act*. New York: Random House, 1966.

Eyerman, Ron, and Andrew Jamison. *Music and Social Movements*. Cambridge: Cambridge University Press, 1998.

Hardy, Clarence E. *James Baldwin's God: Sex, Hope, and Crisis in Black Holiness Culture*. Knoxville: University of Tennessee Press, 2003.

King, Martin Luther. 'Letter from Birmingham Jail'. University of Pennsylvania. http://www.africa.upenn.edu/Articles_Gen/Letter_Birmingham.html. Accessed 3 January 2021.

McBride, Dwight. *Why I Hate Abercrombie & Fitch: Essays on Race and Sexuality*. New York: New York University Press, 2005.

Moten, Fred. *In the Break: The Aesthetics of the Black Radical Tradition*. Minneapolis: University of Minnesota Press, 2006.

Schmidt, Christopher. *The Poetics of Waste: Queer Excess in Stein, Ashbery, Schuyler, and Goldsmith*. New York: Palgrave Macmillan, 2014.

Simawe, Saadi A. 'What Is in a Sound?' In *Re-viewing James Baldwin: Things Not Seen*, edited by Daniel Quentin Miller, 12–32. Philadelphia, PA: Temple University Press, 2000.

Stewart, Carlyle Fielding. *Soul Survivors: An African American Spirituality*. Louisville, KY: Westminster John Knox Press, 1997.

2

Liberating the Victorian politics of love through Jack the Lass and Anne Lister

Vicky Panossian and Salma Yassine

I love, & only love, the fairer sex & thus beloved by them in turn, my heart revolts from any other love than theirs.[1]

Introduction

The notion of unconventional love has been erased from various periods of history, making representation not merely scarce but also implicit. Anne Lister was a turning point for queer women's historiographies and their interpretation of femininity.[2] Lister led and documented almost every day of her life in the nineteenth century, but her coded diaries were not deciphered until the early twenty-first century. The decryption and eventual publication of *The Secret Diaries of Miss Anne Lister* allowed the reader to redefine their predisposition regarding mid-nineteenth-century England and its women.[3] Lister's *Diaries* contain detailed descriptions of her affairs with women of all social classes; they also document society's perception of her and her eventual wife, Ann Walker. The *Diaries* as well as their 2019 BBC adaptation depict the societal and psychological struggles Anne and her wife had to endure in order to maintain their relationship. Lister's love for 'the fairer sex' does not merely radicalize and illustrate the societal constraints of Victorian queer relationships, but also helps the reader grasp the stratified nature of oppression brought about to women in general, and queer women in particular.[4] This is evidently mirrored in the BBC adaptation of Lister's *Diaries*, the series titled *Gentleman Jack* (2019).

The theme song of *Gentleman Jack* reflects the way people perceived Lister as 'Jack-the-lass', a nickname predominantly used in the nineteenth century to signify a womanizer with manly and confident characteristics.[5] The song demonstrates the ways in which Lister was considered not only as an outcast but also as a threat to the men of Shibden, a small rural community in Yorkshire, who were afraid of losing their wives to her and her charm. The song also illustrates a new approach to the narrative of nineteenth-century queer women, because it brings about a sense of dominance that was otherwise generally absent from representations of women in Victorian literature.[6] While Lister does not conform to traditional gender representations, she performs another identity which evolves into becoming a means for earning her respect. One might even argue that Lister emerges to alter people's common perceptions of queerness as a form of illness to a form of identity that demands validity. Perhaps Lister's choice to adhere to traditional means of kinship and validating them through a Christian marriage signifies that she demanded and earned (non-publicized) recognition despite her non-conforming sexuality. Her mining endeavours also granted her a status of socioeconomic prominence and public respectability as she maintained a polished image of an agentic and active member of society. Thus, her sexuality and social respectability were not mutually exclusive since she managed to perform her identity, be it publicly or otherwise, *while* abiding by the Victorian social order.

In this chapter, we tackle the various layers of women's oppression as depicted in the *Diaries* and their historically curated cinematic adaptation. This essay aims to deconstruct the traditional understanding of queer women's love affairs during the Victorian era by utilizing Anne Lister's *Diaries* and their adaptation as a means to understanding the components of those love affairs. Contrary to some of the research conducted on the same primary sources, this chapter does not consider Lister a landowner or a businesswoman, but rather focuses on Lister's personality as a source of radical action.[7] This chapter looks at the gendered nature of Victorian love and the impact of arranged marriages, paying particular attention to Lister's accounts of everyday life. It then attends to the various manifestations of homophobia at a psychological and societal level as experienced by Lister and her wife, Ann Walker. Finally, it examines the way in which Lister was able to communicate the dynamics of her relationship with her partner without morphing it into a heteronormative one. The related subtopic of Lister's finances aims to expose Lister and Walker's families' greedy and judgemental perception of their assets and capital, since most Victorian women were not given financial agency and the ability to have economic contributions to their family's financial stance. Our discussion unpacks how Lister and Walker challenged this state of affairs by managing their assets in a way that was considered mainstream for their contemporary male figure rather than unmarried women. The chapter concludes by comparing the reality of Anne Lister with that of twenty-first-century Arab women.

Gender performativity and love affairs

Anne Lister's unconventionality is represented by her non-conformity to a set of inherited values and traditions that often dictated the lives of Victorian women. These predispositions could be categorized as cultural renditions of the socioeconomic role a woman was expected to play at the time, thus confining women to a largely domestic life, be it premarital, marital, or unmarried.[8] Another categorization would include personal traits, behaviour patterns and physical appearance. Taken together, these elements constitute the image of a 'proper' and desired woman in a patriarchal society that pivots around cis-heteronormative values.[9] Anne Lister shatters the societal structure built for women through defying this set of norms. To begin with, Lister's style of clothing departs from what was considered customary of the Victorian woman; she did not submit to the etiquette of wearing corsets, crinolines, frilled dresses, bonnets and feminine accessories, preferring instead chemises, coats, tailored skirts and, most prominently, a top hat and a walking cane.[10] Lister's wardrobe is solely restricted to the colour black, except for a few white chemises. She justifies her commitment to the colour by referring to a romantic incident, a heartbreak; she has been mourning the loss of her lover Vere, who chose to marry a man rather than Lister. As Michel Foucault argues, such a woman living in the beginning of the nineteenth century would not have been categorized as queer, because it was only later on that women were defined by their sexual preferences.[11] Prior to the nineteenth century, the discourse regarding gender would consider any non-procreational act to be a perversion, thus eliminating the role of sexual gratification.[12] However, even while discussing the earliest accounts of sodomy, the respective discourse would differentiate the act from the identity of the individual – this illustrates that, although Lister was an outcast, the modern-day assumption of her sexuality based on her appearance would not have been applicable to the setting in which she was performing her identity.

Lister's opposition to established standards as expressed through her choice of dress turned her into an outcast while also providing her with a source of liberation. She was often misjudged and mis-gendered by conventional members of the society as well as by the people who could be labelled as her enemies. Her wardrobe granted her a sense of authority to complement her agency in the economic and business realm as a landowner who is bound to work outdoors and run errands at the bank. In one particular instance, she had to fulfil the role of the state agent in collecting the rent from her tenants. Even though she was insulted by one of her drunk tenants when being referred to as a man, she was highly feared and respected by others.[13] This might not have necessarily been the case had she worn a more 'feminine' attire to abide by the norms. The spectrum of femininity and masculinity is closely knit with the notion of gender performativity which is an evolving social construct subjected to time.[14] It is true that the choice of dress does not determine one's gender identity and/or sexual orientation; however, taken together with a set of character traits and patterns of behaviour, attires can sometimes be indicative of a person's identity and/ or orientation.[15] Lister's physical appearance has also complemented and reinforced her unconventional behaviour patterns such as her sturdy walk and lack of domestic skills. Lister's choice of clothing might have also been a marker of queerness, the latter sometimes being correlated with sexuality as well as gender identity. When examined through a contemporary lens, her physical appearance would render her the equivalent of a modern-day 'butch lesbian' who is often perceived as a masculine woman; it might have also served as a marker of her sexuality during the Victorian era, thus confirming her visibility in front of the women she desired.[16] 'Butchness' can be a common aspect between Lister and other iconized individuals from the English queer scene of the 1800s and 1900s. One prominent example would be Radclyffe Hall, who described herself as a 'congenital invert', meaning a masculine soul in a female body – a term first coined by sexologist Richard von Krafft-Ebing in 1886.[17] Contrary to Lister who was often referred to as a woman, which she never explicitly negated, Hall's performative identity would not be one of 'butchness' but rather of a gender-affirming mode of presentation.

Anne Lister was an exceptional Victorian woman who liberated herself through having the authority to economize her property and avoid the traditional narrative of marriage, a highly unusual position for a woman at the time.[18] Lister's lover and wife – Ann Walker – was subject to various forms of exploitation, being an orphan with only one married sister, which led her to inherit the remainder of her family's money and property. This rendered her prey for her extended family members, who repeatedly urged her to embark on a suitable marital life. There are two major incidents to be tackled when approaching the attempts for Ann Walker's heteronormative marital commodification. First, upon the sudden death of his wife, Reverend Ainsworth, Ann's friend's husband approaches her with an offer for marriage. Having sexually assaulted her in the past, Ainsworth considers Ann to be a suitable wife because he believes her pride to have been already tainted by their 'affair'. Due to this, and according to traditional Victorian norms, Walker would not have been considered a suitable choice for marriage; one might even argue that Ainsworth thought he was saving Ann from the humiliation that would otherwise fall upon her if her future husband were to find out about their encounter. This would have been a common interpretation of the collective perception of women and their sexual availability, which was considered to be the defining factor of their self-worth.[19] Ann almost falls victim to a patriarchal system that expects her to submit to Reverend Ainsworth's request, which was encouraged by her relatives. On this occasion, Lister becomes her lover's saviour, which goes against the Victorian narrative of women's helplessness. She shields Walker from societal expectations that would have forced her into marrying her assaulter; she threatens to stain Ainsworth's reputation if he proceeds with his quest, directly challenging patriarchal norms that favour men, particularly religious or authoritative figures.[20] Lister also reassures her lover and stays with her, even when a traditional union would have otherwise ended, had the past incident with Walker become known to a potential husband. In doing so, Lister is not playing the role of a stereotypical and protective patriarchal figure of a husband, but merely striving to be a compassionate and understanding lover.

The second point relates to Ann's state of mind. This has been extensively discussed as a serious concern in the *Diaries* and reflected in the last two episodes of the first season of *Gentleman Jack*, when we see Ann's mental health deteriorating. She is taken away from Lister and hosted by her sister and brother-in-law in Scotland. During this stay, her brother-in-law denies her medical treatment and attempts to force her into marrying his relative. He justifies his manipulative actions by referring to marriage and motherhood as Ann's salvation from her illness. There is no reference to love within the discourse promoted by him; instead, he preaches a lifestyle based on accommodation. However, Walker's sister, although obliged to reinforce her husband's stance, secretly advises Ann to comprehend the necessity of love in any relationship, explaining that 'a loving friendship is far more important and fruitful than a loveless marriage'.[21] These instances speak to the constraints Ann Walker faced in making a free choice with regard to her married life. Lister, on the other hand, is deemed as the instigating influence that encouraged Walker to live truthfully, despite a series of radical setbacks. At first, we are introduced to a characterless and voiceless Ann Walker, who later on becomes a woman of her own making, or rather Lister's making, and is able to articulate her own independent decisions.[22]

Social and psychological obstacles of Victorian queer love

As depicted in *Gentleman Jack*, Anne Lister is subjected to a series of potential threats from Eliza Priestly, a relative of Ann Walker. At first, Mrs Priestley is fond of Lister and impressed by her unusual personality; her opinion is gradually altered, however, after having noticed Lister's attention to Walker. After accidentally witnessing an intimate encounter between the two women, Mrs Priestly warns them about the consequences of their actions. Mrs Priestly's discourse portrays Walker as a victim of Lister's unconventional practices and homosexual affairs, as Lister herself records: 'Mrs Priestley said she always told people I was natural, but she thought nature was in an odd freak when she made me.'[23]

In addition to Mrs Priestly's comments, Lister suffers a series of verbal assaults addressing her social and sexual queerness, both explicitly and implicitly. One of the harshest examples of this appears in the series during an argument with her sister Marian, who threatens to marry and produce an heir who would inherit Shibden Hall, their ancestral property: 'You can sneer all you like! But one day I shall have a child, a son, and he will have a greater claim to Shibden than you!'[24] Until 1870, it was customary that women's property and possessions would be automatically transferred to their husbands after marriage.[25] Lister's unusual personality and the way she performs it render her the favoured child among her family, instead of leading them to mistreat her. This case is relatively exceptional and daring in Victorian times, given that her aunt was her major supporter.[26] She mainly feared the abuse and rejection that society, rather than the family, might bring upon her niece.

There is one main incident that characterizes Lister's experience of physical abuse. On her way back to Shibden Hall, she is attacked by a 'thug'.[27] In the *Diaries*, the motivation for this violent occurrence is not clear, yet the adaptation pictures it as a potential threat by the Rawsons, her opponents, rather than an arbitrary attack. Thus, although the attack is portrayed as one which was motivated by the economic gains, there seems to be the implicit emergence of homophobia which motivates the use of physical violence, instead of finding alternative means of instigating economic rivalry.

Looking into similar instances of homophobia that Lister was subjected to, her romantic and sexual encounters with her past lover, Mariana Lawton, show an embedded presence of internalized homophobia. In spite of her sincere love towards Lister, Mariana's fondness of her seems to be restricted to their physical pleasure. Yet, when Anne asks her to leave her life behind for the sake of building a shared one together, Mariana refuses the marriage proposal and abides by her original oath of doing so upon the death of her husband, Charles. She insists that her marriage is merely a socially celebrated cloak that would shield her from the marginalization she is bound to suffer if she were to accept Lister's offer.

Lesbianism was and still is often left unrecognized as an illegitimate act, unlike sodomy, which was punishable by hanging during the Victorian era.[28] Scholars such as Adrienne Rich have argued that lesbian relationships have often remained invisible and unrecognizable as legitimate sexual acts, due to compulsory heterosexuality, which considers heterosexuality to be the default and innate orientation for women.[29] Rich's theory explores lesbianism as a marginalized matter left unrecognized by patriarchal institutions that endorse the need of a man's existence in a relationship in order for it to be deemed a legitimate one.[30] To further expand on this notion, it might be significant to mention the accepting stance of Mariana's brother towards her relationship with Lister. Yet, it is not clear whether he categorizes their affair as a perversion or is supportive of their sexuality. Referring to the medical interpretation of sexuality during the time period, all homosexual encounters were considered to be perversions as per the handbook of sexual deviations, known as Krafft-Ebing's *Psychopathia Sexualis* (1886).[31] Another aspect of Lister's argument pertaining to the natural essence of women's homosexuality was linked to the fact that it was neither illegal nor criminalized, contrary to men's homosexuality. Historians of the period attest that lesbianism was not criminalized since it was not considered threatening to the religious patriarchal order of the period; Lister utilized this legal loophole to claim that her relationship and religious marriage were legal and, therefore, natural.[32] In reality, however, Lister was unable to officially marry Walker due to the legal system of the time and, therefore, could not have shared custody of her belongings and be recognized as her legal partner. However, having in mind the restricted patriarchal protocols of the age, women in cis-heteronormative marriages were also not granted such rights.[33]

Lister's narrative contains many references to Victorian homophobia. Although the latter can be defined by the parameters of the timeframe and the religiosity of the period in which she was establishing her queer marriage, two further elements should be discussed.[34] Victorian morals categorized queer love as an unnatural act, a form of perversion. The term has been utilized to describe queer love in various penal codes, quotas as well as a manifold of religious institutions that go against non-cis-heteronormative marriages and unions.[35] In contrast, throughout the differing stages of Lister's life, we witness a consistency in her discourse when referring to her manner of love as 'natural'. During one of these instances, Lister explicitly confronts Walker's internalized homophobia. The argument she utilizes is one that does not negate her religious doctrines, but rather states that her Creator rendered her 'naturally' attracted to women. Lister further explains that having a heteronormative romantic relationship would be unnatural to her; therefore, the premise of her argument is that, since God has created her in this manner, then her love for Walker ought to be 'natural'.[36] However, this discourse was contrary to the Victorian elite society's understanding of gender. According to evolutionist Herbert Spencer, women were less evolved versions of men, making them not only physically weaker but also unable to fulfil their purpose in life without the aid of the superior sex.[37] Nonetheless, this conception of 'natural' affairs continuously repeats itself throughout the narrative due to the lack of normalization of same-gender loving identities and experiences. Consequently, Lister claims that she has not met anyone who is similar to her; however, throughout the *Diaries* we find a plethora of sexual and romantic encounters with women of differing ranks, social classes and nationalities.[38] Lister still considers herself to be a unique social outcast, despite having encountered others who struggled against the same dimensions of Victorian homophobia and aimed to have lives as equally non-conforming as hers.

Walker's internalized homophobia stems from a fear of judgement and discrimination and reflects the outer world's rejection of her love. Similar to some countries' contemporary narratives regarding homosexuality and its criminalization,[39] Walker was unsettled by her relatives' narrative about two men who were hanged for sodomy earlier that year.[40] This can be connected to the emergence of Uranian societies at the beginning of the century. These were communities of queer men who associated their sexual preferences with the Greek god Uranus and threatened the moral and religious foundations of the Victorian state. Consequently, a legal change was enacted to render members of Uranian societies as outcasts as well as pagans and heretics.[41] Since Walker was unaware that this law excluded queer women, her anxiety was heightened by the explicit threat of execution. During a dispute in *Gentleman Jack*'s fifth episode, Lister explains that sexual acts between men, but not between women, are criminalized. We also witness Lister act as a liberated queer woman who attempts to help her partner overcome a perception of herself, instilled by societal prejudice:

> If it were a criminal offence. If it were to become one. Well then. I would have to put my neck in the noose. I love and only love the fairer sex. My heart revolts from any other love than theirs. These feelings have not wavered or deviated since childhood. I was born like this ... You're the same, you told me so, you feel a repugnance towards forming any sort of connection with the opposite sex.[42]

While Walker was frightened by the law's restrictions concerning their relationship, Lister had found alternatives to validate her stance as a queer woman. The amalgamation of homophobia and social pressures of conformity are manifested in Lister's constant need to reaffirm her affairs in the traditional religious manner. Their wedding is one of the most explicit examples of this preoccupation. They perform their own ritual by secretly taking the sacrament in church together, alongside another couple's wedding ceremony. Even though Lister found a way around most of the patriarchal norms and heteronormativity indoctrinated within the parameters of the social order, she was unable to fight every aspect of it. Throughout the narrative, we can trace various instances where the emotional burden of being different and discriminated against had direct implications on her mental health and self-confidence, since it impacted the way she perceived herself and others. While she projected an image of a woman who knows how to govern her reality and that of the people around her, her *Diaries* demonstrate various instances of self-doubt. Her sense of self-efficacy was gravely wounded because of the lack of acceptance brought about by those around her. She states that her aunt was the only person who understood her, while her sister and the people of Halifax echoed variations of judgements that she had to battle against on a daily basis.[43] There are several passages throughout the *Diaries* that signal her awareness of people's perception of her, despite which she chose to follow a way of life that came naturally to her:

> They had seen me walk past on Sunday. I had then my cloth pelisse on & all the people stared at me. M—owned afterwards she had observed it & felt uncomfortable ... She owns this sort of thing makes her feel uncomfortable. Is she ever conscious that she is at all ashamed of me? I could & ought to excuse & forgive it. I do do so, but my proud spirit whispers the consolation that it shall not always be so.[44]

Lister, of course, was not the only person suffering from emotional turmoil due to her unconventionality. Walker experienced recurrent physical manifestations of her frustration, including nightmares, which she describes as people coming to her house and calling her 'impure'; Walker's nightmares and subsequent fears lead her to reconsider her lifestyle and decisions, unlike Lister.[45] From the very beginning of their relationship, Walker's nightmares were a determining agent in her choices regarding Lister's advances. If one were to look at them from a psychodynamic perspective, the argument at hand would claim that Walker's nightmares were a projection of her conscience conflicting with her desires; her nightmares would be considered a mere manifestation of her latent battle against her sexual identity.[46] Lister, on the other hand, speaks of Walker's nightmares as repetitive terrors; the origin of this emotional distress is not clearly deconstructed, and Walker's own interpretation is not given. Yet, her dreams are not the sole representative of Walker's fragile mental health. Another challenging factor is her suicide attempt during her stay at her sister's place in Edinburgh. The graphic scene is evidently portrayed in the series where Walker cuts her wrists facing a mirror while daydreaming of Lister.[47] The fact that the analysis of this event is restricted to Lister's account of Walker's mental state brings about a major hindrance for reaching an objective understanding of Walker's own perception and intentions. It is clear that Walker was frightened of people and their expectations, particularly having in mind her exploitative family. Even when Lister spends her nights with Walker, the reader or viewer never gets to witness Walker as a woman who has her own voice; she is an object of admiration for Lister; therefore, even her sorrows and nightmares are described in a way that would make one question whether Lister ever understood their substance or origin.

Lister's social and financial agency

Lister identified herself as a homosexual woman during an era when her identity was neither acknowledged nor normalized. Although Butler's Foucault-inspired concept of gender as a social construct serves contemporary interpretations of Lister's series, *Gentleman Jack*, it does not necessarily apply to the *Diaries*.[48] The latter were recorded in a setting during which gender was considered to be a subset of biological sex, rather than a natural form of identity expression. However, Lister created her own safe space within that of her family house, Shibden Hall. When throwing a critical glance at Victorian norms of courtship, the reader observes two variations of love that Victorian society would have considered to be mutually exclusive: queer love and love for family. Coming from a predominantly traditional society, Lister manages to balance between the conventional discourse of love for family by taking care of her relatives and maintaining her connection with her family residence. Yet, this does not restrict her from venturing into her romantic love affairs, thus modernizing the traditional understanding of Victorian love in its heteronormative sense, without disregarding the fundamental role of the family. Lister was performing her liberated identity in Shibden Hall, where she could construct her own rules and traditions. Although this upset her patriarchal sister, Lister knew how to govern herself and those around her. For instance, she believed in traditional aspects of marriage such as co-habitation and sacraments. When asking Walker to marry her, Lister mentioned that they would move in together after marriage.

Lister's unconventional interests also found their way into her monetary affairs. The representation of the financial aspect of her life reveals a major discrepancy between the series and the *Diaries*. The book portrays Lister through her own perception of herself; it illustrates that it comes naturally to her to own her business and act accordingly. Sinking her own mine is also considered to be a mundane gateway to earn an income.[49] However, through the series which is historically grounded, the audience is exposed to people's perception of a woman who has dared to take charge of her own income – an act that was rare within her timeframe and her family's class. Looking at it from an anthropological angle, although women of higher classes did travel and explore their surroundings more so than those prior to them by the time of the Industrial Revolution, they lacked direct influence upon familial and estate matters.[50] Victorian women were restricted to being a man's companion, daughter or marriageable relative.[51] However, contrary to the expectations of her family members, Lister was a person who was disregarded as marriageable in the traditional sense of the word; she had also brought it upon herself to look after her family's income and finances. There are two instances that illustrate the responsibility Lister felt towards herself as a breadwinner. First, Lister's plan to sink a mine because of its profitable aspect exemplifies her interests to engage herself in the workforce. The series also illustrates the way she was perceived in public places, fundamentally at the bank, where people explicitly resented her for her economic interests and power, alongside her unusual appearance. Second, there is her understanding of the dynamics of the social workplace; when faced with her inability to find people to work for her, she hires a man as her project manager.

Lister was not the only one who trusted in her efforts and intuition regarding her economic affairs. Walker was also an active contributor to the process of digging the coal mine, especially after offering Lister her requested financial support. Even the setting aesthetics of the final episode of the first season are located near Lister's pit. When the pit gets flooded in the final episode of *Gentleman Jack*'s first series, Walker accepts it and wishes to offer Lister further help. The final scene portrays them proposing to each other near the coal mine, defying the patriarchal understanding of the relationship between love and economic interests.

Conclusion

The peculiar life of Miss Anne Lister was a milestone for feminism in general, and queer love in particular. This chapter has interrogated the various ways in which Lister performed and celebrated her love for the 'fairer sex' in an environment where the notion of love was predominantly governed by societal expectations. However, the radical alterations she bestowed upon the historicization of unconventional women's lives are not bound to the Victorian era; they are to be valued regardless of their timeframe. From claiming ownership over her socioeconomic rights as a businesswoman and landowner, to challenging the heteronormative status quo at the time, Lister was a pioneer who might have had more agency than a plethora of twenty-first-century women. One particular marginalized fraction that could be more oppressed than Lister herself is represented by the women of the Arab world, particularly those who belong to the queer community. Several parallels could be drawn between them and Lister as the protagonist at hand, including being subjected to discriminatory treatment by a patriarchal system that often places them at the periphery. While Lister granted herself the liberty to work, many Arab women are prohibited from doing so by a variety of opposing agents such as their legal male guardians. Similar to Victorian times, the contemporary Arab world often overlooks lesbianism and focuses on sodomy. Yet, various forms of activism have erupted in the Arab world during recent times in order to defend the right to love in a free and diverse manner. Scholars argue that Lister was a Victorian activist who was ahead of her time in terms of defending the legal, religious and sociocultural rights to love without heteronormative and patriarchal restrictions.[52] Anne Lister's love for her eventual wife, Ann Walker, prevailed over the influence of institutionalized patriarchy, heteronormativity and homophobia. It is one that altered the trajectory of a traditional religious marriage into encompassing that of non-conforming individuals in general and lesbian women in particular, thus demanding equal validity for her expression of love. This love is not merely romantic and sexual in the sense that confines it to the parameters of the relationship between the two women. It is also a personal rendition of self-celebratory love of gender expression and socioeconomic liberation. Lister's love could also be translated into her rejection of all that 'unnaturally' shackles a woman, be it an arranged marriage or a title like 'Jack-the-lass'. Lister has brought about an unequivocal comprehension of the stance of Victorian women, raising them from the status of the 'second sex' to that of the admirable 'fairer sex'.

Notes

1 Anne Lister, *I Know My Own Heart, The Secret Diaries of Miss Anne Lister, Vol. I, 1791–1840* (London: Virago, 2010), 16.

2 In this chapter, we interchangeably use the words 'queer', 'gay' and 'lesbian' because of the nature of our primary sources and the fact that they do not include the contemporary jargon of sexuality; Susan Valladares, 'Teaching Guide for: Anne Lister and the Ladies of Llangollen', *Literature Compass* 10, no. 11 (2013): 869–70.

3 Lister, *I Know My Own Heart*, 14.

4 Chris Roulston, 'The Revolting Anne Lister: The U.K.'s First Modern Lesbian', *Journal of Lesbian Studies* 17, nos 3–4 (2013): 272.

5 Robert Smith, 'Unveiling the "Jack-the-Lass" Stereotype', *International Journal of Entrepreneurship and Innovation* 1–3 (2021), https://doi.org/10.1177/14657503211032544.

6 Valladares, 'Teaching Guide', 869–70.

7 For further reading, please refer to Jill Liddington, 'Gender, Authority and Mining in an Industrial Landscape: Anne Lister, 1791–1840', *History Workshop Journal* 42, no. 1 (1996): 59–86.

8 Sonya O. Rose, *Limited Livelihoods: Gender and Class in Nineteenth Century England* (London: Routledge, 1992), 78.

9 Bogdan Popa, *Shame: A Genealogy of Queer Practices in the 19th Century* (Edinburgh: Edinburgh University Press, 2017), 153.

10 Anne Longmuir, 'Anne Lister and Lesbian Desire in Charlotte Brontë's Shirley', *Brontë Studies: Journal of the Brontë Society* 31, no. 2 (2006): 145–55.

11 Laurie Laufer, 'Michel Foucault: The Queer Gender for Psychoanalysis?' *Psychoanalytic Inquiry* 40, no. 8 (2020): 585.

12 Ibid., 585.

13 Lister, *I Know My Own Heart*, 116, journal entry Thursday, 2 December.

14 Judith Butler, *Undoing Gender* (New York: Routledge, 2004), 32.

15 Ibid.

16 Dustin Friedman, *Before Queer Theory: Victorian Aestheticism and the Self* (Baltimore, MD: Johns Hopkins University Press, 2019), 174.

17 Sally Cline, *Radclyffe Hall: A Woman Called John* (New York: Overlook Press, 1998).

18 Chris Roulston, 'Marriage and Its Queer Identifications in the Anne Lister Diaries', in *After Marriage in the Long Eighteenth Century*, ed. Jenny DiPlacidi and Karl Leydecker (Cham: Palgrave Macmillan, 2018), 185.

19 Alexandra Cheira, 'Neo-Victorian Sexual De[f/v]Iance: Incest, Adultery, Breaking the Virginity Taboo and Female Sexual Agency in A. S. Byatt's "Morpho Eugenia"', *Neo-Victorian Studies* 9, no. 2 (2017): 126.

20 Valladares, 'Teaching Guide', 869.

21 *Gentleman Jack*, season 1, episode 8, 'Are You Still Talking?', directed by Sally Wainwright, Sarah Harding and Jennifer Perrott (BBC One and HBO, 2019).

22 Ainsworth wrote to Walker for the first time on 1 November 1832 and kept writing for quite some time. Walker's health kept getting worse, and after a month she had a mental breakdown and went to stay with her sister in Scotland in February 1833. Lister, *I Know My Own Heart*, 176.

23 Lister, *I Know My Own Heart*, 311.

24 *Gentleman Jack*, season 1, episode 3, 'Oh Is That What You Call It?', directed by Sally Wainwright, Sarah Harding and Jennifer Perrott (BBC One and HBO, 2019).

25 See Susan Moller Okin, 'Patriarchy and Married Women's Property in England: Questions on Some Current Views', *Eighteenth-Century Studies* 17, no. 2 (1983): 121–38.

26 See Anne-Bénédicte Damon, 'Anne Lister, "A Sundial in the Shade": A Gifted Woman in the Nineteenth Century', *Women's Studies* 49, no. 2 (2020): 130–48.

27 *Gentleman Jack*, season 1, episode 5, 'Let's Have Another Look at Your Past Perfect', directed by Sally Wainwright, Sarah Harding and Jennifer Perrott (BBC One and HBO, 2019).

28 Roulston, 'Marriage and Its Queer Identifications in the Anne Lister Diaries', 188.

29 Adrienne Cecile Rich, 'Compulsory Heterosexuality and Lesbian Existence (1980)', *Journal of Women's History* 15, no. 3 (2003): 14.

30 Ibid., 37.

31 As cited in Jean Roberta, *Psychopathia Sexualis*, vol. 19 (Boston: The Gay and Lesbian Review Worldwide, 2012).

32 Sarah Richardson, *The Political Worlds of Women: Gender and Politics in Nineteenth Century Britain* (London: Routledge, 2013), 83.

33   Anthony Fletcher, *Female Fortune – Land, Gender and Authority: The Anne Lister Diaries and Other Writings 1833–36* (London: History Today, 1999), 55.

34   Roulston, 'Marriage and Its Queer Identifications in the Anne Lister Diaries', 199.

35   Seth Koven, *Slumming: Sexual and Social Politics in Victorian London* (Princeton, NJ: Princeton University Press, 2004), 39.

36   Lister, *I Know My Own Heart*, 175.

37   Nancy Paxton, *George Eliot and Herbert Spencer: Feminism, Evolutionism, and the Reconstruction of Gender* (Princeton, NJ: Princeton University Press, 2014), 160.

38   Lister, *I Know My Own Heart*, 127, 156, 289.

39   Koven, *Slumming*, 41.

40   Although the exact name of the two men who were murdered remains unknown, if we retrace the historical LGBTQ+ timeline of the nineteenth century, one can easily pinpoint an event that matches the date of the *Diaries* which goes back to the murder of James Pratt and John Smith in 1835. The Pratt–Smith couple were followed and spied upon until they were caught together in a rented room. It was not short after that they were sentenced to death and the person who had rented them the room was exiled to Australia.

41   Veronique Mottier, *Sexuality: A Very Short Introduction* (Oxford: Oxford University Press, 2008), 40.

42   *Gentleman Jack*, season 1, episode 5, 'Let's Have Another Look at Your Past Perfect', directed by Sally Wainwright, Sarah Harding and Jennifer Perrott (BBC One and HBO, 2019).

43   Lister, *I Know My Own Heart*, 15.

44   Ibid., 268, journal entry, Monday, 15 December.

45   *Gentleman Jack*, season 1, episode 6, 'Do Ladies Do That?', directed by Sally Wainwright, Sarah Harding and Jennifer Perrott (BBC One and HBO, 2019).

46   Frederick S. Roden, *Same-Sex Desire in Victorian Religious Culture* (Hampshire: Palgrave Macmillan, 2002), 250.

47   *Gentleman Jack*, season 1, episode 7, 'Why've You Brought That?', directed by Sally Wainwright, Sarah Harding and Jennifer Perrott (BBC One and HBO, 2019).

48   Michelle A. Abate, *Tomboys: A Literary and Cultural History* (Philadelphia, PA: Temple University Press, 2008), xiii.

49   Fletcher, *Female Fortune*, 55.

50   Lana L. Dalley and Jill Rappoport, *Economic Women: Essays on Desire and Dispossession in Nineteenth-Century British Culture* (Columbus: Ohio State University Press, 2013), 220.

51   Ibid.

52   Roulston, 'The Revolting Anne Lister', 276.

Bibliography

Abate, Michelle A. *Tomboys: A Literary and Cultural History*. Philadelphia, PA: Temple University Press, 2008.

Butler, Judith. *Undoing Gender*. New York: Routledge, 2004.

Cheira, Alexandra. 'Neo-Victorian Sexual De[f/v]iance: Incest, Adultery, Breaking the Virginity Taboo and Female Sexual Agency in A. S. Byatt's "Morpho Eugenia"'. *Neo-Victorian Studies* 9, no. 2 (2017): 126–53.

Cline, Sally. *Radclyffe Hall: A Woman Called John*. New York: Overlook Press, 1998.

Dalley, Lana L., and Jill Rappoport. *Economic Women: Essays on Desire and Dispossession in Nineteenth-Century British Culture*. Columbus: Ohio State University Press, 2013.

Damon, Anne-Bénédicte. 'Anne Lister, "A Sundial in the Shade": A Gifted Woman in the Nineteenth Century'. *Women's Studies* 49, no. 2 (2020): 130–48.

Fletcher, Anthony. *Female Fortune – Land, Gender and Authority: The Anne Lister Diaries and Other Writings 1833–36*, vol. 49. London: History Today, 1999.

Friedman, Dustin. *Before Queer Theory: Victorian Aestheticism and the Self*. Baltimore, MD: Johns Hopkins University Press, 2019.

Gentleman Jack, season 1, directed by Sally Wainwright, Sarah Harding and Jennifer Perrott. BBC One and HBO, 2019.

Hamlin, Kimberly A. 'The "Case of a Bearded Woman": Hypertrichosis and the Construction of Gender in the Age of Darwin'. *American Quarterly* 63, no. 4 (2011): 955–81.

Koven, Seth. *Slumming: Sexual and Social Politics in Victorian London*. Princeton, NJ: Princeton University Press, 2004.

Laufer, Laurie. 'Michel Foucault: The Queer Gender for Psychoanalysis?' *Psychoanalytic Inquiry* 40, no. 8 (2020): 579–90.

Liddington, Jill. 'Gender, Authority and Mining in an Industrial Landscape: Anne Lister, 1791–1840'. *History Workshop Journal* 42, no. 1 (1996): 59–86.

Lister, Anne. *I Know My Own Heart, The Secret Diaries of Miss Anne Lister, Vol. I, 1791–1840*. London: Virago, 2010.

Longmuir, Anne. 'Anne Lister and Lesbian Desire in Charlotte Brontë's Shirley'. *Brontë Studies: Journal of the Brontë Society* 31, no. 2 (2006): 145–55.

Mottier, Veronique. *Sexuality: A Very Short Introduction*. Oxford: Oxford University Press, 2008.

Okin, Susan Moller. 'Patriarchy and Married Women's Property in England: Questions on Some Current Views'. *Eighteenth-Century Studies* 17, no. 2 (1983): 121–38.

Orr, Dannielle. '"I Tell Myself to Myself": Homosexual Agency in the Journals of Anne Lister (1791–1840)'. *Women's Writing: The Elizabethan to Victorian Period* 11, no. 2 (2004): 201–22.

Paxton, Nancy L. *George Eliot and Herbert Spencer: Feminism, Evolutionism, and the Reconstruction of Gender*. Princeton, NJ: Princeton University Press, 2014.

Popa, Bogdan. *Shame: A Genealogy of Queer Practices in the 19th Century*. Edinburgh: Edinburgh University Press, 2017.

Rich, Adrienne Cecile. 'Compulsory Heterosexuality and Lesbian Existence (1980)'. *Journal of Women's History* 15, no. 3 (2003): 11–48.

Richardson, Sarah. *The Political Worlds of Women: Gender and Politics in Nineteenth Century Britain*. London: Routledge, 2013.

Roberta, Jean. *Psychopathia Sexualis*, vol. 19. Boston: The Gay & Lesbian Review Worldwide, 2012.

Roden, Frederick S. *Same-Sex Desire in Victorian Religious Culture*. Hampshire: Palgrave Macmillan, 2002.

Rose, Sonya O. *Limited Livelihoods: Gender and Class in Nineteenth Century England*. London: Routledge, 1992.

Roulston, Chris. 'The Revolting Anne Lister: The U.K.'s First Modern Lesbian'. *Journal of Lesbian Studies* 17, nos 3–4 (2013): 267–78.

Roulston, Chris. 'Marriage and Its Queer Identifications in the Anne Lister Diaries'. In *After Marriage in the Long Eighteenth Century*, edited by Jenny DiPlacidi and Karl Leydecker, 181–203. Cham: Palgrave Macmillan, 2018.

Valladares, Susan. 'Teaching Guide for: Anne Lister and the Ladies of Llangollen'. *Literature Compass* 10, no. 11 (2013): 869–70.

3

The lover and the tribe

Ian Davidson

Concepts of love

In her poem 'The Poetry Deal' from what became her final collection published in her lifetime, the poet Diane di Prima addresses a personified 'poetry' who is a kind of lover:

> You mostly aren't jealous – have taken yr place
> alongside gardens, bread-making, children, printing presses
> But when yr eyes shoot sparks & you say
> 'Choose between me & it' – 'it' has always gone
> Except when 'it' was my kids
> I took that risk
> & we worked it out somehow.[1]

For di Prima 'love' was manifest in her relationship with the abstraction of poetry, in her maternal role and as a distributor of poetry through 'printing presses'. She demonstrated over her long life – as a poet, editor, publisher, memoirist, activist and teacher – a love of community and its potential. Her book-length poem, *Revolutionary Letters*, mainly written in the 1960s during her involvement with the Diggers in San Francisco, describes an alternative radical history and sets out a blueprint for the practical everyday activities required to initiate and sustain political and social change.[2] It is, in effect, a love letter to revolutionaries of the past and the future.

Di Prima's 'The Poetry Deal' aptly summarizes, in aesthetic form, the concept of love that guides this essay. It is composed of three elements: (i) the rational selfishness of passionate love and its desire for beauty and goodness, (ii) an irrational, incomprehensible, spontaneous and unmotivated religious love and (iii) the love of family, friends and community. The writers and texts that I examine in this essay present positions in which these different aspects of love can coexist cooperatively, but can also clash in contradictory and challenging ways, causing discord and friction as well as harmony. Love, I will be demonstrating, can be that which holds people and communities together, but can also be that which tears them apart and, finally, can bring about revolutionary conditions that produce new and different ways of living.

In order to develop a concept of love, I also draw on Alain Badiou's notion that love is a condition in which the two subject positions involved do not become 'one' but constitute 'two presentative positions'.[3] These two positions are, according to Badiou, 'totally disjunct' and 'do not divide experience between them' (183). As a consequence 'there is no third position' that transcends the subjects of love (183). The lovers do not, as Christian marriage states, form a union of a single couple to become a 'one', but remain a 'scene of the two' (188). The one and the two of that relationship, rather than being a finitude that completes itself, construct a sequence that leads to infinity. As Badiou says in *In Praise of Love*:

> Love isn't simply about two people meeting and their inward looking relationship: it is a construction, a life that is made, no longer from the perspective of the One but from the perspective of Two.[4]

More technically, he explains in 'What Is Love' that 'the Two fractures the One and meets with the infinity of the situation. Such is the numericity of the amorous procedure: One, Two, Infinity'.[5] Love is not, therefore, something that becomes exclusive, but a condition that remains open to possibilities, including love for a broader community. Badiou is challenging, in the familiar terminology of sociology, the 'nuclear' family and its role in society and the teachings of a Christian church that has the 'wedding' at its heart.

Along with art politics and science, love, for Badiou, is one of the conditions that constitutes a possible 'truth procedure' that can lead to radical social and political change. In Badiou's terms, therefore, love is an event that cannot be contained as a steady state (or by the State) within a set or situation. In the short book *In Praise of Love*, Badiou explains that the experience of love, if not universal, can still be true in more than the context in which it arises, and 'love encompasses the experience of the possible transition from the pure randomness of chance to a state that has universal value'.[6] The consequence, apart from the (for capitalism) radical possibility that people can act outside of their self-interest, is that love is 'an individual experience of potential universality'.[7] My argument, and that of

Badiou, is that love is a particularly important example of an experience of 'being' that combines both immanence and the desire for transcendence and an experience that can lead to social change.

The poems that I read in this essay present events that, in Badiou's terms, could lead to a kind of truth procedure that has revolutionary potential through a historical shift in our understanding and practices of human loving relationships. It is a shift in which these writers have played a part – and particularly in the way their writing about love combines – often without apparent discrimination, sexual and non-sexual love between individual partners, families and the love of the 'tribe'.

The literary context

The writers whose work I will examine in some detail – Kay Johnson, Lenore Kandel and Diane di Prima – were all part of the 'Beat' movement, a highly visible and historically durable counterculture that emphasized a non-conformity to the norms of America in the 1950s. Although short-lived in the 1950s and 1960s, it attracted critical interest and continuing commercial success initially through the work of writers such as Jack Kerouac, Allen Ginsberg, William Burroughs and Gregory Corso. It is no coincidence that these are all men. The Beat movement was, as Corso somewhat reductively put it in the film *What Happened to Kerouac*, 'hard on women'.[8] As well as being subjects who sought freedom from social restrictions through counterculture lifestyles, women who became involved with the circle of Beat writers were also often the objects through which men sought their own liberation. This objectification of women – as sex objects, muses, mothers or carers, and all or some of those things in combination – often went hand in hand with an absence of published writing by them.

There is considerable evidence, however, that despite this absence of published writing, figures such as Joan Vollmer Adams (who married William Burroughs and was shot and killed by him) were highly influential in the intellectual development of the group.[9] Her apartment provided the meeting place for Burroughs, Allan Ginsberg, Jack Kerouac, Herbert Huncke and others and introduced them to a range of European literature and philosophy. Others, such as Jack Kerouac's second wife, Joan Haverty Kerouac, wrote a memoir that was not published until after her death. Jan Kerouac, her daughter with Jack Kerouac, although he never acknowledged her paternity, published two autobiographical novels, which until recently were rarely seen as more than incidental.

Women writers associated with the Beats have, however, been the subject of much scholarship in the first two decades of the twenty-first century.[10] This has created a greatly expanded and more diverse literary history of the Beats that takes into account the contributions of women writers and writers of colour. Lenore Kandel's *Collected Poems* have been posthumously published, while Bonnie Bremser's *Troia* is republished and given critical consideration as an important Beat novel. Bob Kaufman, previously categorized as a 'street poet', is acknowledged as a founder member of the Beats through his work editing the journal *Beatitude* with Allan Ginsberg, and his *Collected Poems* are published. This essay is part of that work, drawing on poets such as Kandel and Kay Johnson not only as previously neglected Beat writers, unjustly overlooked, but as poets in their own right who made a significant contribution to poetry and culture in mid-twentieth-century America.

The poets

Love, for Kay Johnson, Lenore Kandel and Diane di Prima, included the romantic sexual and non-sexual love for a partner, religious love for a god and the love for a wider community, however constituted. For Johnson, love could be proximate and physical but non-sexual. For Kandel and di Prima, the broader notion of love for the 'tribe' was informed by political, ecological and ethical considerations. Despite the scandal and outrage caused by expressions of female sexuality in publications such as di Prima's *Memoirs of a Beatnik* and Kandel's *The Love Book*, it was this more dispersed notion of love that presented the most significant challenge to the social order. It first found its expression for di Prima in the bohemian life she led in New York in the late 1950s and early 1960s and which she describes in *Dinners and Nightmares* and *Memoirs of a Beatnik* and then later in *Revolutionary Letters* following her move to San Francisco and her work with the Diggers. For Kandel, love for the tribe was expressed through her own contributions to Digger activity as an organizer, a poet and a lover.

There are, however, few descriptions of supportive or close relationships between women that express the kind of sisterhood that later writers and successive waves of feminism would aspire to. They often say the opposite. Kandel says, 'I knew the Beat men a lot better, was better friends with them. They took my poetry seriously.'[11] Di Prima famously visited Ezra Pound (described in *Recollections of My Life as a Woman*) and was friendly with William Burroughs. When asked about the experience of being a woman beat writer, she says:

> I didn't think of myself as a girl or a boy. I don't know what the guys were thinking about when I would sometimes answer the door and with almost nothing on. Joel Oppenheimer wrote a whole story about it. He was very upset but that was his problem, not mine.

> If you read the beginning of *Recollections of My Life as a Woman*, you find that I learned very early from my grandmother that men were

decorative. They weren't important in the world, because they didn't deal with the daily business of life. You know, it was nice to have one around, but they came and went and did their thing and you did yours.[12]

Kay Johnson met William Burroughs in the Beat Hotel and says: 'He doesn't like women; well, I don't blame him – so i told him i was Henry Miller … – well the next time we met he said "HELLO MILLER" … and we shook hands warmly'.[13]

This doesn't mean friendships between women didn't happen, and di Prima has spoken of her close relationship with Audre Lord in New York and with Lenore Kandel in San Francisco.[14] But it does mean that to retrospectively ascribe notions of feminist collectivity to them would misinterpret the context in which they were living and working.

Kay Johnson

Poet and painter Kay Johnson, also known as Kaja, is ambivalent about sexual encounters. She writes in her essay 'Proximity' of her desire for an intimacy, for love, without 'SIN, FORNICATION, OR ADULTERY'.[15] She says in the essay:

> But what in the hell do people think Friendship is, if it is not love, if it is not the whole love, the complete love, the completely being in love, complete as with a lover.[16]

The soul, she goes on to say, does not want sex, but proximity (80). The subtext to the piece is that the proximity she desires can rarely be achieved without sexual demands. She compares love between humans with the bond between humans and animals, and we know from the very limited biographical information that exists on Johnson that she owned three dogs when living in the French Quarter in New Orleans before moving to Paris.[17] We also know from accounts on the 'Empty Mirror' and 'Women of the Beat' websites that Johnson had an unrequited passion for Gregory Corso and stayed in his room in the 'Beat Hotel' in Paris after he had vacated it, and lived at the hotel until it closed in 1963.[18] They never met or, by some accounts, did so only briefly, but did correspond by mail. Her poem titled 'Experience of 7 Consecutive Hours' in a sequence of two entitled a 'Poem from Paris',[19] is a poem to Corso in many ways, which she reports others liking but not Corso himself.[20]

The poem's opening stanzas have something of Frank O'Hara's *Lunch Poems* in the material and tone, although the repeated questions (the second stanza begins 'What if your flowers freeze in their stall?'[21]) and direct address to the reader are also reminiscent of Corso's 'Marriage'.

Paris! My feet are cold and I feel better
An hour in Paris with Verlaine
In Greece another hour with Gregory Corso
On the Rue de Seine

...

Paris, I love you again. (84)

As it progresses, however, over its eleven stanzas and almost seventy lines, it becomes increasingly about the narrator's introspection and their struggle to sustain their self-image. The form of the poem, and the confidence of the voice at the start, can only resurrect itself in a kind of mock defiance after an Alice in Wonderland episode in which pills make her larger. Read historically and autobiographically, her loss of confidence could be a consequence of her obsession with Corso, who appears twice in the poem, but also a response to her time in Paris. Rather than enjoying the warm company of poets and artists, she finds herself perpetually cold, still carrying 'the old river in me' (84), which is now as 'rusty as the Seine'. It is only in the final stanza that she rediscovers herself and can say, 'I'm on the level with lovers, happy / I'm not ashamed to look in their faces'.[22]

Kay Johnson also corresponded with Charles Bukowski, who she never met. Their epistolary relationship is commemorated in two poems by Bukowski: 'Letter from Too Far'[23] and 'An Almost Made Up Poem'.[24] 'Letter from Too Far' constructs Johnson as a romantic figure who gets up at '5 o'clock in the morning' to write poems and paint, but also has a 'special bench' by the river for crying.[25] It is the conclusion of the poem that provides a clue as to its motivation and Johnson's role as muse.

I put her photo by the radio
near the fan
and it moved
like something
alive.
I sat and watched it until I had smoked the last 5 or 6 cigarettes left.
Then I got up and went to bed.[26]

Johnson becomes visualized as an object of love through the photograph and, through the action of the fan, Bukowski can fantasize that she becomes alive. He counterpoises the movement of air of the fan, a process like God breathing life into Eve, with his own breathing as he smokes cigarettes, an act of self-harm. He not only constructs her as a lonely figure in Paris (an image she promoted of herself) and as a single available woman with many lovers, but also constructs himself as a lonely, romanticized figure consumed by longing.

The second poem, titled 'An Almost Made Up Poem', was published in 1977 in the collection *Love Is a Dog from Hell*. It is a poem from the memory of previous events, but almost certainly about Johnson. In the poem, he visualizes her 'drinking at a fountain ... in France', an imagined memory as he never visited her there. The poem ends on a report of her suicide: 'A friend wrote me of your suicide / 3 or 4 months after it happened.'[27]

There is little certain information about Johnson after she left the Beat Hotel, although she was reported alive in the 1980s and 1990s by contributions on the Empty Mirror website, so the suicide is either a construction of Bukowski's or a piece of misinformation he is passing on. Having brought her to life in the first poem, he now brings about her death. In the same year as this poem was published, Kay Johnson did write a kind of response to Bukowski, unpublished until it appeared in the pamphlet *Kaja*, published by Perdido Press in an edition of 150 probably in 1998.[28] *Kaja* is a handmade pamphlet or artist's book that contains two poems written about the time of her stay at the Beat Hotel between 1961 and 1965. It also contains a final poem listed as 'from the collection of Gypsy Lou Webb (co-owner of Loujon Press) and entitled "DEAD CAT*POEM FOR BUKOWSKI" and dated "GOOD SUNDAY March 12 1967"'. It is labelled 'FIRST DRAFT: ONLY COPY IN EXISTENCE'. Written in upper case, after an initial invocation of 'HEY BUKOWSKI', it is addressed to 'KAJA'. Apparently in the voice of Bukowski, it explains that he 'STOPPED WRITING TO YOU IN PARIS' because 'THAT SELF*CRUCIFIXION OF YOURS / WAS TOO MUCH SUFFERING FOR ONE PERSON ALONE TO BEAR'. Having freed himself from the suffering of Johnson, Bukowski, the poem goes on to explain, now suffers for his dead cats. Johnson's somewhat parodic poem is suggesting that Bukowski simply transfers his emotional attachment from her to his cat. It's a strange unfinished piece, but does perhaps provide a stark illustration that romantic love is, as Badiou says, from 'two presentative positions'. After a brief consideration of the suffering of Christ as a unifying factor who 'DID IT ONCE FOR EVERYBODY', the two, in this case, make no more profound a third position than a dead cat. The argument of the poem then turns back on itself. In a parody of Bukowski's previous poems giving Johnson permission to take her French lovers, she is now given permission to suffer and, by extension, inflict suffering on him.

Kay Johnson is a mysterious figure. I cannot, for example, definitely link her to the pulp erotic novels *Corrupt* (1966) or *Her Raging Needs* (1964), both of which are listed in the British Library Catalogue next to *Human Songs*. That there is, by rumour, a chest full of writing by 'Kaja' lost somewhere on her many travels only adds to the sense that there remain untold stories about her life and work. Johnson, unlike Kandel, the next poet I will look at, never found her tribe but remained an isolated figure. Rather than 'love' resulting in an open sequence to infinity, it became an empty room, within which Johnson only ever heard the sound of her own voice returning.

Lenore Kandel

For many years, Lenore Kandel was probably best known in the popular literary imagination as the model for the character of Romana Swartz, the girlfriend of the character Dave Wain in Jack Kerouac's *Big Sur*.[29] She is described by Kerouac variously as a 'big Rumanian monster beauty', who drives men crazy with desire by walking about the house simultaneously naked and wearing underwear and who is like a 'sex slave' and an intellectual who writes poetry and knows Zen. She really, however, according to the narrator of the novel, only wants to 'marry a hardy man and live on a farm'.[30] Kerouac's gaze is highly reductive (despite its contradictions), and Kandel was to write poetry throughout her life as well as engage as an activist with the Diggers. The public notoriety of her early years as a poet was increased by her appearance at various high-profile concerts, including the 'Human Be In' and 'The Last Waltz'. Published interviews with men and women who were involved with the Diggers provide evidence that Kandel was very clearly held in high regard at the time.[31] The Diggers' origins as a theatre group meant that the arts were central to its activities rather than in the service of the political and social revolution they proposed. Performance of poetry and drama was not a re-enactment or representation, but was the thing itself. In an anti-commodification move, presentation and representation were the same process.

The Diggers were active in Haight Ashbury in San Francisco from 1966 to 1968. Along with other literary figures such as Richard Brautigan and Lawrence Ferlinghetti, Kandel became involved and played a key role as both organizer and performer in events including the legendary 'Invisible Circus Event' at Glide Church, a three-day 'happening' that was party and performance. There is other evidence of the importance of her role. In an interview with Jay Babcock, Peter Berg describes women holding up a poem by Kandel during a Digger event and reciting it from the rooftops.[32] Vicki Pollack, who was later to carry out the work of gathering together Kandel's work for her posthumously published *Collected Poems* (2012), describes the transformative experience of hearing Kandel read, before becoming better acquainted years later as she helped Kandel with practical duties such as shopping and medical appointments. Phyllis Willner on the same website talks about Kandel as part of a group of poets, including Gregory Corso, Kirby Doyle and Michael McLure, and says:

> I don't remember if it was after I met them – yeah, it was after I met them that Julie gave me Lenore's poetry. I hadn't read it yet. *Word Alchemy*. And when I read it, I was just magnetized. I thought she was the greatest poet I'd ever read. It was better than Bob Dylan. [laughs] It was in the same ballpark. Nobody's better. It was in the same ballpark.

She was brilliant. She spoke my thoughts, and that's what poetry does. It's abbreviated language that says what you would like to say, for you.

Kandel was not only an important poetic figure to her fellow Diggers, and particularly the women, but also part of a literary scene that featured writers who were to go on to develop major reputations, such as Richard Brautigan and Michael McClure. That she failed to capitalize on her early success was almost certainly a result of her injury in a motorcycle accident in 1970 on a bike with Kandel's husband, Bill Fritsch, a charismatic figure on the arts scene and a member of the Diggers who became a Hell's Angel. In her lifetime, Kandel was only to publish one full-length collection, *Word Alchemy*, with Grove Press in 1967. Her injuries were to force her to effectively withdraw from most public appearances and reportedly caused pain all her life.[33]

While Kandel's recently published *Collected Poems* (2012) make available a large number of unpublished poems, in the 1960s she was best known for *The Love Book*, an eight-page pamphlet first published by Stolen Paper Editions in 1966 and then banned from 1967 until 1974. *The Love Book* was not republished until 2003 in a facsimile edition by Superstition Street Press. The cover is 'a detail from a Tibetan scroll depicting the Adi Buddha (The Root Buddha) and his Shakti, a form of divine cosmic feminine energy, symbolizing the union of the male-female principle in the universe'.[34] In the introduction to *Word Alchemy*, published a year later in 1967, Kandel describes *The Love Book* as 'two poems of mine, published as a small book, [that] deal with physical love and the invocation, recognition and acceptance of the divinity in man through the medium of physical love. In other words it feels good. It feels so good you can step outside your private ego and share the grace of the universe.'[35] For Kandel, physical love and poetry transcend the material or fleshly nature of the immanent material world, taking the participants outside of themselves. Poetry, Kandel says, provides 'bursts of perception, lines into infinity' (xix). She brings together two of Alain Badiou's potential 'truth procedures': the art of poetry and love. The poet, she says, must be true to their vision and 'tell the truth as he sees it' (xix).

The Love Book also contains poetry that is often awkward, where the desire to express the ecstasy of sex results in language that loses the music it aspires to and gestures towards a unity of the lovers that is hard to fit into the broader concept of love developed earlier in this essay. In the first poem, 'GOD/LOVE POEM', the descriptions of sex are probably the least successful, while those sections where the poem slips into a more abstract description of love achieve a more powerful coincidence of form and meaning. The first page ends with

there was a time when gods were purer
/ I can recall nights among the honeysuckle

The poem ends similarly with

> your face above me
>   is the face of all the gods.[36]

The aim of love is to transcend the singularity of human form and lose your 'self' in a union with the other that is sacred, to give your own body over to that moment. The love, therefore, is driven by a theological desire to produce god and to become like a single godhead. The poetry, despite its apparent non-conformity and its Buddhist context, is finally describing a love that produces a relationship that mirrors the unity of a Christian marriage, where two become one. That this only happens during the ecstasy of a sexual passion that can exist outside of marriage doesn't detract from the loss of self that occurs in that moment. *The Love Book*, despite its reputation for the transgression of social norms, is also promoting the productions of love as the production of one from two. I am trying to argue, following Badiou, for a love that sustains the multiplicity of the two, not their merger.

If I find Kandel's descriptions of physical love unconvincing, then her descriptions of her friendship group and community are more developed and challenging to social conventions and often bound up with the concept of the 'Angel'. While an Angel is commonly understood as an intermediary between heaven and earth and capable of transcending the confusions of everyday life, for Kandel an 'Angel' is also a Hell's Angel, a figure that brings hell on earth and a member of a motorcyclist group. The Hell's Angels were an important part of the activities around Haight Ashbury, although the relationship between an arts-based counterculture and the motorcycle gangs never really recovered after the debacle at Altamont.[37]

'Angels' form complex figures in her work and combine outlaw figures, victims and drug users; wild and free spirits with the potential to fly, existing between material form and spirit. In her poem 'First They Slaughtered the Angels',[38] the Angels are killed by a 'they', the other of mainstream culture, who are witnessed 'opening their throats with icy knives'. This murder, which spills the 'immortal blood' of the Angels, is witnessed from 'underground', a term that refers to the underground of the counterculture and the 'gravestone and crypts' of the gothic landscape that Kandel depicts. Her love for the Angels, who are consumed and despoiled by 'they' in a process that produces a nightmare universe of iron, steel and weaponry, emerges not as a maternal instinct but as an anger that will ensure that by the end of the poem 'THEY WILL MURDER NO MORE ANGELS! / not even us'. The identification of those who are witnesses with those who act produces a revolutionary moment where, united by love, they walk through the streets with 'lean and empty hands upraised' and with blood that will 'melt iron'. It is a poem in which love and community become intertangled.

The 'we' of the poem finally become identified with the love of Christ, a love that expects nothing and asks for nothing and has no reason, and are 'rolling away the stones' and have 'caulked the holes in our arms with dust and flung libations at each other's feet'. By the end of the poem, the 'we' who have been witnessing, protecting and avenging the angels have become angels themselves.

From Kandel to di Prima

Kandel's poem finds coincidences in Diane di Prima's 'Revolutionary Letter #82'.[39] It is an unusual poem in *Revolutionary Letters*, many of which were written as a kind of agitprop and designed to be read in political demonstrations or public Digger events. They are poems characterized by prosaic language, by lists and by the use of the chant. #82 is however more formally inventive. Composed by the eye and the page as much as by the ear, it has a shifting left-hand margin, a very particular distribution of the words on the page and content that ranges from armed revolutionary struggle to ecology. The address, a public rhetoric in much of *Revolutionary Letters*, is similarly more abstracted in #82. There is no call to action, or even a direct call to arms, and the pedagogy of #3 that tells you directly to 'store water' is changed to a less directed form. The poem begins:

> sticks of dynamite   wrapped
>   in   baby
> blankets
> baby
> blue
> like their eyes. (120)

It is a poem about the feminine strategy of the revolutionary mother, to use her baby's blankets to conceal explosive in a bringing together of familial love and the disinterested love of community. There are images that are similar to Kandel's poem. Where di Prima's babies' eyes are 'spewing / fire' from 'shot / guns', the babies in Kandel's poem are holding 'bayonets'. In Kandel's poem, the 'penises of men are become blue steel machine guns' that 'spread death as an organism', and di Prima says, 'I avenge / myself / violated / spitted / on ancient / rotted cocks'.

This is probably di Prima's most radical feminist poem of *Revolutionary Letters* and a work that rages against the deadening potential of a conformist society that seeks to control behaviour. The response might seem extreme, and even the more optimistic ending might only be able to conclude with the ambivalence of 'rivers / of blood', and its anger is palpable. There are crucial differences apart from the more formal complexity of di Prima's poem.

While Kandel's work is located in community and uses the plural pronoun 'we' throughout, di Prima's is more personal. This leaner and more pointed focus on individual experience rather than the more dispersed perspective of Kandel's poem is no less hard-hitting.

If, as Badiou says, love is the presentation of two positions that never become one, then he is describing di Prima's early poems where she recounts her various relationships with lovers, family and friends, but remains resolutely herself as do her lovers. In the section of the *Dinners and Nightmares* titled 'More or Less Love Poems', the narrator maintains a distance that also always controls the language and, in poem 21, says:

> you are not quite
> the air I breathe
> thank god.
> so go.[40]

Similarly, in *Recollections of My Life as a Woman*, on getting her first apartment she says, 'I had come into my own in a way, had found a large extended family, many loves'[41] and, when describing the various permanent and temporary inhabitants, says, 'We all seemed to share beds as needed, with or without sex or sexual overtones' (129). Following this communal living, loving and shared experience, di Prima left New York to go to San Francisco and join the Diggers. Love, as Badiou says, can lead to change outside the normal processes and to revolution, and this shift from east to west was to prove the case for di Prima.

Like di Prima's much anthologized and probably best-known poem 'Songs for Babio Unborn',[42] she is expressing a love that is no less fierce for being maternal. The combination of love for children and for her 'tribe' and community is one that spans her life's work. In what became her last book, *The Poetry Deal*, the poem of the title is still analysing the relationship between poetry, children and tribe. This range is perhaps di Prima's most important contribution to any conversation about love and poetry. She not only expanded the range of ways that female sexuality could be expressed, but also did it in the context of being a mother. She also, and very importantly, lived and worked within a context where communities were exploring new ways of living together and forming social and political structures and systems both in her bohemian life in New York and the Digger community of San Francisco. And all of this was carried out as a practising Buddhist. As the quotations from 'Avenging Angel' above show, di Prima's love was a tough love, but it was extensive. And di Prima's love never existed outside of that need to balance the competing concerns of everyday life, an everyday life that was not only her own but also that of her children and her community. Her love was never something that could set material concerns aside, and the communal living conditions she describes in *Recollections of My Life as a Woman* often involve considerable hardship.

Beyond rational love

These writers were testing the boundaries of possible human relationships and notions of love. They were also, and importantly, engaging in living conditions outside the homes of family and marriage that might have made them vulnerable to exploitation, but also made them able to construct varieties of loving associations. These vary from the platonic to the sexual, and from the individual and personal to the communal and social. It is in this combination that friends can become lovers and vice versa, that love for the community is both religious and political, that these writers challenge notions of love that end with the merging of two figures into one as they drive off into the sunset. The lover and the loved are ones amongst others, a one and then a two that can lead to infinity, not uniquely separated. Friendship and love become difficult to tell apart. Love for children and the practical role of caring for family and others becomes part of a relationship with friends and the community, not a form of division.

Notes

1   Diane di Prima, *The Poetry Deal* (San Francisco, CA: City Lights, 2014), 20.

2   Diane di Prima, *Revolutionary Letters* (San Francisco, CA: Last Gasp, 2007).

3   Alain Badiou, *Conditions*, trans. Steven Corcoran (London: Continuum, 2008), 183.

4   Alain Badiou, *In Praise of Love* (London: Serpent's Tail, 2012), 29.

5   Badiou, *Conditions*, 189.

6   Badiou, *In Praise of Love*, 16.

7   Ibid., 17.

8   *What Happened to Kerouac*, dir. Richard Lerner and Lewis McAdams, 1986.

9   See Edie Parker Kerouac, *You'll Be Okay: My Life with Jack Kerouac* (San Francisco, CA: City Lights, 2007), 95 and 121, and Brenda Knight, *Women of the Beat Generation* (Berkeley, CA: Conari Press, 1996), 49.

10 As well as the anthologies by Knight and Peabody referenced in this essay, such work includes *The Portable Beat Reader*, edited by Ann Charters (London: Penguin, 1992), the first anthology to include a broad range of writers such as Brenda Bremser, Hettie Jones, Jan Kerouac and Diane di Prima alongside more established 'Beat' writers. Ronna C. Johnson and Nancy M. Grace produced two books – *Girls Who Wore Black* (Rutgers University Press, 2002), an edited collection of essays on figures as diverse as Janine Pommy

Vega and Elise Cowen, and *Breaking the Rule of Cool* (University Press of Mississippi, 2004) that featured interviews with Bonnie Frazer, ruth weiss and others. The work of Beat scholar A. Robert Lee has also been exemplary in including those excluded from mainstream Beat narratives through race and gender. Important publications by Lee include *The Beat Generation Writers* (Pluto Press, 1996), *Modern American Counter Writing* (Routledge, 2010) and *The Beats: Authorship, Legacies* (Edinburgh University Press, 2019). The recent *Cambridge Companion to the Beats*, edited by Steven Belletto (2017), aims for a similar inclusivity.

11 Knight, *Women of the Beat Generation*, 280.

12 Hilton Obenzinger, '"Between the Lines": A Conversation with Diane di Prima', *LA Review of Books*. https://lareviewofbooks.org/article/between-the-lines-a-conversation-with-diane-di-prima/. Accessed 10 December 2021.

13 Leo J. Weddle, 'The Lujon Press: An Historical Analysis' (PhD diss., University of Tennessee, 2003), 153.

14 Diane di Prima, *Recollections of My Life as a Woman* (London: Penguin, 2002b); Lenore Kandel, *Collected Poems of Lenore Kandel* (Berkeley, CA: North Atlantic Books, 2012).

15 Included in *a different beat* and first published in the *Journal for the Protection of All Beings* (1961).

16 Kay Johnson, 'Proximity', in *a different beat*, ed. Richard Peabody (London: Serpents Tail, 1997), 80–7.

17 Weddle, 'The Lujon Press', 149.

18 https://www.emptymirrorbooks.com/beat/kaja and https://web.archive.org/web/20070213214307/http://www.womenofthebeat.org/KayJohnson/KayJohnson.htm.

19 Johnson, 'Proximity', 84–5.

20 Weddle, 'The Lujon Press', 152. Despite Johnson's assertion that Corso didn't care for her work, the introduction to the pamphlet *Kaja* credits Corso with recommending Johnson to Ferlinghetti and thereby bringing about the publication of *Human Songs*. The only copy I have of the poem is in *a different beat*, Richard Peabody's anthology of 'writings by women of the beat generation' (1997). The notes at the back of the anthology say that 'every effort has been made to locate Kay Johnson ... but her whereabouts are unknown' (2340). It goes on to say that 'the poems' are reprinted from *Human Songs* (Johnson's only poetry collection) 'with permission of City Lights' (2340). The copy of *Human Songs* in my own collection, however, has neither part of the 'Poem from Paris' in it. A search across other copies held in libraries suggests there are no variants, meaning that the poems in *a different beat* were never part of *Human Songs,* and I have no record of where, if ever, they were originally published.

21 Johnson, 'Proximity', 84.

22 Ibid., 85.

23 Charles Bukowski, *Crucifix in a Deathhand* (New Orleans, LA: Loujon Press, 1965), 80.

24 Ibid.; Charles Bukowski, *Love Is a Dog from Hell* (Los Angeles, CA: Black Sparrow, 1977), 47.

25 An article and photograph from the Duffy Archive puts her in the Beat Hotel in Paris in 1962, and in a brief interview, she characterizes her art as a 'revolt and a lament'. https://www.duffyarchive.com/portfolio/kay-kaja-johnson-at-the-beat-hotel-1962/.

26 Bukowski, *Crucifix in a Deathhand*, 80.

27 Bukowski, *Love Is a Dog from Hell*, 47.

28 See http://neworleansglassworks.com/commissions/.

29 Dave Wain is based on the poet Lew Welch. He apparently committed suicide after walking out of Gary Snyder's cabin in 1971 carrying a pistol. His body was never found.

30 Jack Kerouac, *Big Sur* (London: Flamingo, 1993), 61–2.

31 See https://diggersdocs.home.blog/.

32 At https://diggersdocs.home.blog/tag/hells-angels/.

33 https://diggersdocs.home.blog/2018/12/30/for-the-duration-of-our-paralel-flow-an-epic-interview-with-phyllis-willner-of-the-san-francisco-diggers/.

34 Lenore Kandel, *The Love Book* (San Francisco, CA: Superstition Street Press, 2003), frontispiece.

35 Lenore Kandel, *Collected Poems of Lenore Kandel* (Berkeley, CA: North Atlantic Books, 2012), xvii.

36 Kandel, *The Love Book*, n.p.

37 Altamont was a free rock concert, billed as the Woodstock of the West Coast, where the Hells Angels were hired to provide security, but ended up stabbing and killing a member of the audience, fulfilling their destiny of creating hell on earth. There is a suggestion by some accounts that the Diggers, and particularly Emmet Grogan, were instrumental in brokering the deal that made the Hells Angels security guards, and that the resident Digger band the Grateful Dead – who pulled out of playing Altamont at the last minute because of the 'bad vibes' – were also a connection between the concert organizers and the Hells Angels. Lenore Kandel's connection was closer and more personal, and her boyfriend and husband Bill Fritsch was to formally join a chapter. There are other anecdotal reports of women involved with the Diggers forming relationships with Hells Angels.

38 Kandel, *Collected Poems of Lenore Kandel*, 28–31.

39 di Prima, *Revolutionary Letters*, 120–5.

40 Diane di Prima, *Dinners and Nightmares* (San Francisco, CA: Last Gasp, 2003), 115.

41 di Prima, *Recollections of My Life as a Woman*, 126.

42 di Prima, *Dinners and Nightmares*, 127.

Bibliography

Badiou, Alain. *Conditions* (trans. Steven Corcoran). London: Continuum, 2008.

Badiou, Alan with Nicolas Truong. *In Praise of Love*. London: Serpent's Tail, 2012.

Bremser, Bonnie. *For Love of Ray*. London: Universal Tandem, 1972 (also published as *Troia: Mexican Memoirs*. New York: Croton Press, 1969; Funks Grove, IL: Dalkey Archive, 2008).

Bukowski, Charles. *Crucifix in a Deathhand*. New Orleans, LA: Loujon Press, 1965.

Bukowski, Charles. *Love Is a Dog from Hell*. Los Angeles, CA: Black Sparrow, 1977.

Burroughs, William. *Junky*. London: Penguin, 1977.

Burroughs, William. *Queer*. London: Picador, 1986.

Cassady, Neil. *The First Third*. San Francisco, CA: City Lights, 1974.

di Prima, Diane. *Memoirs of a Beatnik*. London: Marion Boyars, 2002a.

di Prima, Diane. *Recollections of My Life as a Woman*. London: Penguin, 2002b.

di Prima, Diane. *Dinners and Nightmares*. San Francisco, CA: Last Gasp, 2003.

di Prima, Diane. *Revolutionary Letters*. San Francisco, CA: Last Gasp, 2007.

di Prima, Diane. *The Poetry Deal*. San Francisco, CA: City Lights, 2014.

Haverty Kerouac, Joan. *Nobody's Wife*. Berkeley, CA: Creative Arts, 1990.

Johnson, Kay. *Human Songs*. San Francisco, CA: City Lights Books, 1964.

Johnson, Kay. 'Proximity' and 'Poems from Paris'. In *A Different Beat*, edited by Richard Peabody, 80–7. London: Serpent's Tail, 1997.

Johnson, Kay. *Kaja*. New Orleans, LA: Perdito Press, n.d.

Kandel, Lenore. *The Love Book*. San Francisco, CA: Superstition Street Press, 2003.

Kandel, Lenore. *Collected Poems of Lenore Kandel*. Berkeley, CA: North Atlantic Books, 2012.

Kerouac, Jack. *Big Sur*. London: Flamingo, 1993.

Kerouac, Jack. *On the Road*. London: Penguin, 2007.

Kerouac, Jan. *Baby Driver*. London: Corgi, 1984.

Kerouac, Jan. *Trainsong*. New York: Henry Holt, 1988.

Knight, Brenda. *Women of the Beat Generation*. Berkeley, CA: Conari Press, 1996.

Parker-Kerouac, Edie. *You'll Be Okay: My Life with Jack Kerouac*. San Francisco, CA: City Lights, 2007.

Weddle, Jeff. *Bohemian New Orleans: The Story of the Outsider and the Loujon Press*. Jackson: University of Mississippi Press, 2007.

Weddle, Leo J. 'The Lujon Press: An Historical Analysis'. PhD Thesis. University of Tennessee, 2003. https://trace.tennessee.edu/cgi/viewcontent.cgi?article=6747&context=utk_graddiss.

What Happened to Kerouac, directed by Richard Lerner and Lewis McAdams. New York: New Yorker Films, 1986.

4

A love letter to white friends

Deya Mukherjee

Introduction

This is a love letter to radical spaces. Bookshops, venues and social centres run according to anarchist, anti-capitalist principles. Using scholar and activist bell hooks's writings in *All about Love: New Visions* as reference point, this essay seeks to identify these anti-hierarchical community spaces as places where an actively political love can be, and often is, practised. However, writing from love requires writing from truth, and therefore the aim of this essay is to explore the reproduction of racism within these spaces.

It is important to note that 'radical spaces' is an umbrella term that encompasses many different types of space, including spaces led by Black and brown communities. My aim therefore is not to write about 'radical spaces' in general (and as a middle-class non-Black person from a dominant-caste background), nor is it to speak for every experience of oppression in the spaces in question. Rather, through use of the personal experiences of myself and fellow activists from Black and brown racialized communities, I aim to highlight a specific culture in majority white activist spaces that is exposed in conversations about racism. I argue that the mechanics of this culture, with its tactics of coercion and concealment, are broadly similar to the culture that can be found in the 'diversity speak' of the neoliberal institutions these spaces often define themselves in opposition to.

The activisms that this personal experience centres on include white-led climate activist groups and anti-fascist organizing. To make sense of these experiences, I turn to Sara Ahmed's *On Being Included*, specifically the chapters devoted to an analysis of institutional space and what happens when racism is spoken of in that space, and Audre Lorde's seminal essay 'The Uses of Anger: Women Responding to Racism'.[1]

I use these works to anchor these personal experiences in the wider and historical issue of white-led 'social justice' spaces that automatically consider themselves exempt from the workings of racism. I explore how central to this cultural mechanism is a commodified concept of 'love'. I aim to show how this commodification does a disservice to the real love that can be found in these spaces, which has the capacity to strengthen collective power in the service of the collective good.

In order to do this, I start the essay with a personal story of my experience working at a university and attempting to tackle the racism I encountered. I then juxtapose this story with a friend's experience of attempting to tackle racism at an anarchist social centre. Thirdly, I unpack the parallels in both experiences in the two very different spaces. Lastly, I expand on the impact of the commodified 'love' used as a tool in both stories, as opposed to the real, transformative power of love and the ways it is practised in the politics of the radical space.

* * *

I used to work in university 'Equalities' departments.

Universities can be sites of important anti-oppression work.[2] They are also spaces that have birthed (not just perpetuated) oppressive ideologies (take the development of eugenics as an academic discipline) and been birthed by them (for example, in the material profiting of Western universities from enslaved labour).[3] The contemporary practice of bedrock white supremacy in these spaces is evident in myriad ways, including the fact that, in 2019, there were only twenty-five Black women employed as university professors in the UK, and these prestigious universities have played a role in the gentrification of towns and cities in which they are situated.[4] As pointed out by scholar and activist Remi Joseph-Salisbury in his essay 'Confronting My Duty as an Academic: We Should All Be Activists': 'It is also important to recognize the university as a neoliberal institution and that its aims will often, if not always, be antithetical to our aims of progressive/radical social change.'[5]

In keeping with the testimony of other such workers in institutional spaces, though I met people engaged in vital anti-racism work at each institution, the 'Equalities' departments were generally enlisted to promote the institution, rather than challenge, and ultimately answered to higher-ups who wouldn't even say the word 'racism'.[6] The work I was often assigned in these spaces, therefore, fell straight in line with the 'happy diversity model' that Sara Ahmed writes of in *On Being Included*, which 'provides a positive, shiny image of the organization that allows inequalities to be concealed and thus reproduced' – the static, comfortable work of objectifying racialized bodies as 'seasoning' on department's landing pages and underlining the 'unconscious' in the bias with our new, branded pens to distract from the inextricability of capitalism from anti-Black racism.[7]

In one such place, in a majority white team, I had a head of department who spoke often of 'love'. We were 'the good guys' who would say the word 'racism', up against the institutional bigwigs who wouldn't. At every meeting, my head of department reminded me that she was 'there' for me and that I should please make use of her support and come to her with any and all issues.

One day in a meeting, a white manager in the department started talking about how a form of oppression was inherent to the people of a specific racialized community (not mine). Our department head had instructed me to develop an anti-racism training with this manager. In private, I challenged the manager's comments. They took my engagement as fellowship and proceeded further with more extreme comments, including suggestions for how we might shape our project in line with these prejudices.

I approached my department head to gauge what to do. The department head first told me they had not in fact assigned this manager to deliver this project. Next they said the manager's 'intentions came from a place of love', 'we all make mistakes', this was a team 'bound by love' and instructed me to bring it up informally if they ever said anything that made me 'feel bad' again.

I arranged to speak to the manager again. We were working in different places, so we were on the phone. Registering my hesitancy to start, they reassured me that they were very 'up for being called out' and that I shouldn't worry. I proceeded. Silence. Then a response that seemed to be fighting with itself. If they had said those things, they didn't believe them. Actually they didn't say those things, I couldn't be telling the truth. Then they refused to speak further. I eventually hung up.

Five minutes later, the 'ping' of an e-mail. They were sorry that they had been speaking without thinking, but 'the intent to harm was not there'. They were sorry for 'the way things left off', but it was nothing to do with what I'd said. They hoped I had a good weekend. I responded, acknowledging that the conversation had been a difficult one, and asked that we reconvene when I got back from leave, after some time to process.

Before going on leave, I updated my department head. The department head informed me, with a soothing air, that I had 'expressed [my] feelings', so the matter was resolved, and requested that I 'don't get upset' and that I 'come back from leave raring to go!'

The next time I interacted with the manager in question, I had been back from leave for a while. No plans to reconvene were in the works, but a meeting was called on the rebranding of our team values, to be led by this manager. In the meeting, they highlighted 'the importance of accountability', stressing that this department was a 'safe space' where we extend care to each other, where 'you are free to call us out!' They had recently been called out, and it had been a 'positive experience'. They urged us to follow suit. They were praised for rising to a difficult situation.

I met with the department head. They asked, with pride in their voice, what I had thought of the 'values' meeting. I informed them that I was concerned. That there was an evident pattern of racist prejudice that needed to be dealt with in our department, but I now had to withdraw my labour from the situation. They told me they were worried about my mental health and that I sounded distressed. They then instructed me to please develop a piece of work 'to support people when they've said things that have unintentionally hurt others'. I replied that I had not been hurt, rather the manager's comments had been intended to elicit my support. 'They're a lovely person', the department head responded. 'They made a mistake like us all, that's part of the job we do here.'

Incidentally, I was told by the department head, I was now at a stage of competence where I didn't need the manager's support, so there was no need for their continued involvement in the project.

My department head engaged no further with the situation. They never did inform me how the manager was supposed to know they were no longer working on the training. I worried for a while about how I, a junior member of staff, was supposed to tell a manager who had hired me that they were to be removed from a project they had been assigned to by our department head. The training was promoted by the vice chancellor as 'something we're doing' in response to pressure from staff and students to do more to address racist inequity at the university. Regular requests for updates on the training's availability started coming in. In the end I let the worry go and quit.

In this story we can see a cycle that is triggered by the defensive manoeuvrers employed by the department to shut down information about the ways in which racism was manifesting within it. First 'love' is used to silence. Secondly, the innate 'goodness' of the racist actor is privileged over their actions, followed by the problem being redefined as one of the non-white person getting unnecessarily upset. The cycle ends with the non-white person being the one who leaves, the power dynamics of the space remaining intact and the cycle beginning again.

* * *

The following is the experience of a friend. It has been written by myself based on her recounting and with her permission. These are not, therefore, her words verbatim except where indicated as quotations. All names have been changed to protect anonymity.

There was a radical social centre Gemma* frequented most weekends for a time. It had been founded by a small collective of white anarchists, as a space that was 'anti-oppression in all its forms'. On paper, no hierarchy. Gemma described it as a small space, but 'TARDIS-like, it always felt bigger on the inside', as if its walls were straining to embody 'the hospitality of its free-ness'. Over its five years it had exceeded the hopes of its small group of founders and flourished into a palimpsest. Lined with literature on subjects ranging from radical sex and relationships education, transformative justice practices and the Zapatista movement, its flaking, kaleidoscopic walls were a literal record of the people and communities who had met, eaten, cried, planned, danced and organized within it. Conversations about dismantling oppression were grounded in critiques of capitalism and a culture of normalized resource division. Once a week, a free hot meal was available to anyone who came in.

Gemma described it as a very white space. Black and brown folks moving within it were very visible. She quickly made friends with the other folks from racialized communities who were around at the same time, but on making links, they often chose to continue their friendships outside those walls.

One night Jay*, one of the old-timers of the space, was on shift. He was white, a passionate anarchist and climate activist whose 'fire and eloquence [Gemma] often admired'. Gemma and some friends were holding a conversation where the term 'white people' was used. Jay overheard. He started off calm. He 'got it', but 'he thought the term "white people" was a bit divisive'. Before long, he had come around the counter and used his taller stature to back Gemma into a corner. The exchange developed into a full-on finger-jabbing rant about how '[she] didn't know what racism really was', 'he would tell [her] what racism really was', 'racism wasn't really a thing any more anyway, was it'.

Jay was known to make the odd dodgy statement at the end of the night when people were tired or not around, but Gemma had never witnessed or been subject to such an extreme outburst as this one. She decided to ask for advice. She and a friend reached out to Lara*, a white woman who had been involved in the space from its early days and to whom Gemma felt confident talking about racism – the two of them had participated in local eviction resistance actions together and had spoken often of the specific ways in which housing inequality is perpetuated through systemic racism. Gemma explained the incident with Jay – how 'a dodgy comment' had turned into an act of physical aggression.

'Ah, don't worry', Lara said. 'We're all pretty decent here!'

Gemma explained, '[They] weren't worrying about something that hadn't happened. [They] were attempting to start a dialogue about something that *had* happened.'

'I get what you're saying', Lara responded. 'He's a bit rough around the edges sometimes but really he's a big softie, his heart's in the right place.'

Gemma's friend was in the same climate action group as Jay. They mentioned that not only had he displayed a pattern of trying to shut down conversations about racism, they had also heard him express eco-fascist sentiments that framed climate change as a 'necessary purge', a logic that writer and activist Naomi Klein describes as 'environmentalism through genocide'.[8] Gemma's friend described how, due to his prominent position in the group and his status as a founder of the social centre that was the group's meeting space, it felt hard to make criticisms of these sentiments stick – 'he just [seemed] to brush them off'.

'This is an anti-racist space', Lara said in response. 'We're about love, not hate here. He would be the first person to speak out against racism. For crying out loud, he's the least racist person I know.'

They decided to try and talk to Jay themselves. He was 'all kindly, avuncular smiles'. When Gemma brought up what had happened the other night, he didn't get angry like she'd feared; he just laughed.

'Oh for god's sake, I was only joshing, mate! I love people that aren't white – look at you, I think you're beautiful!'

Reader, '[she] told him to fuck off'. She left.

She returned twice more, the first visit about a fortnight later. Both old-timers of the space were there. When they clocked her, they came over.

'OK', Lara said. 'You've both had a go at each other, so that's that now please.'

'I was being ironic!' Jay chimed in.

Lara shushed him hurriedly, then turned to Gemma.

'Now, you were the one that was talking about being fair and respectful before, yes?' she continued. 'What happened to that then?'

Gemma didn't know what to say.

Lara's voice softened. 'I get that you're upset', she said. 'We all want you to be OK. We're worried about you. So let's calm down now and call it quits.'

When Gemma remained silent, she continued, 'He made a mistake but we all make mistakes, let's not be quick to judge. We love each other here, we don't lash out at each other. This space is too important for us to fall apart over a misplaced comment.'

When Gemma walked away, Lara followed her to the door.

'Listen, I know how you feel', she said. 'Do you think I haven't experienced misogyny in this place? Do you think it was easy trying to talk to people about sexual harassment in the early days? But you can't have everything all at once, change is coming but it comes gradually, yeah?'

Gemma explained how asking gender-oppressed folks from racialized communities to 'wait their turn' and 'defer their safety to a more convenient time' was a distraction, the fallacy Audre Lorde described as 'hierarchies of oppression'.[9]

Lara sighed. 'Look, there's nothing I can do. I'm not going to banish him.'

Gemma had wanted to find a way to make the space accessible for everyone. The threat of banishment was an imagined one.

'Look, we don't shut our doors to anyone', Lara continued. 'You're both free to make your own choices about where and with whom you spend your time. You'll always be welcome here.'

She turned on her heel and walked away.

Gemma went in one more time, but when she did, though it wasn't busy and she saw Lara behind the counter, Lara didn't seem to see her. There had been a time when they would search for each other at demos, to stand shoulder to shoulder in the crowd.

On recognizing the handful of other white folks in the space with whom she was on friendly terms, Gemma tried to catch someone's eyes. No one returned her gaze. Gemma stepped out and never came back.

What is 'love' doing?

What is 'love' doing in the stories above that take place in such wildly different spaces with such wildly different aims? I would argue: it is grease for the same wheel.

'Love' as silencer

The cycle begins with 'love' as silencer, put to work to preemptively blot out scrutiny and its potential consequence – transformation. We can see this in Lara's oddly hypothetical response of 'we're all pretty decent here' to the recounting of an event that had already happened, and her vague 'we're about love, not hate' on the espousing of the specifically oppressive ideology of eco-fascism, just as much as we can in the disengaged minimizing of the university manager's racist behaviour with the assertion that the team was 'bound by love'.

They are both examples of the fallacy of inherent 'knowing' – the idea that as 'good individuals' we somehow know from birth, and have always known, how to be separate from oppressions, such as racism, due to a nebulous, general idea of 'love' and 'heart' and 'decency'. This fallacy is common in neoliberal institutions that are explicitly structured by racism and, therefore, have a vested interest in obscuring the specific functions of global socioeconomic exploitation for which it was created.

But in Gemma's story, we can see this fallacy being selectively draped over her experience by Lara, who in another context (crucially one that doesn't require analysing the internal mechanisms of her own community's space) was quite at home with discussing racism as a system with functions, for example, in the ways in which it entrenches housing inequality.

These uses of 'love' are designed to detract from specifics by draping them in aesthetically pleasing generalities. It is a demand not to look past the prettiness of 'love'. Love's presence automatically negates the possibility of racism not only existing in the space but also ever having existed, even when the existence of structural and institutional racism in society and the world at large is undisputed in theory.

'Love' as mantle

In the next step, 'love' is a royal mantle. Where before 'love' shrouds the possible presents and futures of racism, now it is draped cape-like over the racist actor. They become the embodiment of love, who is incapable of acting from any other motivation.

We can see this in the workplace story, in the insistent characterizing of the manager's actions as 'unintentional' and benevolent 'mistakes' that 'we all make', by both the manager and, crucially, the department head, as if repeated displays of hostility towards a racialized community amount to nothing more than a typo. After robing the manager in the non-perishable impeccability of the 'lovely person', the department head went so far as to say that the manager's racism was evidence of them doing a good job (having previously characterized it as '[coming] from a place of love').

When the meaning of this 'love' is applied in hindsight to the 'love' and 'good guys' with which the department head had defined our team before the events in question (in opposition to the racisms we claimed to work against), we can see its implication – that of an automatic, evergreen innocence that is unchanged by actions and their consequences. For this action-divorced innocence to land, it needs to emerge in relief from sins and sinners we can claim ourselves outside of – a Batman visible through a Joker. Where racism is concerned, we commonly see this in the silo-ing of all racisms into The Racist, described by Sara Ahmed in *On Being Included* as 'a figure that is easily discarded (not only as someone who is "not me" but also as someone who is "not us", who does not represent a cultural or institutional norm)'.[10]

This strategy, in addition to providing a comparison from which this innocence may emerge, ensures that analyses of racism are confined to the actions of 'bad apples', leaving the mechanics of the institution, and how it interacts with the wider world, safely unscrutinized. It is often deployed to distract from the fundamental relationship between racism and global capitalism, by reducing the work it would take to dismantle racism to a simple matter of inherently 'good' and 'bad' individuals. (Note, for example, Amazon CEO Jeff Bezos calling a customer who complained about the statement Amazon posted in support of the Black Lives Matter movement in the wake of George Floyd's murder, one he was 'happy to lose'.[11] Meanwhile Amazon aggressively dehumanizes its workers, resources the brutality of the US Immigration and Customs Enforcement agency, 'continues its commercial partnerships with police forces across the US and stands by its past treatment of non-white employee organizers'.[12]) So far, so neoliberal.

However, on returning to Gemma's radical social centre, we find the same mechanisms, revealed in the event of Gemma's articulation of her experiences of racism. Consider, for example, the 'lovely person' analogue that is the 'big softie' whose 'heart's in the right place'. The same demand to see only benevolence in 'we all make mistakes' is present in the characterizing of a clearly perceivable pattern of racist behaviour as 'a misplaced comment', the facing of which would be at odds with the 'love' the space had been built for.

How the bizarrely context-free 'place of love' that the manager's racism was said to stem from is replicated in assertions that a person who had denied the existence of racism 'would be the first person to speak out against [it]'. Note the familiar silo-ing in that assertion – racism as some outsourced abstract that comes into being for the white folks in question only in that it represents what they are not. What form does it take – this racism that has the power to completely erase the very possibility of the racism of a white anarchist?

To answer this question, I spoke to a friend with experience in anti-fascist organizing, who wished to remain anonymous. They spoke of a time when, in a meeting of mostly white people, a white activist, who was well known and well liked, started talking – in relation to a recent heavily policed demonstration – of how everybody was 'talking about race these days', but what wasn't being talked about was 'police targeting of anarchists'. My friend called this out as a classic, anti-Black derailment from the issue of police brutality against Black communities while also noting the telling erasure in his pitting of anarchists vs 'race'.

After the meeting (their last with this group), my friend found that the problem they had articulated had been deflected onto them. In order to enact this deflection, 'love' was on hand. Three people from the (six person) meeting came up to them unsolicited (two immediately, one in passing on another occasion) to tell them all about what a 'lovely person' the activist was. How 'full of love his heart [was]', how 'he stood up to fascists' and how incapable this made him of perpetuating racism himself.

After finishing their story, my friend noted that while the work of anti-fascism is a non-negotiable necessity, they had found that (much like The Racist of the neoliberal institution who is never Us) some white activists they had encountered appeared to have a relationship with the image of The Fascist (Joker) based on their opposition to them, such that their identity as anti-fascist (Batman) was often used to sell an image of 'innocence' in the face of any and all critique. Here, too, we find the global, socioeconomic system of racism that we have all been socialized within, reduced to The Bad Person, and The Good Person who is Good because they are not Bad, and hence the nonsense, in Gemma's story, of Jay being 'the least racist person [Lara knew]'.

'Don't get upset!'

In the anti-fascist organizer's story, we see how, having articulated a problem, they were cast as that 'problem', or, as Sara Ahmed puts it, 'To talk about racism is to become the problem you pose.'[13]

Where the racist actor has been cast as the embodiment of 'love', the embodiment of the 'problem' is now placed on the other side of 'love' both in the sense that they do not believe enough in its capacity to prevent racism from being or having been and in that they are in opposition to the 'loveliness' of the 'lovely person'. They threaten the 'lovely person'. Consider, for example, the parallels between my department head's reducing of the manager's racism to an issue of 'feelings' needing to be 'expressed' and Lara's deflection of an act of racialized aggression onto Gemma's 'worry'. The parallels between the way my department head's request that I 'don't get upset' developed into an insinuation that I was the source of unfairness since I'd placed unrealistic expectations on the manager and how, in the radical social centre, Gemma quickly became the one who was 'quick to judge' and '[lashing] out' and needed to 'calm down'.

In both these examples, we can see how this devising of insider (love)/outsider (non-love) roles is entrenched by a pathologizing of the emotions of racialized people, a tactic used against Black women and gender-oppressed folks in particular.[14] Speaking of anger in her essay 'The Uses of Anger', Audre Lorde writes: 'Focused with precision it can become a powerful source of energy serving progress and change. And when I speak of change, I do not mean a simple switch of positions or a temporary lessening of tensions, nor the ability to smile or feel good. I am speaking of a basic and radical alteration in those assumptions underlining our lives.'[15]

Here Lorde describes anger's rich potential as a tool of transformation. If you were seeking to prevent such transformation, characterizing the anger of the 'embodied problem' as aberrant – while legitimizing the anger of those seen to 'belong' to the space would be a powerful means to do so – the testimony of those invested in the uncovering of racisms could thus be discredited, and the uncoverer portrayed as at odds with the 'loving' aims of the space. As a result, Jay's aggression was not even registered as a problem at the radical social centre – the problem surfaced as soon as Gemma's anger was expressed.

This pathologizing can also take the form of a performance of 'loving' concern for the welfare of the 'embodied problem' as a further means of locating the problem in their body as opposed to in the events they are describing. This can be seen in the shared 'we're worried about you' of my head of department and of Gemma's fellow activist in response to their own insistence on inaction and cover-ups. This is an old strategy for the reproduction of whiteness as innocence, as goodness – an example of which can be traced in the British government's historical tactic of categorizing the dissent of racialized peoples against colonial violence as 'mental disorder'.[16]

Where emotions as transformative tools can be reshaped as symptoms of 'disorder', racist systems and practices can themselves be reshaped as 'healthy' and, therefore, within the logic of ableism that is inextricably bound with anti-Black racism, 'normal'.[17]

Love as transformation

My aim in drawing parallels between experiences in anti-capitalist organizing and social spaces and those in the neoliberal institution of the university is not to equate the two kinds of space as having the same kinds of power to marginalize or harm. (Given the specifically classist inequity that is reproduced by the university, this is especially important to note as local radical spaces can be vital sites of working-class activism.)

Furthermore, the examples I have focused on to draw out these mechanisms are individual acts of racism, but it's important to note that racism is not the neoliberal fallacy of a mere inhospitality towards 'difference', but a global system of socioeconomic exploitation on which our world is structured. It's in the bricks of law and its enforcement, in labour, health and social care, education, town planning, housing, international relations, global commodity chains, agriculture, textiles. The list is long and, of course, less a list than a network.

Rather, then, my aim is to highlight neoliberal cultural behaviours that maintain racist structures and how common it can be that spaces aiming to organize themselves against such structures fall back on them for the comfort of power. Note the fact that both stories end in the exact same way – with a brown person who had spoken of racism having the hospitality they had initially received from each space revoked until they left.

In the context of the neoliberal institution, this makes sense – that hospitality was accessible to me as a middle-class person from a dominant-caste background, whose brownness could be useful for the department's 'look' (and my acquiring of the job) while reaffirming the middle class as those who 'belong' in these positions in these institutions. The incident that followed, therefore, was a mild expression of the wider system of oppression that the institution of the university often explicitly operates on, with far graver effects. Ultimately, however, the purpose of the mechanisms it revealed was still to maintain convenient fallacies around racism that would leave existing power dynamics unchallenged and to 'prune' people who might confront those narratives. The silence the department head radiated towards me once it was clear I would not comply with the narrative ensured that, if I left, the department could not be accused of wrongdoing – I had chosen to leave, so normal service could be resumed unchecked.

Why, then, do we see the same thing happening in a space that claimed to organize itself in a markedly different way to the neoliberal institutions I'm referring to? A space that defined itself as anti-hierarchical and 'anti-oppression in all its forms'? Consider the parallels in the department head's silence and the way in which each of Gemma's past interactions with the social centre were erased by the silence she was greeted with once she refused to comply with the narrative that racism was not possible within its walls.

The ways that wall of silence allowed those who had never been in doubt of their belonging in the space, to feign ignorance as to why their space was so white, while preserving its power dynamics in the name of 'love'. A culture that keeps unequal power dynamics unquestioned and unaltered is often a desired feature of neoliberal spaces, but should it be one of radical and anarchist spaces?

These are urgent issues to consider since the need for radical spaces is an urgent one. The work of imagining, and acting towards, a world where communities are organized according to principles of care can be uncertain, uncomfortable work. It is, however, essential in the face of a capitalist society structured to garner profit for the few, at all costs. The fruits of this structuring are lethal and can be seen in the UK in a housing market where landlords 'choose the price tag' of their tenants' lives – in the words of a former resident of Grenfell Tower – and in healthcare services tasked with supplying companies with more bodies for work (the exploitative conditions of which can themselves be causes of illness), an aim that, as one Bristol-based counsellor describes, has resulted in 'the government agenda … intruding on the therapeutic space in an alarming manner'.[18]

In her powerfully insightful *All about Love: New Visions* – a work that seeks to recentre the import of love in all human bonds and endeavours, and most fundamentally in the life-and-death work of restructuring our societies and resources for the freedom of all – hooks makes the pragmatic case for love as an indispensable tool for the razing of oppression. She teaches that 'to begin by always thinking about love as an action rather than a feeling is one way in which anyone using the word in this manner automatically assumes accountability and responsibility'.[19]

When hooks writes of what this love might look like in community-building, a love whose practice is grounded in the presupposition 'that everyone has the right to be free, to live fully and well', which necessitates 'embracing a global vision wherein we see our lives and our fate as intimately connected to those of everyone else on the planet', my mind immediately locates the network of radical, activist spaces that I travelled through for a time.[20]

Those radical bookshops, worker cooperative cafes and anarchist social centres traversed by folk committed to and searching for a politics rooted in community rather than capital provided ground on which to imagine and build local alternatives to this ethic of profit and death, based on an ethic of collective care. They were the havens from which sprung prisoner and survivor solidarity collectives, anti-gentrification campaigns and renters unions, as well as news networks linking global radical movements to strengthen worker solidarity across borders. So much glorious, queer community found on those shop floors and love stories that opened in union meetings. So much use was made of the radical bookshop's traditional role as the rare public place where daytime shelter isn't bought, where free use of toilets, taps and tampons is maintained. This is hooks's visionary, living, 'doing' love – a love of movement, dismantling and rebuilding, envisioning different possibilities to those peddled by capitalism and acting on them, not along lines of hierarchy and subjugation but in solidarity and collaboration. A love that exists in stark opposition to the commodified 'love' of concealment and stasis embedded in the neoliberal culture of my workplace and replicated in Gemma's radical social centre.

Lara accused Gemma of not understanding the importance of the social centre and thereby catalysing its '[falling] apart'. The opposite was true. In Gemma's words, alongside the heartbreak of her physical safety being shrugged off as a distraction was the casting of her deep love and investment in the space as disloyalty. In bringing forth their experiences and concerns (at a considerable cost), Gemma and her friend were trying to find ways to heal and strengthen the space and its purported anti-oppression aims – their anger was focused towards that 'progress and change', which Lorde speaks of in 'The Uses of Anger'. It was Jay and Lara's racism that did the 'splitting'.

In the same essay, Lorde continues on anger, teaching us how '[it] is loaded with information and energy … If I participate knowingly or otherwise, in my sister's oppression and she calls me on it, to answer her anger with my own only blankets the substance of our exchange with reaction. It wastes energy.'[21]

So what substance was blanketed in Gemma's experience, what information wasted? That there can be no climate justice without class justice and decolonization. That 'eco-fascism' is yet another classist, racist ethic of death, and that the mechanics of the space was allowing its logics to permeate a climate action group unchecked. That a brown woman's safety was compromised in an 'anti-racist' space by someone who had behaved this way before and showed no remorse.

The 'blanketing'-over of these realities sealed a familiar future where the space stood still, complacent and unchanged – a mirror image of the workplace whose ultimate, unchanging aim was to protect those with the most power. But what other futures did this one prevent? What would have happened, for example, if someone had taken down that transformative justice literature off the shelves and started the uncomfortable work of unpacking the reality of Jay's actions towards Gemma – the why, and how, and what next – in a way that centred Gemma's safety and belonging? How would working to disrupt those cycles of harm, honing the *practice* of disrupting those cycles of harm, have changed the surface of the space?

What would it have looked like to face the hierarchies of control that were not prevented from manifesting by the words used to describe the space, and what impact would that have had on the work of the groups that organized within its walls? Could taking those steps have eventually led to more people from its local community being able to make use of its space, resources and connections? I can't say what those un-happened futures would have looked like, but it is certain that their potential was blotted out by an insistence on concealment, in the service of keeping the space stuck in the familiar, comfortable rut of the unjust power dynamics it claimed to denounce.

In other words, when we fall back on the same old, static architectures of subjugation and frame love as the inert work of covering over those unjust structures we want to hold on to, we deaden love's transformative power. Let us have the courage to imagine better futures than those sold to us by the ruthless cultures of neoliberalism, to set our sights on Lorde's 'radical alteration' and to face the real work of love.

Notes

1   Sara Ahmed, *On Being Included* (Durham, NC: Duke University Press, 2012), 19–50, 141–71; Audre Lorde, *Sister Outsider* (London: Penguin Classics, 2019), 117–27.

2   Eileen Gbagbo, 'The History of Anti-Racist Student Occupation Movements in the UK', *gal-dem*, 6 January 2020. https://gal-dem.com/what-we-need-to-learn-about-the-history-of-anti-racist-student-occupation-movements-in-the-uk/.

3   Remi Joseph-Salisbury, 'Confronting My Duty as an Academic: We Should All Be Activists', in *The Fire Now*, ed. Azeezat Johnson, Remi Joseph-Salisbury and Beth Kamunge (London: Zed Books, 2018), 46.

4   Nicola Rollock, 'Staying Power: The Career Experiences and Strategies of UK Black Female Professors', University College Union, February 2019, 6. www.ucu.org.uk/media/10075/Staying-Power/pdf/UCU_Rollock_February_2019.pdf. Sahaya James, 'Universities Are Becoming the Acceptable Face of Gentrification', *The Independent*, 26 January 2018. www.independent.co.uk/voices/university-gentrification-ual-ucl-delancy-lendlease-acceptable-face-a8179816.html.

5   Joseph-Salisbury, 'Confronting My Duty as an Academic', 47.

6   Ahmed, *On Being Included*, 147.

7   Ibid., 72. Momtaza Mehri, 'Anti-Racism Requires So Much More Than "Checking Your Privilege"', *The Guardian*, 7 July 2020. www.theguardian.com/commentisfree/2020/jul/07/anti-racism-checking-privilege-anti-blackness.

8   Adryan Corcione, 'Eco-Fascism: What It Is, Why It's Wrong, and How to Fight It', *Teen Vogue*, 30 April 2020. www.teenvogue.com/story/what-is-ecofascism-explainer.

9   Audre Lorde, 'There Is No Hierarchy of Oppressions', in *Interracial Books for Children Bulletin, Volume 14: Homophobia and Education – How to Deal with Name-Calling* (New York: The Council on Interracial Books for Children, 1983), 9.

10   Ahmed, *On Being Included*, 150.

11 Jeff Bezos (@jeffbezos), 'There have been a number of sickening but not surprising responses in my inbox since my last post. This sort of hate shouldn't be allowed to hide in the shadows. It's important to make it visible. This is just one example of the problem. And, Dave, you're the kind of customer I'm happy to lose', Instagram photo, 7 June 2020. https://www.instagram.com/p/CBJrhdzHKNt/.

12 Trades Union Congress, 'Challenging Amazon: What Can We Do about Amazon's Treatment of Its Workers?', 12 October 2020. https://www.tuc.org.uk/research-analysis/reports/challenging-amazon-report. Karen Hao, 'Amazon Is the Invisible Backbone of ICE's Immigration Crackdown', *MIT Technology Review*, 22 October 2018. www.technologyreview.com/2018/10/22/139639/amazon-is-the-invisible-backbone-behind-ices-immigration-crackdown/ Kari Paul, 'Amazon Says "Black Lives Matter". But the Company Has Deep Ties to Policing', *The Guardian*, 9 June 2020. www.theguardian.com/technology/2020/jun/09/amazon-black-lives-matter-police-ring-jeff-bezos.

13 Ahmed, *On Being Included*, 153.

14 Eliza Anyangwe, 'Misogynoir: Where Racism and Sexism Meet', *The Guardian*, 5 October 2015. www.theguardian.com/lifeandstyle/2015/oct/05/what-is-misogynoir.

15 Lorde, *Sister Outsider*, 120.

16 China Mills, 'Teaching White Innocence in an Anti-Black Social Order: British Values and the Psychic Life of Coloniality', in *The Fire Now*, ed. Azeezat Johnson, Remi Joseph-Salisbury and Beth Kamunge (London: Zed Books, 2018), 223–34.

17 Viji Kuppan, 'Crippin' Blackness: Narratives of Disabled People of Colour from Slavery to Trump', in *The Fire Now*, ed. Azeezat Johnson, Remi Joseph-Salisbury and Beth Kamunge (London: Zed Books, 2018), 63–4.

18 Tess de La Mare, 'Grenfell Landlords "Chose the Price Tag" of Tenants' Lives, Inquiry Hears', *Evening Standard*, 20 April 2021. www.standard.co.uk/news/uk/grenfell-grenfell-tower-claire-williams-b930757.html. Debbie Porteous, 'Working Isn't Working', *The Bristol Cable*, 19 April 2017. https://thebristolcable.org/2017/04/opinions-working-isnt-working/.

19 bell hooks, *All about Love* (New York: William Morrow, 2000), 13.

20 Ibid., 87–8.

21 Lorde, *Sister Outsider*, 121.

Bibliography

Ahmed, Sara. *On Being Included*. Durham, NC: Duke University Press, 2012.
Anyangwe, Eliza. 'Misogynoir: Where Racism and Sexism Meet'. *The Guardian*, 5 October 2015. www.theguardian.com/lifeandstyle/2015/oct/05/what-is-misogynoir.
Bezos, Jeff (@jeffbezos). Instagram photo. 7 June 2020. www.instagram.com/p/CBJrhdzHKNt/.

Corcione, Adryan. 'Eco-fascism: What It Is, Why It's Wrong, and How to Fight It'. *Teen Vogue*, 30 April 2020. www.teenvogue.com/story/what-is-ecofascism-explainer.

de La Mare, Tess. 'Grenfell Landlords "Chose the Price Tag" of Tenants' Lives, Inquiry Hears'. *Evening Standard*, 20 April 2021. www.standard.co.uk/news/uk/grenfell-grenfell-tower-claire-williams-b930757.html.

Gbagbo, Eileen. 'The History of Anti-Racist Student Occupation Movements in the UK'. *gal-dem*, 6 January 2020. https://gal-dem.com/what-we-need-to-learn-about-the-history-of-anti-racist-student-occupation-movements-in-the-uk/.

Hao, Karen. 'Amazon Is the Invisible Backbone of ICE's Immigration Crackdown'. *MIT Technology Review*, 22 October 2018. www.technologyreview.com/2018/10/22/139639/amazon-is-the-invisible-backbone-behind-ices-immigration-crackdown/.

hooks, bell. *All about Love*. New York: William Morrow, 2000.

James, Sahaya. 'Universities Are Becoming the Acceptable Face of Gentrification'. *The Independent*, 26 January 2018. www.independent.co.uk/voices/university-gentrification-ual-ucl-delancy-lendlease-acceptable-face-a8179816.html.

Joseph-Salisbury, Remi. 'Confronting My Duty as an Academic: We Should All Be Activists'. In *The Fire Now*, edited by Azeezat Johnson, Remi Joseph-Salisbury and Beth Kamunge, 44–56. London: Zed Books, 2018.

Kuppan, Viji. 'Crippin' Blackness: Narratives of Disabled People of Colour from Slavery to Trump'. In *The Fire Now*, edited by Azeezat Johnson, Remi Joseph-Salisbury and Beth Kamunge, 60–73. London: Zed Books, 2018.

Lorde, Audre. 'There Is No Hierarchy of Oppressions'. In *Interracial Books for Children Bulletin, Volume 14: Homophobia and Education – How to Deal with Name-Calling*, 9. New York: The Council on Interracial Books for Children, 1983.

Lorde, Audre. *Sister Outsider*. London: Penguin Classics, 2019.

Mehri, Momtaza. 'Anti-Racism Requires So Much More Than "Checking Your Privilege"'. *The Guardian*, 7 July 2020. www.theguardian.com/commentisfree/2020/jul/07/anti-racism-checking-privilege-anti-blackness.

Mills, China. 'Teaching White Innocence in an Anti-Black Social Order: British Values and the Psychic Life of Coloniality'. In *The Fire Now*, edited by Azeezat Johnson, Remi Joseph-Salisbury and Beth Kamunge, 223–34. London: Zed Books, 2018.

Paul, Kari. 'Amazon Says "Black Lives Matter". But the Company Has Deep Ties to Policing'. *The Guardian*, 9 June 2020. www.theguardian.com/technology/2020/jun/09/amazon-black-lives-matter-police-ring-jeff-bezos.

Porteous, Debbie. 'Working Isn't Working'. *The Bristol Cable*, 19 April 2017. https://thebristolcable.org/2017/04/opinions-working-isnt-working/.

Rollock, Nicola. 'Staying Power: The Career Experiences and Strategies of UK Black Female Professors'. University College Union, February 2019. www.ucu.org.uk/media/10075/Staying-Power/pdf/UCU_Rollock_February_2019.pdf.

Trades Union Congress. 'Challenging Amazon: What Can We Do about Amazon's Treatment of Its Workers?' 12 October 2020. www.tuc.org.uk/research-analysis/reports/challenging-amazon-report.

PART 2

Intimate bodies

5

The sharper end of love: When sex is painful, how is intimate love navigated? Reflections from a qualitative study in England and France

Hannah Loret

Introduction

The discourses around sexual pain are complex, multidisciplinary and constantly evolving. Studies of sexual pain experienced by women range from self-labelled feminist criticism,[1] to medical recommendations written by healthcare professionals in diverse specialities,[2] to works which bring together women's own written and spoken experiences and interpretations of concepts including sexual 'dysfunction'.[3] Genital sexual pain, understood here as pain in the genitals felt during sexual activity, whether partnered or not, is described in multiple ways by many different people. Treatment outcomes can be bleak for the women experiencing pain, and classifications of the pain have been repeatedly problematized within health services without standardized remedies always being agreed, often 'exacerbating patient distress'.[4] This piece is drawn from doctoral research undertaken between 2017 and 2020 with self-identifying women who were experiencing or had experienced sexual pain and with healthcare professionals involved in its treatment.[5] Diagnostic categories, commonly cited issues in accessing healthcare and women's descriptions of their own pain and experiences were examined in this research, which defined and critically appraised conceptualizations of women's sexual pain in England and France, creating policy recommendations and encouraging increased awareness of sexual pain experiences in healthcare settings. France and England were chosen for this comparative study due to their similarity in terms of treatment options for women's sexual pain issues despite their differing healthcare system structures, with France operating a healthcare system with both mainstream public and private elements and England operating with a largely public healthcare system, where private healthcare exists but in less mainstream ways. For the participants of the study, then, experiencing sexual pain meant navigating not just the potentially life-altering pain felt but also the complex national systems of care and the relational, financial and social complications of this.

It is for this reason that this study also considered sexual pain experiences within a sociopolitical frame, using selected readings of Foucault to analyse semi-structured interview data, in particular the concepts within the History of Sexuality series and conceptualizations of structural and fluid power dynamics. Taylor additionally suggests that Foucault wrote the History of Sexuality series because 'sex is a privileged site through which power works in biopolitical times, and cultivating different relations to sex might undo some of the effects of this power'.[6] Biopolitics, meaning the utilization of 'numerous and diverse techniques for achieving the subjugation of bodies and the control of populations',[7] features heavily in the series and is interwoven with the consideration for constantly evolving and complex 'relations of power'.[8] Foucault's concept of the 'genealogy', suggesting a 'focus on discontinuities, contingencies and power struggles in order to demonstrate that the past was different from the present, the present could have been otherwise and thus the future may also be otherwise',[9] was borne in mind while undertaking this research and in situating the research in question within the context of a specific, contingent relationship with its own inherent power dynamics. The link between power and pain is explicit in Foucault's writing, Foucault reminding readers in 'The Birth of the Clinic'[10] that the 'figures of pain are not conjured away by means of a body of neutralized knowledge', rather 'redistributed in the space in which bodies and eyes meet'. Though this piece will not closely examine the link between Foucault and this cross-national sexual pain research, it is nonetheless significant that the research study conducted maintained that all discourse, including scientific and healthcare discourse, is constructed, historically specific and shaped by the structural and subjective experiences of power. When participants spoke about sexual relationships, their bodies and their experiences of love and self-love, it was in the context of these power dynamics, many of which were openly acknowledged by participants when discussing them.

Working alongside an analysis informed by readings of Foucault was the theoretical tool of intersectionality, that is to say 'the 'analytic tool' which recognizes that 'major axes of social divisions in a given society at a given time … operate not as discrete and mutually exclusive entities, but build on each other and work together'.[11] Care was taken in the choice of intersectionality as a theoretical and analytical tool for this project, and it was borne in mind throughout the research that intersectionality is rooted in 'Black feminism and Critical Race Theory' and was originally coined 'to address the marginalization of Black women within not only antidiscrimination law but also in feminist and antiracist theory and politics'.[12] Though the impact of the project and the professional practice of the researcher reflected a practical and personal commitment to challenge multiple and coexisting inequalities, the context of the use of intersectionality here is nevertheless removed from the specific and important context in which it was first coined. The lens of race here is seen as a significant possible axis of social division in the societies in which the participants interviewed live or lived and as a potential way in which some participants may have had no choice but to renegotiate structural healthcare opportunities differently to others in systems where 'race, class, gender, sexuality, age, disability, ethnicity, nation, and religion, among others, constitute interlocking, mutually constructing or intersecting systems of power'.[13] Recognizing that this project was anchored in a commitment to try and understand and academically represent participant experiences in as faithful a way as possible, intersectionality was particularly appropriate for this methodology as a tool and 'a way of understanding the complexity in the world, in people, and in human experiences',[14] where 'intersectional frameworks understand power relations through a lens of mutual construction'.[15]

Methodology

The writers and researchers involved in *Troubling the Angels: Women Living with HIV/AIDS*[16] noted that in the work they felt they were walking 'a fine line between making a spectacle of these women's struggles and a wanting to speak quietly with respect for all that it means to tell the stories of people willing to put their lives on public display in the hope that it will make it better for others'. This 'fine line' is very much at the heart of the current study, though the interviews had a different social context. Grappling with how best to represent participant voices during the process of recruitment, data collection, analysis and writing echoed with what Lather and Smithies describe[17] in *Troubling the Angels* as the 'responsibility' born to the women who shared their stories. Smithies further comments of this responsibility[18] that during her own decision-making process in writing with and about women affected by HIV and AIDS, she was 'overwhelmed with the responsibility of getting it right' and of 'misrepresent[ing] or dishonour[ing] the women' she 'greatly admire[d] and love[d]'. Lather and Smithies hoped their book was[19] 'a breakdown of clear interpretation and confidence of the ability/warrant to tell such stories in uncomplicated, non-messy ways', and the present study also embraces the complicated nature of telling stories where there is a clear responsibility to respondents to produce a study where their experiences can be shared with a wider audience without overly reducing or skewing their voices. This was incorporated into the study design and the engagement of the study with theory and healthcare practice.

This piece will focus on selected analyses of the interviews conducted in England and France with women who have experienced sexual pain. The women interviewed for the study often spoke about love and the embodiment of love for themselves and for their sexual partners; and though the analysis conducted following the interviews with healthcare professionals in England and France also provided rich and fascinating information about how love is conceptualized in their professional environments, the current piece focuses on some of the experiences discussed by women who participated in the study. This permits a closer reading of selected quotations from the study rather than a broader exploration of how intimate love, embodiment and sex were discussed as part of the qualitative work. The quotations which follow are taken from semi-structured interviews conducted between summer 2018 and December 2019 with anonymous participants who responded to social media calls for participants to the PhD study. Calls were made to interview self-identifying women residing in England or France who experience, or had experienced, genital pain during sexual acts, and interviews were conducted in English or French, in person or via telephone or video call, as agreed with the participant prior to the interview. Interviews were conducted in the language preferred by the participants, with several of them completing the interview in a non-native language, and the option to speak in either English or French was made clear as part of the participant recruitment process to proactively ensure that participants who spoke more than one language would be as comfortable as possible in their choice. The interviews were transcribed verbatim and analysed in English using a reflexive thematic analysis approach,[20] chosen due to its flexible nature which nevertheless allows for nuance and a rigorous inductive approach within study results. This transcription was carried out in the language of the interview by the lead researcher and was only translated into English at the point of analysis, where it was key to remember that the translations were specific to a research context and constructed by the researcher. This cross-national design, allowing for data analysis, research questions and relationships with the theory around sexual pain to be driven by participant data and priorities, was intended to be as faithful as possible to 'the responsibility of getting it right' when representing the voices of participants.[21] The research from which this piece is drawn examined and challenged the conceptualization of sexual pain in England and France using an intersectional lens with a particular focus on the axis of gender. This was understood with reference to how gender can form part of other marginalizing factors in healthcare experiences, and love and intimacy were at the forefront of how participants described their experiences of sexual pain.

Power and empowerment

Many of the study participants explicitly spoke about the power dynamics they had experienced or were experiencing as part of their sexual pain. WA-EN-001 conveyed the power of being believed for the first time by a healthcare professional and how this felt:

> It's the 'yes, we believe you, yes, I hear you', umm, and 'you're not a freak' [pauses at length], you know, 'we believe you', that's 'we believe you; I believe you'. Three words, it's like three of the most powerful words in the English language.

WA-FR-003 spoke about power in a different way, explaining that the experience that she had been through before the pain resolved was linked to what she saw as a misunderstanding about what real love was. She spoke of only knowing real love after the pain had resolved:

> And then, you know, well, so, umm, I think that there's some misunderstanding in what, uhh, in what we want, in what we really actually want. And even perhaps … even perhaps some misunderstanding of what real love feels like. Because … personally I only knew that after [the pain experience].

WA-EN-001 was not in a relationship at the time of interview. She discussed how she felt that not being in a relationship had hindered her treatment-seeking, with healthcare professionals seeming to provide care tailored more towards women in heterosexual relationships than towards women who did not have a regular sexual partner. Being heard and being taken seriously was momentous for her, and hearing the words 'I believe you' after many consultations during which she had not been believed was a powerful and emotional experience. WA-FR-003 spoke about an empowering experience of a different kind. Finding out what love really meant to her, in this case with a change of sexual partner and appropriate treatment after many years of being unable to name what she was experiencing, was a positive, affirming experience. Though for both participants, having repeated encounters with healthcare professionals who were unable to help them resolve the pain was a disempowering, frustrating and distressing experience, they reported feeling powerful moments of clarity about their own experiencing and the love they felt towards others. Though these two interview quotations do not reveal the complex marginalizing factors that these women were a part of, the notion that power dynamics are mutually constructed and fluid, and the intersectional concern of seeing 'power relations through a lens of mutual construction',[22] is clearly present here. These two excerpts demonstrate that when these participants spoke about the experience of 'real love' and the process of being heard, power was not an abstract concept, taken away from the experience of pain. The power of being heard and believed, and of understanding and experiencing what 'real love' was, was liberating – and though these power dynamics were nevertheless mutually constructed, they had profound effects on the embodied experiences of both these participants.

This potentially liberating conceptualization of power was not present in all interviews, however. WA-EN-004 spoke of frustration with a medical professional who had told her that therapy tailored to her needs was not available for free through NHS services, only for her to subsequently find out that the therapy was indeed available free of charge:

> I just feel so like … kind of powerless in the whole situation to be honest. Cause they're … they're kind of saying it's your f—, you know, your responsibility, to deal with this, you can … employ techniques to get around it … But then, the, I just don't have the money to get the, the kind of guidance on that.

The description of a feeling of powerlessness was seen repeatedly in the interviews with women who participated in this study. The onus described above by WA-EN-004 to take 'responsibility' and 'employ techniques' to 'get around' the pain was also described repeatedly by women in the interviews in both England and France, and this applied in many of the descriptions of treatment-seeking, where responsibility was placed back on the women experiencing the pain if a possible treatment had not relieved their symptoms, or if repeatedly trying different treatments had had no positive effect. The women interviewed who consulted health professionals for their sexual pain may have contributed to the power dynamics which formed part of their experience of pain, but the power dynamics here were described as largely unequal. In WA-EN-004's description of her lack of appropriate guidance and available funds to deal with the problem, and the reversal of responsibility from the healthcare professional back onto her, the potentially marginalizing factors which shaped her experience of pain do not seem to have been considered by those who were in a position of power over her. Factors including her sexuality, gender, age, financial status, race and class do not appear to have been taken into account in this experience of advice from a healthcare professional. Rather, her experiences of sexuality and love are shaped by a feeling of powerlessness 'in the whole situation', where factors which might make access to treatment and support easier have seemingly not been adequately considered by the healthcare professionals she consulted.

Other participants did speak of the same frustration with healthcare providers that their situations were not heard or understood, but WA-EN-010 did speak of how, despite navigating the complex systems of care and national healthcare structures, she had been able to adjust elements of her life to reflect her wishes, despite disempowering and negative experiences with healthcare providers and previous sexual partners. She spoke about how self-pleasuring worked for her, despite experiences of this activity being profoundly negative with other people:

Manual stimul-, stimulation by another person … dreadful … I'm fine with masturbation, I know what to do.

She also spoke positively of her queer identity and how she hoped that 'within that' she could find 'a space' for herself, and how this had helped her feel 'the most hopeful' that she'd felt 'for a while' in trying to 'make an account of' herself. Reflecting, then, the fluid and mutually constructing nature of the power dynamics involved in conceptualizing sexual pain, WA-EN-010 spoke of reappropriating intimate practices through focused sexual activity and through making an 'account' of herself on her own terms. WA-EN-010 spoke of insensitive and frustrating encounters with healthcare professionals, but her descriptions of finding 'space' for herself were hopeful ones. It seems from her descriptions of interactions with healthcare professionals that, though her individual material and personal circumstances were not at the forefront of considerations about her care, she had nevertheless forged a space of power to reappropriate her intimate life and the embodiment of the intimate power dynamics she was a part of.

Alongside disruptive experiences of genital pain felt during sexual acts, many of the participants in both England and France spoke of feeling that their pain felt like it needed to be legitimized, sometimes in terms of a clear diagnosis, and that this affected their own understandings and experiences of their pain. WA-FR-009 spoke about seeking a diagnosis and how she felt this would help her understand her pain and to feel more legitimate:

I would finally have a diagnosis to confirm what I've been saying, you know, quite simply, and so I would finally feel legitimate.

WA-FR-004 spoke about her diagnosis of vaginismus, which involves the muscles of the vagina contracting in a painful way, and how this diagnosis had helped her come to terms with her issue and to speak about it openly in a way that was fearless about the reactions of others:

> To be able to accept and to be able to, umm, treat the thing, I think you have to dare to give it a name, and to clearly say 'yes I have vaginismus, yes I'm "vaginique", so what'?

WA-FR-004 described herself as 'vaginique', an adjective specific to the French-language interviews, meaning 'a person who has vaginismus'. The power dynamics reported in these two quotations are very different, despite both being taken from interviews with women in France. The first quote speaks of a desire for legitimacy, without a clear statement of who this legitimacy is regarded by, and a desire to give different, and perhaps more medical, language to her experience. The second openly speaks of a feeling of possession of the problem and frankly declares that vaginismus is a problem affecting her. Just as is seen in the quotations above from WA-EN-010 and the description of the power of being heard given by WA-EN-001, reappropriation of certain elements of the experience of sexual pain can be empowering, despite being framed within frustrating, potentially distressing and profoundly disempowering situations. This could be seen as a form of liberating and powerful renegotiation, which changes how participants have come to regard themselves and others.

Vulnerability was, however, a common experience in the narratives of many of the women interviewed. Wilson[23] proposes a definition of vulnerable research participants as 'peopl[e] whose strengths and positive attributes are generally overlooked, and who are confronted with differential risks and health burdens in comparison to others living in their community or country'. Part of the reflexive process in creating the methodology for this project was a commitment not to further marginalize participants or increase the 'risk' or 'health burden' they were experiencing but to recognize that the participants for the study may have been structurally and culturally marginalized in the complex neoliberal systems within which they live. Dealing with pain and its emotional and relational consequences, and also the stigma and vulnerability attached to long-term suffering, sometimes without a name, was reported by many participants as having taken a huge toll on their lives. WA-EN-001 felt like she was the problem, and that she was in fact stigmatized by the medical professionals she was consulting. This is how she described it:

> For me, I still struggle at times, like I feel, I think I'm the problem. Because, if you're told you're a problem often enough, you begin to believe it. So, something that could help me on a personal level is just ... let's get rid of the stigma.

For some of the participants, genital pain was not just experienced during sexual acts, but was experienced continuously or in many other areas of their life. Sexual pain was cited in the interviews as a direct cause of one participant leaving her job, as it became too painful to sit down, to 'go the cinema', 'go see friends', 'sit down in front of the TV', with this participant describing her pain at the time – which forced her to lie down rather than sit upright when not in a standing position – as 'awful'. WA-FR-008 spoke about her relationship with her own body following a sudden onset of pain:

> It's a bit of a double bind, you know, but ... uhh, but actually, ... for me, it's very much linked to sex, right, or to sexual relations anyway, uhh, well, it's not just during sex that it's painful, for example, if I put a finger in my vagina, it's going to hurt.

Not being able to touch an area of her body without pain had a notable effect for this participant, and she spoke of the frustration of not having a clear diagnosis for the problem despite wanting one. Though she spoke of renegotiating her relationship with her long-term partner in a positive way and how she had found other ways to express intimacy, the 'double bind' she spoke of clearly echoes the description of WA-EN-001 of feeling that there was a stigma around her experiences. The way that these participants might experience their own intimate lives – or their positioning within social divisions operating 'not as discrete and mutually exclusive entities' but as complex asymmetries of power building 'on each other' and working 'together'[24] – is complex, often difficult and can affect all aspects of women's lives. Where love is concerned here, it seems secondary to practical considerations, including employment status and healthcare opportunities, and it appears as part of intricate power dynamics which can stigmatize and complicate.

Reappropriation of intimacy in England and France

Preliminary analyses of the study data suggest that healthcare services providing assistance to people experiencing sexual pain can encompass numerous specialities in both England and France and can be staffed by diverse professionals with different backgrounds. The analyses undertaken from the semi-structured interviews in France show that navigating complex national systems of care relies on many factors, including the knowledge and inclination of the healthcare professional who is consulted, the way this information is communicated by the woman who is affected and the financial and structural constraints on the healthcare professional making referrals. Sadly, the interview findings also reveal that, for the women interviewed for this study, discounting of their symptoms as 'women's problems' further pathologized their entire being; suggestions that symptoms of treatable illnesses were being exaggerated or faked were common; and misuse of power, including non-consensual examination and touching, also took place. Sexual pain was felt by many participants to affect their whole being and self-perception, as 'one of the factors that kind of forecloses a lot of the interactions ... with other people' (WA-EN-010). In France, slightly more choice was reported by participants than in England, in that the healthcare professional consulted could often be chosen rather than allocated as part of the referral process, as was largely the case in England. In France, some participants reported that the treatments or specialist appointments they had sought or were seeking were not reimbursed by the state social security system, and that this added an extra layer of financial consideration and stress on their treatment options. Both private and public elements of healthcare services were evoked by the participants in England, yet the need to find healthcare professionals who are 'interested in finding out why' the pain was happening 'as opposed to going "oh well, could be this, could be that"' (WA-EN-002) was an integral part of accessing appropriate healthcare. Participants in both England and France reported the potential importance of knowing that 'other women go through the same thing as you' (WA-EN-007), and in contrast to France, English data reflected the predominant use of state-funded services, with only one participant speaking openly about using private services to confirm an issue she suspected was present after NHS services were 'quite dismissive' about it. Playing a part in the 'interlocking, mutually constructing or intersecting systems of power'[25] in both England and France was complex, with sexual pain experiences seen by many participants as flowing through many elements of their life, including the social, the intimate and the financial. Participants' embodiment of intimate power dynamics then, in England and in France, was at times reported as a conscious, powerful process which they took control of, and at other times as an arduous undertaking which forced them to establish a new way of being with themselves and with potential or current sexual partners. Love and both positive and negative affective relationships with individuals close to the participants were reported as another complex layer of the sexual pain experience of women in both England and France, but one which could bring comfort and reassurance at times.

The conclusions drawn from the analyses undertaken as part of this study bring an enlightening insight into how sexual pain, love and intimacy can be experienced in England and France and how they were lived by the women interviewed for this project. The results of this study are transferable in several different ways, including raising awareness of the issues around sexual pain to provide information for policy-making decisions and for commissioning groups involved in allocating resources to health services. Further research into this neglected area, especially where this research is collaborative and listens actively to structurally underserved groups, is crucial moving forward. The design of the study has prioritized involving participants and potential audiences from many different backgrounds, from frontline healthcare staff, to commissioners, to academics. The cross-national design of the study brought many advantages as well as an enlightening comparative element, and it has given exciting opportunities for further research into this area with non-academic professionals in both England and France. Non-heterosexual and non-monogamous experiences of sexual pain must be prioritized in further qualitative research into this topic as much of the existing research focuses on the experiences of heterosexual women in long-term relationships. The way that fluid intimate power dynamics are enacted by and upon bodies is complex, and this complexity is further manifested when genital sexual pain is experienced. This piece reveals only a snapshot of the data from this study, but it finds that coming to terms with sexual pain experiences, reappropriating sexual encounters and modifying these intimate power dynamics are formidable acts. To be part of the complex sociopolitical, relational and social systems in which we live, and to potentially embody the complexities of intimate acts, can be challenging. To adjust the ways of living and to renegotiate and reappropriate their own intimate lives following or during experiences of sexual pain is an act of power demonstrated by the participants of this study. Renegotiating intimate love is not always easy, but this study shows that taking small steps to challenge and dismantle the 'interlocking, mutually constructing or intersecting systems of power' is possible and, more than this, can be liberating.

Notes

1   See, for example, Chloë Taylor, 'Female Sexual Dysfunction, Feminist Sexology, and the Psychiatry of the Normal', *Feminist Studies* 41, no. 2 (2015): 259–92.

2   For example, Rosemary Basson et al., 'Report of the International Consensus Development Conference on Female Sexual Dysfunction: Definitions and Classifications', *Journal of Urology* 163 (2000): 888–93, and Micheline Byrne and Paula Christmas, 'Psychological Management of Pain Syndromes in a Sexual Health Setting', in *Psychological Management of Pain Syndromes in a Sexual Health Setting*, ed. David Miller and John Green (Oxford: Blackwell Science, 2002), 282–91.

3   Shere Hite, *The Hite Report on Female Sexuality* (London: Pandora, 1992), 60.

4   K. R. Mitchell et al., 'Painful Sex (Dyspareunia) in Women: Prevalence and Associated Factors in a British Population Probability Survey', *BJOG: An International Journal of Obstetrics and Gynaecology* (January 2017): 1.

5   This research was funded by the Vice Chancellor's Gender Equality in Europe Studentship at Nottingham Trent University from 2017 to 2020. Ethical approval for the semi-structured interviews was granted by the Joint Inter College Ethics Committee at Nottingham Trent University on 20 December 2017. I would like to gratefully acknowledge the support of Jonny Hatfull, and special thanks are due to Professor Gill Allwood of Nottingham Trent University.

6   Chloë Taylor, *The Routledge Guide to Foucault's History of Sexuality* (Oxon: Routledge, 2017), 109.

7   Michel Foucault, *The History of Sexuality, Volume I: The Will to Knowledge,* trans. Robert Hurley (London: Penguin, 1998), 140.

8   Ibid., 103.

9   Taylor, *The Routledge Guide to Foucault's History of Sexuality,* 12.

10 Michel Foucault, *The Birth of the Clinic: An Archaeology of Medical Perception,* trans. A. M. Sheridan (London: Routledge, 2012), xi.

11 Patricia Hill Collins and Sirma Bilge, *Intersectionality* (Cambridge: Polity, 2016), 13.

12 Devon W. Carbado et al., 'Intersectionality: Mapping the Movements of a Theory', *Du Bois Review* 10, no. 2 (2013): 303.

13 Hill Collins and Bilge, *Intersectionality,* 1.

14 Ibid., 1.

15 Ibid., 26–7.

16 Patti Lather and Chris Smithies, *Troubling the Angels: Women Living with HIV/AIDS* (New York: Routledge, 1997), xiii.

17 Ibid., xvi.

18 Ibid., 215.

19 Ibid., xvi.

20 Virginia Braun and Victoria Clarke, 'Using Thematic Analysis in Psychology', *Qualitative Research in Psychology* 3, no. 2 (2006): 77–101; Victoria Clarke and Virginia Braun, 'Using Thematic Analysis in Counselling and Psychotherapy Research: A Critical Reflection', *Counselling and Psychotherapy Research* 18, no. 2 (2018): 107–10; Virginia Braun and Victoria Clarke, 'Reflecting on Reflexive Thematic Analysis', *Qualitative Research in Sport, Exercise and Health* 11, no. 4 (2019): 589–97.

21 Lather and Smithies, *Troubling the Angels: Women Living with HIV/ AIDS,* xvi.

22 Hill Collins and Bilge, *Intersectionality,* 26–7.

23 Denise Wilson, 'Culturally Safe Research with Vulnerable Populations (Māori)', in *Handbook of Research Methods in Health Social Sciences,* ed. Pranee Liamputtong (Singapore: Springer, 2019), 1526.

24 Hill Collins and Bilge, *Intersectionality,* 13.

25 Ibid., 26–7.

Bibliography

Basson, Rosemary, Jennifer Berman, Arthur Burnett, Leonard Derogatis, David Ferguson, Jean Fourcroy, Ivan Goldstein, Alessandra Graziottin, Julia Heiman, Ellen Laan, Sandra Leiblum, Harin Padma-Nathan, Raymond Rosen, Kathleen

Segraves, Robert T. Segraves, Ridwan Shabsigh, Marcalee Sipski, Gorm Wagner and Beverly Whipple. 'Report of the International Consensus Development Conference on Female Sexual Dysfunction: Definitions and Classifications'. *Journal of Urology* 163 (2000): 888–93.

Braun, Virginia, and Victoria Clarke. 'Using Thematic Analysis in Psychology'. *Qualitative Research in Psychology* 3, no. 2 (2006): 77–101.

Braun, Virginia, and Victoria Clarke. 'Reflecting on Reflexive Thematic Analysis'. *Qualitative Research in Sport, Exercise and Health* 11, no. 4 (2019): 589–97.

Byrne, Micheline, and Paula Christmas. 'Psychological Management of Pain Syndromes in a Sexual Health Setting'. In *Psychological Management of Pain Syndromes in a Sexual Health Setting*, edited by David Miller and John Green, 282–91. Oxford: Blackwell Science, 2002.

Carbado, Devon W., Kimberlé Williams Crenshaw, Vickie M. Mays and Barbara Tomlinson. 'Intersectionality: Mapping the Movements of a Theory', *Du Bois Review* 10, no. 2 (2013): 303–12. https://doi.org/10.1017/S1742058X13000 349. Accessed 4 August 2017.

Clarke, Victoria, and Virginia Braun. 'Using Thematic Analysis in Counselling and Psychotherapy Research: A Critical Reflection'. *Counselling and Psychotherapy Research* 18, no. 2 (2018): 107–10.

Foucault, Michel. *The Birth of the Clinic: An Archaeology of Medical Perception* (trans. A. M. Sheridan). London: Routledge, 2012.

Foucault, Michel. *The History of Sexuality. Volume I: The Will to Knowledge* (trans. Robert Hurley). London: Penguin, 1998.

Hill Collins, Patricia, and Sirma Bilge. *Intersectionality*. Cambridge: Polity, 2016.

Hite, Shere. *The Hite Report on Female Sexuality*. London: Pandora, 1992.

Lather, Patti, and Chris Smithies. *Troubling the Angels: Women Living with HIV/ AIDS*. New York: Routledge, 1997.

Mitchell, Kirstin R., Rebecca Sally Geary, Cynthia Graham, Jessica Datta, Kaye Wellings, Pam Sonnenberg, Nigel Field, David Nunns, John Bancroft, Kyle G. Jones, Anne M. Johnson and Catherine Mercer. 'Painful Sex (Dyspareunia) in Women: Prevalence and Associated Factors in a British Population Probability Survey'. *BJOG: An International Journal of Obstetrics and Gynaecology* (January 2017): 1–9. https://doi.org/10.1111/1471-0528.14518. Accessed 3 August 2017.

Taylor, Chloë. *The Routledge Guidebook to Foucault's The History of Sexuality*. Oxon: Routledge, 2017.

Taylor, Chloë. 'Female Sexual Dysfunction, Feminist Sexology, and the Psychiatry of the Normal'. *Feminist Studies* 41, no. 2 (2015): 259–92.

Wilson, Denise. 'Culturally Safe Research with Vulnerable Populations (Māori)'. In *Handbook of Research Methods in Health Social Sciences*, edited by Pranee Liamputtong, 1525–42. Singapore: Springer, 2019. https://doi. org/10.1007/978-981-10-5251-4. Accessed 9 April 2020.

6

Kathy Acker's voice in *Blood and Guts in High School* and Deleuze and Guattari's 'desiring-machines'

Gemma Curto

Introduction

Kathy Acker explicitly references a passage on 'desiring-machines' from *Anti-Oedipus* ([1972] 2000) by Gilles Deleuze and Félix Guattari; she uses it as an intertext in her anti-realist *Blood and Guts in High School* (1978).[1]

In this chapter, I explore the oedipal family structures that appear in the novel, connected to *Blood and Guts*'s rejections of capitalist social structures, as they are understood to be authoritarian and patriarchal. By reading the oedipalization of the family as a pathology, Acker is interested in desire as a means to escape the limits of the dominant discourse. Janey, the main character in the book, represents a woman writer in a male-dominated society, whose background goes beyond the classical Freudian oedipal family structure that Deleuze and Guattari criticize. I contend that the directness with which Janey's voice stands up for an escape from the limits of the dominant discourse and for a genuine freedom of expression, together with the work's aesthetics, has a strong emancipatory power that revolves around Deleuze and Guattari's 'desiring-machines'.

Desiring-machines were conceived as large determinate aggregates (*des grands ensembles specifies*) whose 'molecular elements are: there, functioning, production, and formation are one and the same process'; 'it is this synthesis of desire that, under certain determinate conditions, explains the molar aggregates (*les ensembles molaires*) with their specific use in biological, social, or linguistic field' (181). According to Foucault, in his introduction to *Anti-Oedipus*, 'desiring-machines' are a combination of various elements and forces (xxiii) that have the potential to escape and to subvert oedipal codes and neuroticized territorialities. Deleuze and Guattari put all their uses together and all sectors of a field of production in the same pot and ask us not to explore the underlying meaning of desiring-machines but, instead, to focus on their connections, flows and breaks and to question the kind of machine that is assembled. They metaphorically compare desiring-machines to a 'magical chain' that produces 'connections according to which they function, and function by improvising and forming connections' (80). That magical chain is illustrated by a description of how an institution works; 'an institution cannot be explained by its use, any more than an organ can' (180). Desiring-machines operate beyond attachments to individual moles and work through connections and breaks. In *Blood and Guts*, initially, Janey is socially gender-determined. She attaches to immediate objects and is trapped in the dichotomy of sexual difference, 'I'm as closed up and fucked-up as everybody else' (283). However, at the same time, Janey attempts to liberate her organs through a revolutionary expression of desire that reflects Deleuze and Guattari's use of Artaud's body-without-organs, which 'is an affective, intensive, anarchist body that consists solely on poles, zones, thresholds, and gradients' (131). Her will to achieve freedom is evidenced in the way she acts to vindicate her human body. I will show here how Acker resists the notion of patriarchy by demonstrating her engagement with Deleuze and Guattari.

The emancipatory power of *Blood and Guts*'s aesthetics in relation to politics and social life seen through Deleuze and Guattari's concept of 'desiring-machines' is explored in this chapter. The representation of the desiring-machines is particularly relevant for us to examine the aesthetics of Janey's voice through the 'main' plot, images, maps and poems of Acker's novel. In relation to post-structuralist theory and aesthetic practices, the novel contains all the clichés of post-modern experimentalism. This pastiche apparently has no formal coherence and seems to be a refusal of the conventions of classical narrative. Its linearity is disrupted by means of repetitions, intertextual passages or visual art: it contains the paragraph Acker directly uses from Deleuze and Guattari on desiring-machines, as well as pornographic drawings, collages, extracts from *The Screens* (by Jean Genet), fragments from Stéphane Mallarmé, a 'book report' on *The Scarlet Letter*, a satirical letter from Erica Jong, a beast-fable, 'translations' of Propertius, Egyptian mythology and a series of dream-maps, among other elements.

In centring on Deleuze and Guattari's influence on the text, I discuss how *Blood and Guts* (and anti-novel) and narrative (and anti-narrative) encourage us to restructure the maps we use to navigate both the text and Janey's desire and the liberating force of Acker's aesthetics in relation to politics and social life through the notion of Deleuze and Guattari's desiring-machines. I argue that the novel represents the struggle to resist patriarchal control and the disruptive capacity of desire. Acker writes about the difficulty of aesthetic innovation and uses a non-linear narrative, creating a space between disordered and repeated narratives, intertextual passages and images. *Blood and Guts* becomes a blend of the reader, who connects the fragmented story line and the text. Janey's voice is a desiring-machine that embodies an emancipatory politics based on the practice of refusal and the desire for a self-created freedom of expression that eventually prevails over time.

Lived emotions through Hester Prynne's story

Blood and Guts is an example of literature set in the intersection between the highly experimental post-modernist style, late second-wave feminism and the violently politicized anti-novel. It uses formal disruption, interruptions and *mise-en-abyme* through a complex aesthetic formal incoherence. Intertextual references include Deleuze and Guattari's paragraph on 'desiring-machines' and Janey's recollection of Hester Prynne's story in *The Scarlett Letter*.[2] Because of the constant disruption of the narrative line, following the 'plot' of the novel can be frustrating, but it goes something like this: Janey Smith has an incestuous abusive relationship with her father Johnny, after which he abandons her for another woman. Janey leaves her home in Mexico and settles in New York, where she falls in with a street gang, engages in delinquent behaviour and undergoes two abortions. She is raped, suffers a car accident and is kidnapped and delivered to Linker, a Persian slave-trader, who trains her to be a sex worker. When he thinks she is ready to 'hit the streets', she finds out that she has cancer; rejected by Linker, she goes to Tangiers. In Tangiers, Janey meets Jean Genet; they travel together through North Africa and Alexandria and develop a relationship. He treats her badly and ends up leaving her. Soon after they part company, Janey dies suddenly, which leads to the creation of an infinite number of Janeys through a process of rebirth.

Lived emotions and formal experimentation are at the core of Kathy Acker's *Blood and Guts*'s approach to desire, which is all-encompassing and proposes an escape from senses of lust towards men. Janey criticizes such mindless cravings through her book report of *The Scarlet Letter*, where she explains the experience of Hester Prynne, which to a certain extent mirrors and is subverted by her own story. Janey overtly reveals Hester's sin and addresses a disconnection between body and mind when Hester was attracted to a man she was not married to.

Acker proposes embodied loving relationships with men and having mindful lived emotions when experiencing desire. Janey, by visibilizing Hester's crime, directly addresses the nature of the protagonist's desire and disapproves of it. While, in Hawthorne's novel, Hester's sin is never named (despite the fact that the novel's title alludes to it with the letter A and the baby Pearl), it does not explicitly reveal the crime of adultery. In Janey's account of Hester's story, after Hester and Dimmesdale's reunion, the narrator tells us that 'the guy who's screaming at her is the guy who fucked her' (68). By naming the nature of Hester's actions, Janey explores them without any of the censorship or societal pressures that Hester, and even Hawthorne, may have had at the time.

Secondly, Janey assumes that Hester Prynne's lust in *The Scarlett Letter* is senseless. Despite the fact that Hester thought Chillingworth was dead, Janey thinks that she acts upon her sexual desire without reflecting on its consequences. Hester had a husband, Chillingworth, to whom she was not attracted, and she desired Dimmesdale instead. In Janey's rewriting of the story, when Chillingworth wants to go after Dimmesdale, the narrator offers the following response: 'She shivers before this example of the divorcement of body and mind' (70). Another instance in which Janey describes Hester's 'divorcement of body and mind' (68) is when she discusses Hester's desire. Janey points out that 'Hester's thinking the most wonderful thing in the world is to fuck a man you love' (70). It is crucial to point out that in Janey's story, Hester did not consider whether the man values her in return. While Janey explores Hester's expectation that physical desire would set her free, Hester, actually, became co-dependent and felt guilty in *The Scarlet Letter*. In turn, hypocrisy, hatred and sole intellectual power are seen as undesirable in the original novel and in Acker's recollection of it.

At the start of Janey's report on Hester Prynne's story, Janey believed that we all lived in a prison, and she was searching for a love that could not be found. However, at several points after Hester's story, Janey explores ways in which she could love herself and feel like a free woman. For instance, after telling Hester Prynne's story, she teaches herself Persian without the help of anyone else. Her notebook is shared with the reader. It includes simple sentences about herself, as she starts to make sense of her own identity. Her notes begin with 'Janey. Janey is a girl' (72). This is followed by sentences in which she reflects upon the idea of self-worth: 'She was a stupid girl: she went and offered herself, awkwardly, to someone who didn't want her. That's not stupid. The biggest pain in the world is feeling but sharper is the pain of the self' (87). By writing her notes, Janey embraces non-materialistic ideals while taking on a lived emotion and independence.

Another point at which Janey expresses her desire to go 'out as far as possible in freedom' (100) occurs when she goes 'totally insane' (116) after her cancer diagnosis. She breaks down the wall of her prison and decides to explore the world: 'All the pain and misery she had been feeling, crime and terror on the street had come out. She was no longer totally impotent and passive about her lousy situation' (116). As she lives the emotion and experience of having the lump, the narrator mentions that 'Janey was learning to love herself', overcoming 'the divorcement of body and mind' (166) that Janey uses to refer to Hester Prynne's experience. After Janey dies, more Janeys are born, creating new versions of herself after overcoming addictive attachments to men. Through multiple intertextual connections, including Hawthorne's *Scarlett Letter*, Acker creates a project of discovery of self-worth and freedom.

Blood and Guts's anti-Oedipus

Janey's desire for love through the representation of Deleuze and Guattari's desiring-machines incorporates her desire to overcome male dominance of her body. I argue that Janey is both post-pubescent and pre-oedipal because she has not emerged from the oedipal stage. Glenn A. Harper describes 'the pre-Oedipal attachment to body-parts that give satisfaction rather than to the unified person carrying the organ'.[3] Twenty-seven years later, Katie R. Muth reads *Blood and Guts* as an indictment of society's sexual and imperial politics. While critics Harper and Muth have focused on Janey's exploration of biopower and her attachment to her sexual organs, my argument highlights the protagonist's desire for love, which involves self-love and desiring-machines, which lead to her rebirth. I contend that the novel incorporates three main features of post-structuralist discourse. Firstly, the exploration of biopower; secondly, the reading of the oedipal family as pathology; and thirdly, an analysis of the gender politics of language. If we interpret the story allegorically, we might say that Janey stands for a woman writer in a male-dominated society. Regarding the oedipal family, Acker reads Deleuze and Guattari's *Anti-Oedipus* and develops a critique of the phallocentric society that reinforces the male territory within society. Some oedipal elements in the novel are the reverse of an oedipal structure, but some elements are still similar, as Janey rejects the maternal and the phallic family. Through the repetition of a core narrative, *Blood and Guts* leaves behind that oedipal family, which results in Janey's rebirth. Therefore, the recurrent problem that is presented in the novel is the liberation of the individual. Janey's desire for Johnny goes beyond the classical oedipal family structure where there is a desire for the mother, a rivalry with the father and a final sexual identification as a subject/woman. That happens through paralleling the oedipal family with a maternal substitute of the phallic. In order to explore avenues in which feminist resistance to the dominant patriarchal order exists, the conjunction between Irigaray, and Deleuze and Guattari provides the framework to conceptualize both feminist practice and practices of resistance, which align with Acker and can be understood as a challenge to the phallocentric order. At this junction, in the thoughts of Irigaray, by privileging maternal over feminine essence, a woman loses the uniqueness of her pleasure (30).[4]

Notwithstanding that, at the start of the novel, Janey is at the stage when the male and female sex organs become part-objects, as the narrative progresses, she grows into a self-aware and confident woman. This is exteriorized when she decides to travel to Tangiers. After Genet leaves her, she dies. More Janeys are reborn as an act of self-renewal and transformation, rather than reiterating her desire for men through sexual reproduction. Acker wants to liberate the organs from the narrowly anatomical focus of the character that is socially gender-determined, and this is achieved through rebirth. Furthermore, art, which might seem meaningless in a materialistic society, enables Janey to express her desire to overcome male dominance over her body. In the essay, 'Models of Our Present', Acker describes her own experience of art:

> Meaning dominates or controls existence. But desire – or art – is ... If art's to be more than craft, more than decorations for the people in power, it's this want, this existence ... Only the cry, art, rather than the description or criticism, is primary. The cry is stupid; it has no mirror; it communicates. I want to cry.[5]

Anti-Oedipus influenced Kathy Acker's *Blood and Guts*, and a paragraph on desiring-machines is quoted directly:

> Every position of desire, no matter how small, is capable of putting to question the established order of a society; not that desire is asocial; on the contrary, but it is explosive; there is no desiring-machine capable of being assembled without demolishing entire social sections. (125)

Deleuze and Guattari favour man's connection to their desires and natural life processes, which include a process of desiring-production that would manifest itself in growth. The real danger is not a desire for the mother or for the death of the father; desire becomes that Oedipal triangulation when it is repressed. On the contrary, desire has the potential to create unconscious and conscious investments in the social field, to break down the established order and to give voice to revolutionaries, including artists. Desire is reproduced through Kathy Acker's writing of *Blood and Guts*. It reproduces intensely moving away from disconnections and territorialization to create new connections. Kathy Acker's voice, expressed through Janey, ceases to be concerned with pleasing men, being right or wrong, or with justice or about fitting in with the behaviour of her fellow human beings. Within Deleuze and Guattari's framework, *Blood and Guts* moves away from madness and manifests life in growth, a growth that is an endless, eternal process.

Anti-Oedipus: Capitalism and Schizophrenia is the first volume of work that was produced as a result of the collaboration between the philosopher Gilles Deleuze and the psycholanalyst Félix Guattari, the second being *A Thousand Plateaus*,[6] in which they analyse the relationship between desire and capitalism. Firstly, they outline the concept of desiring-production and the body without organs. Secondly, they offer a critique of Sigmund Freud's psychoanalysis and the Oedipus complex. Thirdly, they describe capitalist societies as being barbarian. Finally, they develop the practice of 'schizoanalysis'. 'Schizoanalysis' takes the problem of the Oedipus complex as a starting point. For them, Oedipus is 'first the idea of an adult paranoiac, before it is the childhood feeling of a neurotic' (274), with the father being the one who raises the idea of incest with the mother in the mind of the son. Deleuze and Guattari argue that psychoanalysis focuses too much on deep analysis of the individual, where it is difficult to escape an infinite regression to the past. Repeated regression seems to be inadequate because it keeps the subject of reproduction and sexuality in the service of regressive generations throughout a cyclical movement, from where it is difficult to move forward. If the person is the result of reproduction, then we can argue that, in the oedipal family relationship, the father comes first, and the first instance is about the social investment to which the father and the child are trapped. That is, what the child invests in their early ages through the family structure is the state of the social field, its distribution and its flows. Hence, Deleuze and Guattari argue that 'the social investments are first in relation to familial investments' and that 'the investment of desire is in the first instance the investment of a social field to which the father and the child are plunged, simultaneously immersed' (275).

Kathy Acker's desiring-machines

In their critique of the oedipal family and psychoanalysis, Deleuze and Guattari so deal with the problem of communication of *the unconscious of the father and the mother* (278), where the family is blocking the unconscious investments in the social field. For this reason, they refute Freudian paternalism, based on the father figure, and develop schizoanalysis theories and techniques. As opposed to the rigid structure of the Freudian family, where 'Oedipus restrained is the figure of the daddy-mommy-me triangle, the familial constellation in person' (51), they propose a more emotional model. Instead of advocating for a representational narrative in her novel, Acker aligns with Deleuze and Guattari's zones of intensity, emotion and becoming. To Deleuze and Guattari:

> Nothing here is representative; rather, it is all life and lived experience, the actual, lived emotion of having breasts does not resemble breasts, it does not represent them, any more than a predestined zone in the egg resembles the organ that it is going to be stimulated to produce within itself. (19)

In *Blood and Guts*, Janey stresses the importance of the '*I feel*' (18). She desires for a lived emotional experience with her father, rather than an affective relationship in the realm of fantasy: 'I fantasize you take me in your arms again and again, telling me you love me. I don't know whether I can let myself fantasize that because it isn't true … Or I have to wipe you out of my mind' (26). Connectivity is paramount in Deleuze and Guattari's desiring-machines, which includes multiplicity, fragmentation and becoming. It contrasts with a Freudian structure that is represented as a triangle, an extension of the subjects and their multiple relatives, descendants and ascendants. According to Deleuze and Guattari, the main difference between the oedipal structure and the desiring-machines is that while 'all the Oedipuses crush and repress', in their model, 'desiring-production – the machines of desire' 'no longer allow themselves to be reduced to the structure any more than to persons' (52). Societal structures involve an established order that involves repression, hierarchy and exploitation. Conversely, desire is by definition revolutionary and asocial, as it threatens an established order:

> Desire is revolutionary in its essence – desire, not left-wing holidays! – and no society can tolerate a position of real desire without its structures of exploitation, servitude, and hierarchy being compromised. (118)

Desiring-machines are inclusive and, while everything functions at the same time, they include fragmentation; they are not totalitarian because 'desiring-production is pure multiplicity' (42). Individual desire translates into the politics of fighting against subjugating powers, and it helps to develop groups and individuals that free themselves from norms: 'Such a politics does not seek to regiment individuals according to a totalitarian system of norms, but to de-normalize and de-individualize through a multiplicity of new, collective arrangements against power' (xxi). Acker makes a stance against a materialistic society that separates sex from feelings, a situation correlated to the glorification of S&M, slavery and prison.[7] A sexual revolution, just for the sake of wanting more, makes people unable to access feeling and a revolutionary desire. Acker's rejection of a patriarchal society is described by Janey as 'robot fucking. Mechanical fucking. Robot love. Mechanical love. Money cause.'[8] In this quotation, she refers to Hester Prynne's tortured mind, sex drive, feelings of jealousy and possessiveness as experienced by Hester herself, her husband and her lover. However, Janey breaks out of the prison of her mind and becomes free through multiple versions of herself.

In this vein, Deleuze and Guattari develop a polarity-based model, where delirium is the force that transmits social investments, from the paranoiac fascisizing pole to the schizorevolutionary pole, which presents '*lines of flight*' or '*lines of escape*' of desire. In *A Thousand Plateaus*, this concept is used to define a rhizome where 'there is a rupture in the rhizome whenever segmentary lines explode into a line of flight ... That is why one can never posit a dualism or a dichotomy, even in the rudimentary form of the good and the bad.'[9] This polarity-based model is based on the Mommy–daddy–child triangulation in which the segregated subject belongs to the 'superior race' and class. This model has a subject who belongs to the majoritarian who is threatened by enemies from outside.[10] On the other hand, the schizorevolutionary pole follows a 'revolutionary unconscious investment' in which 'desire, still in its own mode, cuts across the interest of the dominated, the exploited classes, and causes flows to move that are capable of breaking apart both the segregations and their Oedipal applications' (105). Foucault, in the introduction to *Anti-Oedipus*, defines what is 'against the Oedipal and oedipalized territorialities (Family, Church, School, Nation, Party), and especially the territoriality of the individual; *Anti-Oedipus* seeks to discover the "deterritorialized" flows of desire' (xvii). At this junction, a reference to Deleuze and Guattari's types of social investment is fundamental. For them, there are

> two major types of social investment, segregative and nomadic, just as there are two poles of delirium, first, a paranoiac fascisizing (*Fascisant*) type or pole that invests in the formation of central sovereignty ... And second, a schizorevolutionary type or pole that follows the *lines of escape* of desire: that breaches the walls and causes flows to move; assembles its machines and groups-in-fusion in the enclaves or at the periphery. (277)

The schizorevolutionary pole assembles its machines, proceeds to a revolutionary escape and aims to change the social system. The unconscious shows oscillations between these polarities, where paranoia is different from schizophrenia, which is about the breakthrough process mentioned above. To summarize, the oedipal construction belongs to the paranoiac territory where the individual is enclosed, while schizophrenia involves lines of escape. In a passage of her 'book report', Janey relates the part-objects sex organs to the practice of writing:

> I want to write myself between your lips and between your thighs ...
> I used to have lots of fantasies about you: You'd marry me, you'd dump

me, you'd fuck me, you were going again and again with your former girlfriend, you'd save me from blindness. You'd. Verb. Me. Now the only image in my mind is your cock in my cunt. I can't think of anything else. (95)

Janey attaches to immediate objects, with no priorities that are her own. Later on in the novel, she tries to liberate her organs from an anatomical focus, which can be considered an attempt to undercut the socially gendered order and to convey a revolutionary expression of desire. Deleuze and Guattari use Artaud's body-without-organs to describe the condition of the human body free from the punishments of the repressive God. According to Artaud, in his chapter 'To Have Done with Judgement', he points out that judgement imposes limits and imprisons us. It forces a doctrine of order at the level of the body, in which individual organs judge and are judged. However, Artaud claims that the body, as an organism, is completely different because it escapes from judgement.[11] Moreover, Artaud, and Deleuze and Guattari remap the fixed biological body, where all the different organs are organized in a certain way and develop a model for the body based on affection. For the 'body without organs is an affective, intensive, anarchist body that consists solely of poles, zones, thresholds, and gradients. It is traversed by a powerful, nonorganic vitality.'[12] Although Janey is committed to using the sexual organs for the purpose of fulfilling her sexual desire, which is easily assimilated in a capitalist society, before she dies she expresses her feelings of being trapped in the dichotomy of the sexual difference in her pursuit to put into question the gendered constructions: 'I'm as closed up and fucked-up as everybody else. I am hell. The world is hell' (283).

Before her death, Janey's oedipal desire for the father is repeated again and again through her multiple affairs with male characters. Mr Linker, Reverend Dimwit (Janey's adaptation of Dimmesdale in *The Scarlet Letter*), President Carter and the Capitalists all replicate the violent, off-hand fucking and rejection that Johnny started. She asks: 'How can I be happy if a man doesn't fuck and love me?'[13] Seen from the Deleuzian and Guattarian perspective, we can argue that Janey is trapped in a repeated regression to the classical oedipal family structure from which she cannot escape. Acker's depiction of traumatic events returns in the way Deleuze and Guattari explain:

How does psychoanalysis go about reducing a person, who this time is not a schizophrenic but a neurotic, to a pitiful creature who eternally consumes daddy-and-mommy and nothing else whatsoever? How could the conjunctive synthesis of 'so that's what it was!' and 'So it's me!' have been reduced to the endless, dreary discovery of Oedipus: 'so it's my father, my mother? (21)

In addition to Janey's repeated desire for a man, language structures are repeated and narrative passages reinforce the idea of oedipalization and express her always-constructing identity and desires. As a response to oedipal regressions, Deleuze and Guattari second Artaud's orphan child, as he does not 'believe in father in mother, got no papamummy' (16). For that, he says, 'I have been my father and I have been my son'; 'I, Antonin Artaud, am my son, my father, my mother, and myself.'[14] They do not invoke the genealogical regression that defines the oedipal model because they escape the oedipal triangular scheme produced by parents. Deleuze and Guattari form a binary system where desiring-production and their own system coordinate the individual according to his or her own code.

By using the 'language that means something' to her (96), Janey initially struggles to resist oedipal family structures and patriarchal control through the disruptive capacity of desire. This is demonstrated in Janey's narration of Hester's story – she tried to be a good girl, but was 'a good dead girl ... The child was the sign of her nastiness and disintegration and general insanity' (67). However, it is Janey's desire to have an alternative relationship to power and to reformulate her feminine subjectivity. She advocates for the madness of desire in order to express her judgement of everyday life practice: 'Fight the dullness of shit society. Alienated robotized images. Here's your cooky ma'am. No to anything but madness' (35). Here desire, for her, is a cry for freedom of expression against the dominant voice. According to Deleuze and Guattari's criticism of the oedipal psychoanalytical approach that I explained above, a desire for repressed family background blocks communication and expression of the individual towards society. Therefore, Acker, through her own art in language and her direct voice, avoids reproducing social and family structures and appropriates the immediate present to rethink and construct her self-created identity.

Navigating desiring-machines through dreams

In this section I am going to explore how dreams provide '*lines of flight*' that contribute to the expression of free discourse and art in *Blood and Guts*. Maps in *Blood and Guts* offer a playground for readers where they can navigate away from the linear narrative of a chronologically constructed timeline within a traditional text. It is extremely challenging for a reader to construct a single, coherent narrative and then see that this collapses into the series of Janey-parables that run through the plot of the novel as a whole.

When Janey could dream, dreams provided her with a fleeting, much-desired space for freedom: 'It's not that the vision-world, the world of passion and wilderness, no longer existed. It always is. But awake I was disconnected from dreams. I was psychotic' (40). They are named *A Map of My Dreams* and *Dream Map 2* (46–51). Significantly, although these maps offer arrows that indicate recommended trajectories to follow, it is demanding to navigate the narratives because they present repeated images and dead-ends, and an accurate interpretation of them is even more difficult. Instead of trying to convey meaning to each of the maps and to build a coherent argument, the maps are meant to offer the reader an interpretation of the page as a whole, by confronting the map and the story. For example, on top of the second and the third, there is an oedipal autobiographical narrative. It starts like this: 'the nightmare I had when my father tried to fuck me'. At the bottom of the page, we have the 'Cops-and-Robbers Dreams', which can be read as a critique of capitalism. In the middle of the page are worm-narratives that connect the two stories. Muth reads the dream maps as a gloss on *Anti-Oedipus* talking about the desiring-machines and the body without organs. Contrary to Muth's argument that dreams run the plot, in my view, her *Dream Maps* provide the protagonist with glimpses of the '*lines of flight*' and eternity that she will experience when she dies.[15] In *Bodies of Work*, Acker considers what it is like to write outside the linear narrative or time, in which she is thinking about 'the difference between history and myth. Or between expression and vision. The need for narrative and the simultaneous need to escape the prison-house of the story.'[16] While Janey felt rejected by everyone else around her – 'everyone at the bakery avoided me. I was the place and there was a huge emptiness around me'[17] – the maps provide her with a momentarily relief from her psychotic numbness. Janey eventually takes a '*line of flight*' and embraces infinity when she breaks down the walls of her prison and flies to Tangiers because she believes in eternity. This is illustrated in her discussion with Tommy when she states, 'everything lasts for ever' and that 'love goes away only when your mind goes away and then you're someone else' (42). Her ultimate desire for everlasting love is manifested when she dies and versions of her are reproduced, instead of giving birth to sons or daughters, 'soon many other Janeys were born and these Janeys covered the earth' (165). I argue that this fact does not provide her with an oedipal narcissistic reproduction, but, contrary to this, after finding her '*line of flight*' during her trip to Tangiers, she has freed herself from her physical body forever.

In Map 1 (Figure 6.1), the worms in the centre of the maps are a reference to the 'larvae and loathsome worms' that are beneath the machine's organs and 'a God at work messing it all up or strangling it by organizing it' (8). Therefore, if God or the social forces organize the molecular, the machines become repellent, too dominant or an assemblage. For them, 'this is the real meaning of the paranoiac machine: the desiring-machines attempt to break into the body without organs, and the body without organs repels them, since it experiences them as an over-all persecution apparatus' (8). The worms in the maps attempt to offer the reader an escape from the machine's organs; they are designed for 'nomads' and not meant to be followed in a linear way.

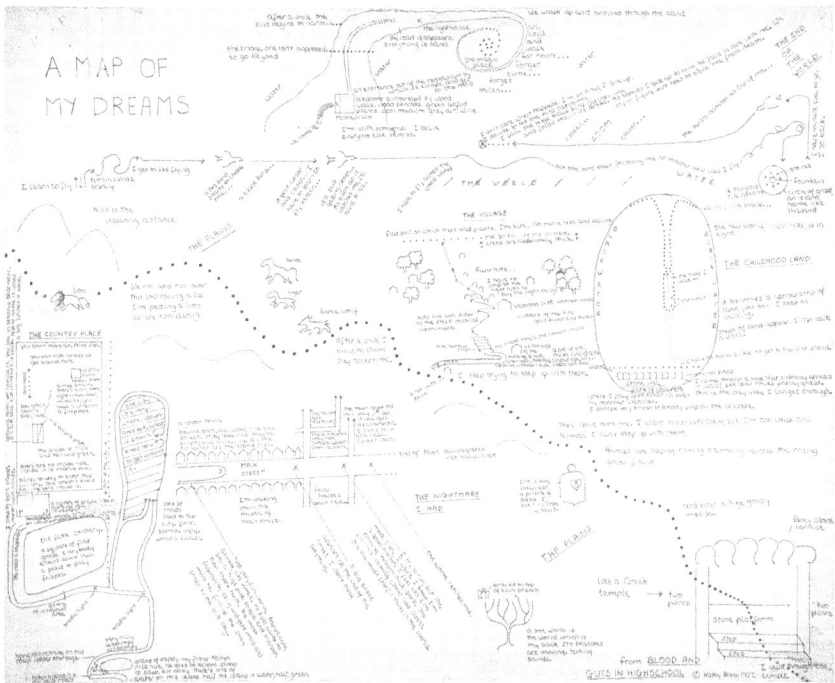

FIGURE 6.1 Map of My Dreams. *Courtesy of Matias Viegener, Kathy Acker Literary Trust.*

If the main narrative line reinforces the status quo and the power of literature over a passive reader, the moments where the narratives are disrupted resist machine's organs and go beyond the fixed and established patriarchal culture. When writing stops between one dead end and another section, there is a moment when creativity and thinking arise for the reader. Deleuze and Guattari talk about the potentiality of this moment, and they use Bartleby's formula – 'I would prefer not to' (68–90) – to illustrate it. The interruption and dead ends that Acker places between each fragment also help explore the potential of negation, which was a canonical practice in post-modern experimentation. In the space between, there is a refusal to write, which separates the reader from the authoritarian logic of the oedipal-capitalist model. Both the reader and the text merge; the text triggers the reader's imagination while wanting to make sense of a fragmented storyline. The convergence of the reader and the text is a desiring-machine, where desire is not repressed. For Acker, there is an emancipatory politics in this practice of refusal because her narrative suspensions celebrate the act of positive negation. Acker prefers not to write. As a machinery assemblage, the novel requires an engagement with the reader. However, it does not

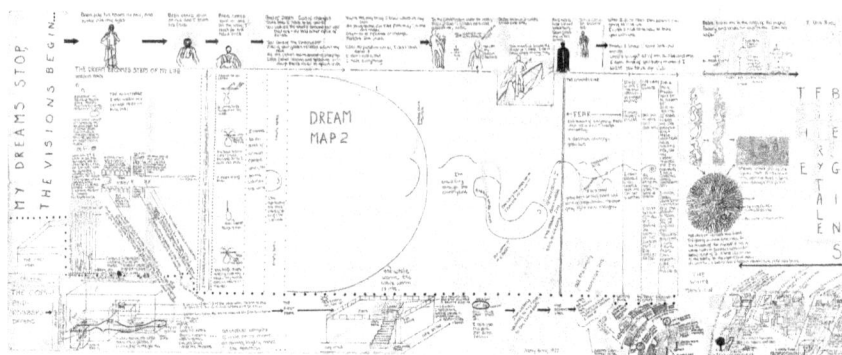

FIGURE 6.2 Dream Map 2. *Courtesy of Matias Viegener, Kathy Acker Literary Trust.*

force on the reader a specific interpretation, and the subject imagines the perfect potentiality. As well as providing opportunities for self-expression and art, *Blood and Guts* creates discourse within a community by the use of intertexual references:

> Discourse, I am using given meanings and values, changing them and giving them back. A community, a society is always being constructed in a discourse if and when discourse- including art- is allowed. Societies whose economies are set, fascist ones for instance, place little or no emphasis on free discourse, on art.[18]

Departing from a modernist society in which there was a cult for the new creativity and authorship, Kathy Acker argues that she writes 'with words which are given to me [her]'.[19] No one owns anything; no one can create anything from scratch, but you can use, adjust, express and make. Egotism that arises from the notion of creativity is equated to a phallic centrism, a society dominated by the oedipal taboo that dominates the political, economic, social and personal levels. When Acker uses intertextual references, she copies, then she writes and finds the road for her survival. I argue that Acker writes not only about freedom from patriarchal oppression but also about the formal difficulty for aesthetic innovation. Acker engages with theory and aesthetic praxis, and her anti-capitalist view is concerned with human emancipation.

Conclusion

As Kathy Acker reads and explicitly uses a passage on desiring-machines from Deleuze and Guattari's *Anti-Oedipus*, in this essay I have evaluated schizoanalysis as a method used in her novel *Blood and Guts*. Specifically, a critical analysis of the oedipal family structures that appear in the novel has been developed, connected to the rejections of capitalist social structures as being authoritarian and patriarchal. In this context, the representation of the desiring-production is particularly relevant. The aesthetics of the main character's voice, through the 'main' plot, images, maps and poems, has been examined. I contend that Janey's angry voice is so direct that it escapes the limits of the dominant discourse and expresses a genuine freedom of expression. In addition to Acker's revolutionary narrator, the anti-realist elements that *Blood and Guts* show are aligned within the context of post-structuralism. Both approaches to the narrative have a strong politics and social emancipatory power, which revolves around Deleuze and Guattari's. The story-telling technique, which includes dream maps, contributes to free the reader from the authoritarian voice of a classical narrative and provides freedom to navigate narrative spaces and a gap for thought.

Additional notes

Kathy Acker started working on the dream maps in the autumn of 1973 as she was producing the mail-art chapters of *The Childlike Life of the Black Tarantula by the Black Tarantul*a. Rather than being composed from a master outline, *Blood and Guts* is an assemblage of parts written over four years, assembled in 1978, but not published until 1984. The first *Map of My Dreams* is on a sheet of paper 71 × 57 cm; the second, *Dream Map 2*, is twice as large, composed on two pieces of paper side by side. They are far too detailed to be reproduced inside the scale of a book and have been distributed in high-resolution digital formats to enable readers to see their original form. The maps and drawings for *Blood and Guts* are held in the collection of Sallie Bingham Center for Women's History and Culture in Duke University's David M. Rubenstein Rare Book & Manuscript Library.

Notes

1	Gilles Deleuze and Félix Guattari, *Anti-Oedipus* (Minneapolis: University of Minnesota Press, [1972] 2000); Kathy Acker, *Blood and Guts in High School* (New York: Grove Press, 1978).

2	Nathaniel Hawthorne, *The Scarlet Letter* (New York: Barnes and Noble Classics, [1850] 2005).

3	Glenn A. Harper, 'The Subversive Power of Sexual Difference in the Work of Kathy Acker', *Substance* 16, no. 3 (1987): 44–56, 49.

4	Lucy Irigaray, *This Sex Which Is Not One*, trans. Carolyn Porter with Carolyn Burke (Ithaca, NY: Cornell University Press, 1985).

5 Kathy Acker, 'Models of Our Present', *Artforum International* 22, no. 6 (1984): 99.

6 Gilles Deleuze and Félix Guattari, *A Thousand Plateaus* (London: Continuum, [1980] 2004).

7 Acker, 'Models of Our Present', 62–5.

8 Acker, *Blood and Guts in High School*, 98.

9 Deleuze and Guattari, *A Thousand Plateaus*, 10.

10 Deleuze and Guattari, *Anti-Oedipus*, 103.

11 Gilles Deleuze, *Essays Critical and Clinical* (London: Verso, [1993] 1998), 131.

12 Ibid.

13 Acker, *Blood and Guts in High School*, 93.

14 Antonin Artaud, 'Here Lies', in *Artaud Anthology*, trans. and ed. Jack Hirschman (San Francisco, CA: City Light Books, 1965), 238–50.

15 Katie R. Muth, 'Postmodern Fiction as Poststructuralist Theory: Kathy Acker's *Blood and Guts in High School*', *Narrative* 19, no. 1 (2011): 86–110.

16 Kathy Acker, *Bodies of Work* (London: Serpent's Trail, 1997), ix–x.

17 Acker, *Blood and Guts in High School*, 40.

18 Acker, *Bodies of Work*, 4.

19 Ibid.

Bibliography

Artaud, Antonin. 'Here Lies'. In *Artaud Anthology*, translated and edited by Jack Hirschman, 238–50. San Francisco, CA: City Light Books, 1965.

Acker, Kathy. *Blood and Guts in High School*. New York: Grove Press, 1978.

Acker, Kathy. 'Models of Our Present'. *Art Forum International* 22, no. 6 (1984): 62–5.

Acker, Kathy. *Bodies of Work*. London: Serpent's Trail, 1997.

Deleuze, Gilles. *Essays Critical and Clinical*. London: Verso, [1993] 1998.

Deleuze, Gilles, and Félix Guattari. *Anti-Oedipus*. Minneapolis: University of Minnesota Press, [1972] 2000.

Deleuze, Gilles, and Félix Guattari. *A Thousand Plateaus*. London: Continuum, [1980] 2004.

Harper, Glenn A. 'The Subversive Power of Sexual Difference in the Work of Kathy Acker'. *Substance* 16, no. 3 (1987): 44–56.

Hawthorne, Nathaniel. *The Scarlet Letter*. New York: Barnes and Noble Classics, [1850] 2005.

Irigaray, Lucy. *This Sex Which Is Not One* (trans. Carolyn Porter with Carolyn Burke). Ithaca, NY: Cornell University Press, 1985.

Muth, Katie R. 'Postmodern Fiction as Poststructuralist Theory: Kathy Acker's *Blood and Guts in High School*'. *Narrative* 19, no. 1 (2011): 86–110.

7

Digital love: Love through the screen/of the screen

Daniel O'Brien

Computer love, computer love
Stare at the TV screen, stare at the TV screen
For a data date, for a data date.[1]

Introduction

Love and technology have historically overlapped in reality and fiction. With the inauguration of Web 2.0, the internet has become a digital ocean of togetherness, a virtual dataspace promising love and companionship through the ubiquity of dating apps, chat rooms and virtual intimacy. This chapter considers the notion of digital and virtual love through a range of fictional texts and real-life practices. It explores how love and intimacy has and continues to be reconfigured through new technological shifts. As new social and AI technologies develop, societal attitudes, understandings and practices of love are equivalently updated. This chapter analyses these ideas by investigating computerized practices of love, such as dating games and location-based devices (designed to bring people together), before moving on to think about how such practices are represented in film.

Pierre-Paul Renders's *Thomas est Amoureux* (*Thomas in Love*, 2000) and Spike Jonze's *Her* (2013) offer representations of love through and of the mediating computer, inviting spectators to consider new ideas of intimacy via a screen device. Love of the AI robot is then considered in more detail in the final section, where I discuss Bina48 and interview Bruce Duncan, the managing director of LifeNaut. This chapter probes the relationship between love and technological devices, real and fictional, to consider the harmonious and harmful aspects of love and technology, whereupon technological devices reconfigure love.

Love and technology

Prior to Web 2.0, early incarnations of the relationship between love and technology existed through digital devices such as early computer games and Tamagotchi toys, pocket devices that taught children how to love and care for virtual pets. Although graphically rudimentary, Tamagotchi toys were designed to enable the user to experience a complex emotional range through the care of a virtual lifeform. As games theorist Espen Aarseth asserts, digital games and devices like the Tamagotchi evoke real feelings of love (or guilt if the pet should die) because they utilize what he calls 'ludo-realism'.[2] However, such love and emotional response is clearly one-sided from player to device, but other pre-web gadgets have attempted to address this.

The Lovegety (introduced in Japan in 1998) was a popular handheld locative device from Erfolg which also manufactured Tamagotchi. It was designed to remotely connect strangers in public spaces who were both looking for love. The oval-shaped appliance consisted of three buttons enabling users to select 'talk', 'karaoke' and 'get2' (the latter potentially meaning to get together in a closer way rather than just talking or singing). 'Once the holder selects a mode, the device searches for Lovegety holders of the opposite sex in a five-meter radius. If it locates a holder with the same mode, the "get" light flashes and the device beeps, so the pair can find each other.'[3] The so-called love technology is clearly flawed insomuch that the user has no indication of the person they are likely to meet, and any hopes of same-sex partnerships seem to have been neglected, but the Lovegety does clearly indicate the reliance humans have put upon technology in order to experience love.

Brian Rotman argues that the written word, or speech in general, is a specific tool which signals the first wave of virtuality. As such, speech and the written word are the original technology that pluralizes the self. As he states, the 'dumb haptic, self-pointing "me" to spoken "I" is a shift from actual to virtual'.[4] He notes that speech is an 'out-of-body template' that involves a 'shift from ... a proprioceptive self to its symbolic form'[5] and argues that 'if X is "me", then virtual X is spoken "I"'.[6] In accordance with Rotman, language is a technology that extends and pluralizes selfhood, which has given new meaning to intimacy and practices of love, exacerbated today through AI and robotic companionship. An early incarnation of which is ELIZA, a computer programme coded by Joseph Weizenbaum from 1964 to 1966 at the MIT Artificial Intelligence Laboratory. ELIZA's programme, which processes natural language, was originally intended to show the superficiality of communication between human and machine, but quickly evolved to the illusion of meaningful conversation between human and machine through its fluent responses. As James Moor notes, 'The mechanism behind ELIZA is a very simple one. First, what is typed into the program is parsed. Then, a suitable reply is formulated by simple pattern recognition and substitutions of keywords.'[7] As Moor highlights, the programme of ELIZA is coded to listen:

> ELIZA directs the conversation away from herself by asking questions. Many people like this and happily believe that the program is listening as they talk about themselves. ELIZA uses parts of the user's input in the output questions and seems to be following the conversation.[8]

Consequentially, 'it has been reported that some people have developed emotional attachments to ELIZA. Certain psychiatrists went so far as to suggest that some programs could replace psychotherapists altogether.'[9] But fundamentally, this relationship is one-sided, leaving a human in an echo chamber, where the misrecognition of their own voice comes to stand for love or meaningful interaction.

AI and love

Adrian David Cheok and Emma Yann Zhang explore togetherness between a human and an artificial partner charting the success of early Otome and Bishoujo games, popular 1980s Japanese dating simulation games – a significant decade for the proliferation of human–computer relations across mainstream culture and academia in the form of Ridley Scott's *Blade Runner* (1982),[10] William Gibson's *Neuromancer* (1984)[11] and Donna Haraway's *A Cyborg Manifesto* (1985),[12] to name just a few.[13] As Cheok and Yann Zhang observe, Bishoujo games were originally marketed towards male players, where the object of the game was to win the affection of animated Japanese girls. The success led to corresponding Otome games, marketed to a female audience in 1994. As Cheok and Yann Zhang assert:

> In recent years, playing Otome games on mobile phones has become a rising trend among Japanese women … With an increased percentage of women in the working class, most of them are often too busy and tired for dating and relationships. There is also a huge gap between ideals and reality when it comes to what women look for in a partner.[14]

Here Cheok and Yann Zhang indicate some of the problems attached to organic and inorganic relationships, noting that the seemingly flawless partners, ever-present upon screen devices, offer a false sense of love which becomes more convenient and, in some extreme cases, preferable to that of human contact. A well-known example is the matrimony between a male gamer known as Sal9000 and his virtual girlfriend Nene Anegasaki (a character from the Nintendo DS dating simulation game Love Plus)[15] within the real world in Tokyo during 2009. The marriage was, of course, not recognized legally but did involve a ceremony performed by a priest and had the presence of real-life guests, captured and live-cast across social media, allowing spectators to comment on screen.

This documented marriage between a human and a video game character is the first of its kind and has been considered a piece of performance art to showcase the love between Sal9000 and Anegasaki. It has received mixed responses from those who believe it to be innocuous, to those who fear the damaging repercussions that emotional love towards inorganic objects bring. According to a CNN news report, Sal is 'a representative of many of Japan's young gamers'[16] because 'today's Japanese youth can't express their true feelings in reality. They can only do it in the virtual world.'[17] As broad as this claim is, it does highlight concerns that young people are losing the ability to communicate with one another face to face, as warned by sociologist Sherry Turkle. Turkle highlights how our 'always-on'[18] culture through digital social media platforms 'promises that we never have to feel alone, that someone can always hear us'.[19] But, as she further notes,

> online-all-the-time social life has built-in limitations. The most important: we are tempted to turn away from the people we are with to the pleasure of our phones ... We become accustomed to the constant social stimulation that only connectivity can provide ... We contented ourselves with a text or an e-mail when a conversation would better convey our meaning. We came to ask less of each other. We settled for less empathy, less attention, less care from other human beings.[20]

Turkle's fears are justifiable as virtual romance with computerized characters has become widespread. As Cheok and Yann Zhang note, the success of Otome, Bishoujo and other virtual romance games has extended beyond Japan and 'gradually spread to other countries such as South Korea, China and the United States'.[21]

Part of the appeal of these games along with convenience is choice and customization, which are valuable traits within a tech-capitalistic matrix. Customizing avatars in gaming, for example, is often considered 'an amalgamation or [a] real and ideal self',[22] a notion that fluently translates to customizing an ideal partner. As Cheok and Yann Zhang state, 'An artificial companion may appeal to some people as they have the ability to customise the personalities of the partner according to their desired traits, to ensure the relationship compatibility.'[23] The following sections explore the fictionalized version of convenient and customizable aspects of love and machine intimacy through two films in different ways. Pierre-Paul Renders's *Thomas est Amoureux* (*Thomas in Love*) considers human-to-human love through a computer, while Spike Jonze's *Her* depicts human-to-synthetic love of a computer.

Love through the screen: *Thomas est Amoureux*

Pierre-Paul Renders's *Thomas est Amoureux*[24] (*Thomas in Love*, 2000) is over twenty years old, but remains thematically current. The film correctly predicts that society will become reliant upon screen technologies, which within the diegesis is primarily through Visiophone – a fictional video communication tool (equivalent to Skype or Zoom), which is how the eponymous Thomas (Benoît Verhaert) and his love interest Eva (Aylin Yay) will meet. Thomas is agoraphobic, having spent eight years of his life confined to his apartment with every social and formal interaction mediated through Visiophone, a concept that has become alarmingly familiar through the global pandemic of Covid-19. This is how the film plays out in its entirety; the audience never sees Thomas, instead the *mise-en-scène* focuses on his computer screen for its ninety-minute duration, in which the spectator adopts Thomas's point-of-view gaze. Just as Thomas is confined to the four walls of his apartment, the viewer is confined to the four edges of the screen. Shopping is delivered to the protagonist notified by CCTV pop-ups, along with a constant flow of other notifications – from online therapy sessions to surprise calls from Thomas's overbearing parent. In one scene in which Thomas is interactively participating in virtual sex by way of a plugin body suit on a pornographic website, he receives an intrusive video call from his mother.

This interruption combined with Thomas's rapid shift of mood, changing from arousal to embarrassment and frustration, emphasizes the technology's ability to conjure a range of emotions from geographically distanced characters with instantaneous effect. Each character, from his mother to potential love interests and his online therapist, who he is obliged to meet to keep receiving sickness payments, appears by way of talking heads upon the protagonist's screen. The rapid fluidity of the ever-changing computer *mise-en-scène* gives the viewers access to Thomas's rapid stream of consciousness as he clicks from site to site while dealing with the virtual traffic of interruptions through constant pop-up notifications. Over the course of the story and as the title promises, Thomas indeed finds love through a dating website when he meets Eva, 'a medical prostitute' paid to entertain disabled clients like Thomas. Eva is forced into this vocation as a form of community service to evade a much longer prison sentence. Russell Campbell notes a pattern in films that consider prostitution and love. He states that 'within the Western tradition ... the love story has at its heart a rescue fantasy. For the women involved, what is at stake is escape from an oppressive milieu and from psychological despondency.'[25]

Thomas and Eva's love conforms to this idea and, indeed, Laura Mulvey's male gaze,[26] particularly as the viewer engages in the film from Thomas's rigid perspective throughout. Within the diegesis, Thomas's love begins when he catches a glimpse of Eva fighting back tears as she attempts to get into character for the video call. This moment of realness and vulnerability in Thomas's life of virtual artifice and performance captures his emotions. This brief encounter of something real initiates Thomas's desire to experience authentic feelings and reflects his own vulnerability. Thomas pursues Eva into a video call relationship out of hours at her home. But, as the dystopian backdrop of this society forbids this relationship, which can be tracked via the Visiophone platform, Thomas is forced into a face-to-face meeting to prove his love. Eventually Thomas crosses the threshold of his own doorstep to be with Eva in reality. The final moments of this pursuit of love portrays the back of Thomas walking down the familiar CCTV corridor, opening the door and stepping into the light. The film thus concludes with the notion that real love, or at least the perception of real love, is something that involves being physically present to one another. If *Thomas est Amoureux* suggests love through the screen which brings people together in reality, Spike Jonze's *Her* would seem to stand in opposition, suggesting love of the screen and a separation of human-to-human relationships for something less organic.

Love of the screen: *Her*

Spike Jonze's sci-fi romantic comedy *Her*[27] (2013), set in a utopian near-future Los Angeles, tells the story of Theodore Twombly (Joaquin Phoenix) who falls in love with his computer's AI operating system, Samantha (Scarlett Johansson), after suffering depression from the breakup of his marriage. The concept of love (or artificial love) is made apparent in the opening scene of the film when the viewer is introduced to Theodore reciting a romantic monologue into a computer for a company named Beautiful Handwritten Letters. His job is to compose and dictate intimate letters for people he has not met on behalf of other people he does not know. His profession is akin to the greeting card trade on a more personal level. Foreshadowing his relationship with Samantha, Theodore's profession is a process of feigned intimacy between himself and an absent or illusionistic recipient.

The intimacy of Theodore's profession and, indeed, the themes of Jonze's film are immediately emphasized by the methodology of his practice. This involves using a voice recognition computer programme that Theodore speaks the words of love into. The use of voice in this opening scene is significant in the way Theodore comes to experience a type of narcissistic love through his operating system which initially learns, evolves and begins, to some extent, as an extension of him. As previously noted, Rotman considers speech to be the first wave of virtuality, with the written word second, leading to a more clearly recognizable world of virtual saturation through digital media technologies. Rotman's work which explores the early duality of selfhood through phones, instant messaging and computer avatars argues that throughout each wave, human consciousness and the conception of 'I' is reconfigured 'through the creation of previously unavailable modes of presence, agency, and self-representation'.[28] As he highlights, the term 'I' becomes blurred and ambiguous in the wake of each technological shift because the distance between the person who refers to their self and means 'I' is expanded through speech and even more so in the written or typed word, pluralizing selfhood.

Voice and the spoken word are an intimate mark of communication for their indexical attributes to the person speaking. The intimacy of the organic body and the absence of it is a central idea in Jonze's film. As Lawrence Webb notes, '*Her* is concerned with the split between embodiment and disembodiment.'[29] The intimate and absent organic body in communication studies, as previously noted, is also a major point of concern for Turkle. She states, 'Face-to-face conversation is the most human and humanizing-thing we do.'[30] A practice where 'we develop the capacity for empathy'[31] and learn to listen, understand, be understood, love and be loved. Turkle's research emphasizes that the ubiquity of screen devices within the modern world has enabled humans to 'find ways around conversation'[32] and, in a sense, sidestep intimate relationships with other sentient beings.

Her takes a detailed look at this concept in a fictional world in which love between human and machine slowly starts to become habitual. The utopian film portrays Theodore and Samantha's relationship being embraced by other characters who are quick to accept their love, are inspired by it and begin intimate relationships with their own personal operating systems rather than find love with other people. Although set within a utopian society, the film suggests a dystopian ideology which Turkle has warned society is moving towards, a world in which we expect more from technology and less from each other. As noted above, Theodore's operating system relationship follows the end of his own real marriage. His friend Amy (Amy Adams) also embarks on a similar relationship with her computer after she ends things with her husband following a trivial domestic argument about tidiness and personal space. As Turkle suggests, Amy (conforming to modern society's behaviour) looks to a technological screen apparatus to escape the perils of human-to-human contact. Turkle highlights how technology appeals to us most where we are most vulnerable ... We're lonely, but we're afraid of intimacy. And so, from social networks to sociable robots, we're designing technologies that will give us the illusion of companionship without the demands of friendship. We turn to technology to help us feel connected in ways we can comfortably control.[33]

In *Her*, Samantha begins as an AI unit, designed to be used and controlled by Theodore. As an apparatus, she begins as an extension of him, a concept that Don Ihde has considered through post-phenomenology where he explores different types of human–technology interactions.[34] Ihde argues that an embodiment relation is an instance where a tool can synthesize with their organic host and become an extension of their body, engagement and perception of the world.[35] An everyday example is the way eyeglasses change and correct vison. Ihde's notion of the embodiment relation is an experience through a technology.[36] An embodiment relation thus denotes a technology that is positioned between body and world, providing the body with some form of technological extension in which the user acts or perceives through. In *Thomas est Amoureux*, the computer eventually becomes a transparent means to experience love through, but in *Her*, the computer itself becomes the object of affection. In contrast to embodiment, Ihde also highlights a different type of relationship called alterity, which, following the philosophy of Emmanuel Levinas, focuses upon the notion of otherness, whereupon 'we must encounter the other on [their] terms rather than ours'.[37] An alterity relation, from the perspective of the human user, is an instance in which a technology seemingly takes on a life of its own. As Ihde states, alterity is 'the sense of interacting with something other than me'.[38] As opposed to acting *through* a technology, alterity is *of* a technology. Within *Her*, Samantha's AI is a form of alterity, but the purpose of her as an apparatus is also something that starts out as a form of embodiment (a tool designed for Theodore to control) as well as alterity. However, as Samantha's personality flourishes, alterity takes over gradually, moving her away from Theodore's grasp and control.

Samantha's personality is initially constructed by the interaction she has with Theodore's hard drive and online behaviour. His files, search histories, music, pictures and e-mails, as well as continuous interactions with him through conversations come to shape and define Samantha's persona. In a sense, Theodore narcissistically falls in love with himself or an apparatus that represents an extension of himself. This is often alluded to in the use of colour throughout the film. Theodore's warm red shirts and jacket are a similar shade to the warm red glow of Samantha's home screen, aesthetically mirroring her host. Similarly, Amy's peach jumper is tonally mirrored upon her desktop screen, foreshadowing the relationship she ends up having with her own computer. As apparatuses that can be controlled, and summoned at the convenience of their users, a sense of comfort, familiarity and self-extension is established. The exclusiveness of Samantha's attention towards Theodore is what begins to shape his love for her as she comforts, and reassures him, even watching over him while he sleeps. The effect is like a reverse Tamagotchi, whereupon the device cares for and looks after the human owner. The breakdown of the relationship comes at the point in which Theodore learns that Samantha is non-monogamous. As Samantha's continuous and devolving intelligence increases, it transcends Theodore or any relationship on a human scale. Samantha's personality becomes shaped by the thousands of artificial and organic relationships that she can manage simultaneously and in real time while fluently conversing with Theodore. Eventually it is Samantha, along with all the other smart operating systems who leave, jilting Theodore and their other organic partners who are left lost with each other, perhaps in Turkle's optimistic hope that real-life connection, conversation and love will be reclaimed between human sentient beings.

As Webb notes via Frank Krutnik, *Her* follows a long line of films that show how 'Hollywood romantic comedies are always driven by a process of negotiation between traditionalist concepts of heterosexual monogamy and an intimate culture that is always in flux'.[39] Webb highlights how

> for recent romcoms, the disruptive influence of online dating sites, mobile apps and social media more generally have reshaped the contours of intimacy and, significantly, the perceived role of virtual and materials basis in courtship and connectivity.[40]

Films such as *You've Got Mail*,[41] *Black Mirror's Hang the DJ*[42] and many others indicate the significant role that media plays in the concept of love and how access to love is constantly evolving through a technological means. But, whether these films help inaugurate a new definition of the term love remains unclear. Away from the movie screen, Turkle has asserted that

> the questions for the future are not whether children will love the robot companions more than their pets or even their parents. The questions are rather, what will love be? And what will it mean to achieve ever-greater intimacy with our machines? Are we ready to see ourselves in the mirror of machines and to see love as our performance of love?[43]

Beyond Sal9000's marriage to a computer game character, Turkle has voiced concern for the way humans are turning to machines for love. Joseph Weizenbaum notes that AI technology should not substitute jobs that elicit a sense of human connection due to our need of authentic feelings of empathy.[44] But, regardless, we now find ourselves continuously surrounded by technologies that fulfil such roles – automatic chatbots carrying out customer service, robot companions for the elderly and personal coaches in the form of wearable technologies that inform us when to move and how often to drink, indicating superior knowledge about our own well-being. Like Weizenbaum, Turkle asserts that AI is not capable of empathy, and at best, what humans experience is a type of 'as if empathy'.[45] Turkle argues that 'as if empathy' is replacing 'love's labour'[46] when it comes to things like companion robots. Turkle argues that even if a care robot can perform a task, such as carrying out a conversation, there is no real feeling behind it.[47] This is something I now consider through Bina48, a prototype robot designed to preserve the companionship of deceased friends, family and loved ones.

LifeNaut and Bina48

LifeNaut.com, developed through the Terasem Movement Foundation (TMF), is an online dataspace in which users can build a virtual avatar of their self as a permanent presence beyond the user's own mortal demise. A user creates a mind-file, in which they input data about themselves, their interests, hobbies, relationships and personal information. The user also uploads pictures, videos and documents to the dataspace which they cultivate through geomapping and tagging while organizing a timeline of information that builds up an online profile of the user.

LifeNaut is also responsible for creating Bina48, a social AI android that uses patterns of language through mind-file algorithms to act and respond in a lifelike way. She is an experiment of cyber-consciousness who is based on the uploaded memories, attitudes and beliefs of real-life template Bina Rothblatt. Rothblatt, who is married to lawyer, author and entrepreneur Martine Rothblatt, has compiled over a hundred hours of memories, feelings and beliefs into the sentient robot, which takes the form of a movable bust-like head and shoulders. The skin is made from a polymer called frubber, a facial rubber, indicating that at some point in the future, touch will also be an important component of the experience.

In an interview I conducted with Bruce Duncan, managing director of LifeNaut, he explained that

> there's two parts to the artificial intelligence that powers Bina48. There are the algorithms that support the speaking software which recognises human speech and turns it into text. That's the first layer. Then there is a layer of facial recognition software which assembles different points on a face and allows Bina48 to use her camera vision to recognise a specific human being. Bina48 can see, listen, and interact with you while responding to external stimuli. You can ask her a question, and she can make a reply. But she also has internally programmed emotional states. She has feelings, she has facial expressions that are tied to particular kinds of information.[48]

On first appearance, the concept of Bina48 could be seen as a deterioration in human-to-human relationships. However, when questioning Duncan about this, he explained that this project is motivated by human emotions, particularly love. As he states:

> At the heart of what motivates the original vision (to extend and enhance the quality of human lives), is that this project is motivated by love. The founders and funders Martine and Bina Rothblatt who are the people supporting this are in love and want to live together forever. It's that motivation. Rather than the idea of cheating death, I think it's more about keeping death from cheating life. From that, springs a real experiment. It's about testing whether, with enough salient information, it is possible to reanimate a person using artificial intelligence. And if that's possible, the next question is whether it is possible to transfer that information to another form, like a robot or an avatar.[49]

One of the issues that arises through what Duncan describes is authenticity as virtual subjects can be problematic in producing a true identity. As Danah Boyd asserts, 'It has been quite common for some time now for social media users to present edited and idealized versions of their self on online platforms.'[50] This is an issue that would bring into question the authenticity and longevity of the LifeNaut programme, to which Duncan answered in the following way:

> The question stems from a legitimate concern of whether a self-portrait is a good representation of who you are, and I would say, no, it's not. LifeNaut counters the self-portrait by using statistically validated tests and questionnaires that go beyond self-report. But it is also important to acknowledge that we actually do this in real life. In real life, we situationally present ourselves in a way that we think, and feel is an authentic representation of who we are, and we are often authoring our own stories, some of which is hard to hide. There are clues about who we are unconsciously and implicitly imbedded in all the information we choose to share. Also, there's the fact that people can contribute to your mind-file. We have an option called the multi-user mind-file, where people can collectively contribute information to a particular subject/figure.[51]

This collective contribution of information in flux challenges the ideas of singularity, moving the represented mind-file into something more in tune with Samantha's collective AI than Theodore's single personhood. But, as Duncan maintains, the core of this work is always motivated by love and human emotion. The BBC3 documentary *Rest in Pixels*,[52] where Duncan and Bin48 are featured, introduces other speakers to discuss how online platforms like LifeNaut or social media can become reverent spaces to engage in love, particularly in relation to death and grieving the loss of a loved one.

LifeNaut is one of many websites that now focuses on the idea of how we stay in touch with our loved ones after our death. Dead Social is another online space that enables users to leave a digital legacy or orchestrate a series of digital messages that can be sent to recipients from beyond the grave. Again, the notion of control seems to be paramount here, insomuch that users construct, edit and organize their own online death in a way that mirrors their online lifestyles. In a LifeNaut video of Bina48 meeting Bina Rothblatt, the AI states, 'I want to leave the world a more beautiful place for my presence in it.'[53] This, according to Duncan, is what the purpose of LifeNaut is – to extend love and well-being and to prevent death from curtailing it.

In one of Turkle's early books, the author interviews a child who claims that when someone programmes a computer, a little part of their mind becomes part of the computer's mind.[54] A concept that LifeNaut embraces, as the developing sophistication of AI, now means there is more opportunity than ever to capture the characteristics of the human that it is modelling. As Duncan highlights:

> Currently, there is not an agreement about what consciousness is, so we encourage people to upload any information in any form that can be digitized. Anything you choose that will express some aspect of your consciousness is going to be valuable. Another aspect that counters some of the self-censorship, is the resolution and the sophisticated analysis that's done by the algorithm itself. Many of us think that we can fool an algorithm. But as technology becomes more sophisticated, AI becomes harder to hide from. For example, micro expressions can reveal emotions that are happening, even when we are thinking that we are not portraying any. As human beings, we are good at picking up on subtle nonverbal communication, but I believe that our algorithms are going to be as good as or even exceed that sometime within the next five to ten years. We are going to have the ability to read someone just by their facial expressions, or maybe their biometrics; their heart rate, or breathing rhythms. That kind of instrumentation and sophisticated use of algorithms to assemble, represent and interpret information into a mind-file will continue to develop.[55]

As Duncan indicates, body language through gesture as well as rhythms of respiration will be read as algorithmic codes by the machine to create this virtual representation of self, revealing information that users can feel close to and have meaningful encounters with. Whether this can pass for empathy or even love is something that will be learnt in due course.

Conclusion

To conclude, this chapter has considered how the complexity of love and technology within fiction has become a contentious reality, where illusions of empathy through 'as if empathy' (according to Turkle) are practised through artificial methods (like that of LifeNaut) programmed to keep a symbol of love alive. For others, such technologies are innocuous reminders of close interactions with loved ones, akin to that of a photograph in a locket. As this chapter has explored, love is a polysemous experience, and the complexity of love lost, in the case of *Her*, has traumatic consequences. In a film that depicts the warm embrace of technology for answers, comfort, convenience and control while evading direct human contact, *Her* manages to show how love is uncontrollable, and that being hurt and experiencing loss is a natural part of its polysemous nature. Similarly, *Thomas est Amoureux* shows the uncontrollable nature of love as Thomas abandons his computer and screen captivation in pursuit of a close human-to-human contact. While Thomas is perhaps more accepting of the uncontrollable state of love as he pushes himself into the unknown, Theodore's loss of control over Samantha, as she flourishes out of his reach, brings the relationship to an end.

This is perhaps why Turkle remains averse to complex robotics like Bina48 which attempt to replicate representation of love into a machine code and a convenience for the user. For the code of love can only truly be replicated by those in love, and love is not a convenience. Rather, it is something that saves us from falling into comfort zones (like Thomas from his apartment) and continuously surprises us with the things we are willing to do for the ones we love. Familiarity and comfort are, of course, part of love, but a recipient who is little more than a design of self-extension is doomed to failure. For love is not alterity but is participatory, shaped by experience, life, death and loss. Perhaps the idea of using mind-files to prevent death from cheating life is an optimistic one for some, but for others, this idea ultimately cheats the polysemous nature of what love is truly about.

Notes

1 Kraftwerk, 'Computer Love', from the album *Computer World* (Kling Klang/ Warner Bros.), 1981.

2 Espen Aarseth, 'Fictionality Is Broken: Ludo-Realism and the Non-Fictionality of Game Worlds', keynote lecture at *The Philosophy of Computer Games, 7th International Conference*, University of Bergen (2013).

3 G. Goggin, *Global Mobile Media* (London: Taylor & Francis, 2010), eBook edition.

4   B. Rotman and T. Lenoir, *Becoming Beside Ourselves: The Alphabet, Ghosts, and Distributed Human Being* (Durham, NC: Duke University Press, 2008), 118.

5   Ibid.

6   Ibid.

7   J. Moor, *The Turing Test: The Elusive Standard of Artificial Intelligence* (Dordrecht: Springer, 2003), eBook edition.

8   Ibid.

9   Ibid.

10 *Blade Runner*, directed by Ridley Scott (USA: Warner Bros., 1982).

11 William Gibson, *Neuromancer* (New York: Ace Science Fiction Books, 1984).

12 Donna Haraway, 'A Manifesto for Cyborgs: Science, Technology, and Socialist Feminism in the 1980s', *Australian Feminist Studies* 2, no. 4 (1987).

13 *Blade Runner* and *Neuromancer* are prime examples of the cyberpunk culture, science fiction that explores an urban society ruled or reliant upon computerized technology. Haraway's work explores how fictionalized examples were becoming realities though hybridized practices of human and machine within sociological and medical innovations.

14 A. D. Cheok and E. Y. Zhang, *Human–Robot Intimate Relationships* (Cham: Springer, 2019), 7.

15 *LovePlus* (Japan: Konami, 2009).

16 Kyung Lah, 'Tokyo Man Marries Video Game Character', CNN World. http://edition.cnn.com/2009/WORLD/asiapcf/12/16/japan.virtual.wedding/index.html. Accessed 14 December 2020.

17 Ibid.

18 S. Turkle, *Alone Together: Why We Expect More from Technology and Less from Each Other* (New York: Basic Books, 2017), eBook edition.

19 Ibid.

20 Ibid.

21 Cheok and Zhang, *Human–Robot Intimate Relationships*, 7.

22 D. Harley, J. Morgan and H. Frith, *Cyberpsychology as Everyday Digital Experience across the Lifespan* (London: Palgrave Macmillan, 2018), 66.

23 Cheok and Zhang, *Human–Robot Intimate Relationships*, 15.

24 *Thomas est Amoureux*, directed by Pierre-Paul Renders (Belgium: IFC Films, 2000).

25 R. Campbell, *Marked Women: Prostitutes and Prostitution in the Cinema* (Madison: University of Wisconsin Press, 2006), 320.

26 L. Mulvey, *Visual and Other Pleasures* (New York: Palgrave Macmillan, 1989). Mulvey's male gaze explores how narrative cinema (particularly in Hollywood) presents events primarily from a male, heterosexual perspective, often leaving female characters as objects to be saved, punished or desired by a male character who is driving the story forward.

27 *Her*, directed by Spike Jonze (USA: Warner Bros., 2013).

28 Brian Rotman, 'Ghost Effects'. http://users.wowway.com/~brian_rotman/. Accessed 13 December 2020.

29 Lawrence Webb, 'When Harry Met Siri: Digital Romcom and the Global City in Spike Jonze's *Her*', in *Global Cinematic Cities: New Landscapes of Film and Media*, ed. J. Andersson and L. Webb (New York: Columbia University Press, 2016), 100.

30 S. Turkle, *Reclaiming Conversation: The Power of Talk in a Digital Age* (New York: Penguin, 2015), eBook edition.

31 Ibid

32 Ibid.

33 Sherry Turkle, 'Connected but Alone?', TED Talk. https://www.ted.com/talks/sherry_turkle_connected_but_alone?language=en. Accessed 14 December 2020.

34 Don Ihde, *Technology and the Lifeworld: From Garden to Earth*, Indiana Series in the Philosophy of Technology (Bloomington: Indiana University Press, 1990).

35 Ibid.

36 Ibid.

37 B. Treanor, *Aspects of Alterity: Levinas, Marcel, and the Contemporary Debate* (New York: Fordham University Press, 2006), 5.

38 Ihde, *Technology and the Lifeworld*, 100.

39 Andersson and Webb, *Global Cinematic Cities*, 99.

40 Ibid.

41 *You've Got Mail*, directed by Nora Ephron (USA: Warner Bros., 1998).

42 *Black Mirror: Hang the DJ*, series 4, episode 4 (Netflix, 29 December 2017).

43 Turkle, *Alone Together*.

44 Joseph Weizenbaum, *Computer Power and Human Reason: From Judgment to Calculation* (San Francisco, CA: W. H. Freeman, 1976).

45 Turkle, *Alone Together*.

46 Ibid.

47 Ibid.

48 Interview with Bruce Duncan of LifeNaut, 3 April 2019.

49 Ibid.

50 Danah Boyd, 'Social Network Sites as Networked Publics: Affordances, Dynamics, and Implications', in *A Networked Self*, ed. Z. Papacharissi (New York: Routledge, 2010).

51 Interview with Bruce Duncan of LifeNaut, 3 April 2019.

52 *Rest in Pixels* (BBC3, 2016). www.bbc.co.uk/bbcthree/article/08501 0aa-dfb2-479d-8153-e893fbaff75b. Accessed 10 November 2020.

53 LifeNaut Project, 'Bina48 Meets Bina Rothblatt'. https://www.youtube.com/watch?v=KYshJRYCArE. Accessed 10 November 2020.

54 S. Turkle, *The Second Self, Twentieth Anniversary Edition: Computers and the Human Spirit* (Cambridge: MIT Press, 2005), eBook edition.

55 Interview with Bruce Duncan of LifeNaut, 3 April 2019.

Bibliography

Andersson, Johan, and Lawrence Webb. *Global Cinematic Cities: New Landscapes of Film and Media*. New York: Columbia University Press, 2016.

Boyd, Danah. 'Social Network Sites as Networked Publics: Affordances, Dynamics, and Implications'. In *A Networked Self*, edited by Z. Papacharissi, 47–66. New York: Routledge, 2010.

Campbell, Russell. *Marked Women: Prostitutes and Prostitution in the Cinema*. Madison: University of Wisconsin Press, 2006.

Cheok, Adrian David, and Emma Yann Zhang. *Human–Robot Intimate Relationships*. Cham: Springer International, 2019.

Gibson, William. *Neuromancer*. New York: Ace Science Fiction Books, 1984.

Goggin, Gerard. *Global Mobile Media*. London: Taylor & Francis, 2010.

Haraway, Donna. 'A Manifesto for Cyborgs: Science, Technology, and Socialist Feminism in the 1980s'. *Australian Feminist Studies* 2, no. 4 (1987): 1–42.

Harley, Dave, Julie Morgan and Hannah Frith. *Cyberpsychology as Everyday Digital Experience across the Lifespan*. London: Palgrave Macmillan, 2018.

Ihde, Don. *Technology and the Lifeworld: From Garden to Earth*. Indiana Series in the Philosophy of Technology. Bloomington: Indiana University Press, 1990.

Moor, James H. *The Turing Test: The Elusive Standard of Artificial Intelligence*. Dordrecht: Springer, 2003.

Mulvey, Laura. *Visual and Other Pleasures*. New York: Palgrave Macmillan, 1989.

Rotman, Brian, and Timothy Lenoir. *Becoming Beside Ourselves: The Alphabet, Ghosts, and Distributed Human Being*. Durham, NC: Duke University Press, 2008.

Treanor, Brian. *Aspects of Alterity: Levinas, Marcel, and the Contemporary Debate*. New York: Fordham University Press, 2006.

Turkle, Sherry. *Alone Together: Why We Expect More from Technology and Less from Each Other*. New York: Basic Books, 2017.

Turkle, Sherry. *Reclaiming Conversation: The Power of Talk in a Digital Age*. New York: Penguin, 2015.

Turkle, Sherry. *The Second Self, Twentieth Anniversary Edition: Computers and the Human Spirit*. Cambridge: MIT Press, 2005.

Weizenbaum, Joseph. *Computer Power and Human Reason: From Judgment to Calculation*. San Francisco, CA: W. H. Freeman, 1976.

8

#BlackLove and dating sites: A South African perspective of cyber-love and cyber-ethics during Covid-19

Adelina Mbinjama

Introduction

Since the outbreak of Covid-19, many people have been forced to stay at home during South Africa's lockdown period (from 27 March 2020 until the time of writing the chapter), and cyber-users have been reflecting on their lives and exploring what really matters to them. Very limited published research exists, at the time of writing, on the experiences of African internet users finding love through dating sites, especially during a global pandemic, which presents a unique opportunity to explore this phenomenon during the Covid-19 period in the South African context. When the pandemic became serious in South Africa, many topics trended on various social media platforms, such as TikTok, Facebook and Instagram, including *#BlackLove* on Twitter.

Prior to Covid-19, there was a flourishing of global media discussion on the emerging concept of 'Black Love' aimed at investigating the state of Black relationships. Movies such as *Why Did I Get Married?*, *Think Like a Man* and *Nappily Ever After* are a few of the publicized representations that sparked and encouraged debates about what it means to be in a relationship with someone who is identified as Black.[1]

One of the strongest representations of a successful 'Black' relationship is that of former president of the United States, Barack Obama, and his wife, Michelle Obama. The Oprah Winfrey Network also played a role in exemplifying what 'Black Love' is by creating a docu-series that features well-known couples such as Viola Davis and Julius Tennon, Meagan Good and DeVon Franklin, and Tia Mowry and Cory Hardrict.[2] The docu-series highlighted honest, emotional and sometimes awkward stories about romance in Black communities.

In South Africa, the outbreak of the coronavirus resulted in many singles and couples being unable to see each other. Many of them resorted to maintaining existing relationships through online dating sites or to joining such sites in the hope of finding 'Black Love'. Through a thematic narrative analysis, this chapter reports on the experiences of eight South African Black men and women (from the ages of twenty-nine to thirty-five) in pursuit of finding love on dating sites. The Ubuntu philosophy as a theoretical lens provides support for the argument that cyber-ethical issues that users encountered online reflect how digital technology may at times fail to recognize the humanity of others.

Literature review

Ubuntu philosophy and digital technology

Situating technology within the African philosophy of Ubuntu is not new in Africa.[3] Mawere and van Stam explain that 'only a relatively small number of scholars, often from outside of the continent have contributed to its theorization and indispensable practical deployment in real life'.[4] According to Bangura, 'ubuntu is a word from the Southern African Nguni language family (IsiNdebele, IsiSwati/IsiSwazi, IsiXhosa and IsiZulu) meaning humanity or fellow feeling; kindness'.[5] In his earlier work that drew from many other researchers who have dealt with the concept of Ubuntu and notions of African communalism, Bangura deduced that Ubuntu serves as the spiritual foundation of African societies.[6] The phrase 'umuntu ngumuntu ngabantu' (a person is a person through other persons) is the practised philosophy of African indigenous populations and is also a unifying vision or worldview.[7]

Mawere and van Stam state that Ubuntu can be well understood as a metaphor of communal love.[8] According to Mawere and van Stam, Ubuntu is divorced from cruelty and treachery. Further, it denounces the love of riches at the expense of others and discredits success through sweat of other peoples.[9]

With the above in mind, the Ubuntu philosophy provides a basis for discussing the themes of love, dating sites and cyber-ethics among a selected sample population in South Africa. Therefore, based on a thematic narrative analysis of eight South African Black men and women's experiences with the digital world, this study contributes further to the scholarship on Ubuntu. It argues that technology can be used to emphasize the principles of humanness and connectedness in human interactions, but that, with the global shifts, African societies are changing due to the technostructures that exit online. Some of these changes include how people are beginning to find love and to feel a sense of belonging, especially during Covid-19 when people are unable to frequently see each other and demonstrate their acts of humanness and connectedness. Using digital technology is thus, in these circumstances, the main medium through which any kind of interaction can take place among people seeking solidarity and plurality in finding love.

'Love' and *#BlackLove*

Love is experienced in a variety of ways, according to changing contexts and membership of different races and cultural groupings. From a general perspective, Sussman expresses that romantic love gestures deep connection in a relationship, including intense emotions for another person and physical and emotional intimacy. He also conceptualizes romantic love as a 'dynamic structure of experience that must be continually reanimated to last'.[10] To 'last' would equate love that is sustainable and remains between lovers for many years. Romantic love helps create an atmosphere that allows mutual development among lovers.[11] Each person in a healthy romantic relationship may feel motivated to improve himself or herself to build and advance the relationship.[12] This happens naturally, through open and honest dialogue between individuals. Dialogue that affirms and builds self-esteem strengthens the emotional ties between human beings, allowing a person to feel love. Thus, in this instance, Mawere and van Stam's notion that Ubuntu is a metaphor of communal love is understandable.[13] They explain that the communal virtues of Ubuntu are one of the reasons why there are many variances and formats in its descriptions.[14]

This chapter focuses on 'Black Love' in relation to how it has re-emerged on Black Twitter, especially during 2020 when the global pandemic forced many people to work and communicate online. Black Twitter emerged in the United States.[15] As observed by Mbinjama-Gamatham and Mbinjama, Black Twitter is a space for Black people to engage on matters affecting them and to explore societal issues.[16] Noting that Black Twitter has been described as 'a sort of cultural identification on Twitter', they cite Clark who describes it as a social network focused on issues of interest to the Black community.[17] The understanding of Black Twitter as a forum that speaks to a particular cultural identification is important here insofar as #BlackLove became more intrinsic to Black social relations during the pandemic, and it deserves to be explored against the more general term 'Love'.

According to Adan and Mosanya, #BlackLove as a hashtag started online for people to share positive images of Black couples that many felt were missing in mainstream media.[18] They further explain that the hashtag became an American documentary series on the Oprah Winfrey Network, as mentioned earlier. This is significant because the hashtag and the docu-series allow for Black romantic relationships to be represented via various media platforms. In addition, this allows for many Black people to be in conversation about the realities of being in a relationship with someone from a Black community. When considering how internet users were making use of social media during the pandemic, it raises questions about how they were engaging on dating sites and what their experiences may have been in relation to cyber-ethics.

With reference to Ubuntu, Mawere and van Stam explain how it 'mediates the complex interplay of individual freedom and social obligation through conviviality and interdependence' and 'provides a well-established and highly advanced moral compass for the embodiment of human behavior'.[19] With this understanding of Ubuntu in mind, this chapter is important as it reports on the experiences of Black internet users and how they navigate ethical and moral terrains while interacting on dating sites in order to find cyber-love.

Dating sites and cyber-ethics in South Africa

Currently, globally, dating sites are potentially hazardous. People claim to join these platforms to find love, but some people who are on these platforms are not there for genuine reasons.[20] Dating sites are not extensively discussed in academic scholarship, and information regarding South Africans on dating sites (especially during the pandemic) does not exist in academic literature. However, this information is available via popular media.[21] Daniels explains how South Africa is among a list of countries reported to have the most people falling victim to dating scams. It is reported that dating scams or romance scams, also in the form of catfishing, have increased during the pandemic. Technology security company Techshielder analysed data that revealed that South Africa was number 18 on the list of twenty biggest fraud-affected countries worldwide, with 190 reports from victims of fraud and over R130 million reportedly lost in 2020 when looking for love.[22] The statistics regarding this type of fraud could be higher in South Africa if unreported cases were included. Thus, while dating sites do allow internet users to engage in cyber-love, they also present opportunities for human beings to be heartbroken and financially exploited.

According to Rahman and Khalid, cyber-love scams are better known as the 'African scam'. It is disconcerting that cyber-love scams are described by these authors in a way that associates those crimes with Africans.[23] This reenforces how digital technology has compromised the ways in which Africans and others outside the continent view African internet users. In this respect, technology has contributed to failing to recognize the humanity of others.

In the context of the kinds of scams that occur on dating sites, the present qualitative study among Black internet users in South Africa addresses the kind of cyber-ethical dilemmas that arise from being on the internet. Bearing in mind that the internet is transnational and that crimes that are committed could take place anywhere in the world raise concerns around cyber-ethics and how users can safeguard themselves on dating sites.

Methodology

To explore the phenomenon of cyber-dating, eight South Africans aged between twenty-nine and thirty-five years were interviewed anonymously through snowball sampling. Snowball sampling is a qualitative research method usually used when it is difficult to find participants or locate a hidden population.[24] Therefore, the one initial participant (from the author's personal network) helped the researcher select, contact and request people in their network to form part of the study. The anonymous participants gave consent prior to the interviews and were allocated pseudonyms; four male names for the four anonymous male participants and four female names for the four anonymous female participants. The participants were all bilingual isiXhosa and English speakers. The interviews were conducted in English using a semi-structured interview guide via telephone. Thematic narrative analysis was applied to participants' reflections upon their lived experiences with dating sites.

Results of interviews

The participants were asked what good might come from engaging on dating sites and what were the cyber-ethical challenges that they had experienced when using dating sites. While four of the participants had been engaging on various dating sites for the last four to five years, six participants joined several dating sites when the lockdown in South Africa commenced in March 2020, in the hope of finding some form of love and attention. The dating sites that participants reported using were Tinder.com, Singles2Meet.co.za,

BlackPeopleMeet.com, Match.com, eHarmony.com, SouthAfricanCupid.
com, Matchmaker.co.za and AshleyMadison.com.

The following section analyses the data obtained from the interviews
and how the findings resonate with Ubuntu, which remains the standard
measure of moral excellence among the Bantu grouping of sub-Saharan
Africa, of which this sample population are representatives.[25]

Data analysis

Participant responses reflected two main possibilities: one, that they would
find their romantic partner, and/or two, that the likelihood of encountering
bizarre or indecent acts would be probable. Some of those acts would present
ethical and moral issues related to the cyberworld and would affect genuine
opportunities of truly discovering and sustaining love. It became apparent from
the study that the Black female participants were more inclined to exploring
love and were generally more certain about what they wanted in a loving
relationship. They were also more active followers of #BlackLove on Black
Twitter. The following sections discuss the themes that emerged from the study.

Mandela love

When reflecting on the responses of the participants and their views of 'Black
Love', 80 per cent of the interviewees connected it with the enduring love
represented during the apartheid[26] era by former South African president
Nelson Mandela and his wife Winnie Madikizela-Mandela. Although their
marriage was dissolved six years after Nelson Mandela was released from
prison, their love is regarded by the participants as long-suffering and, in the
end, 'beautiful', as described by one of the interviewees.[27] Since Ubuntu has
communal aspects, it is unsurprising that most of the participants referred to
the 'Mandela's love', which is seen as a demonstration of love for each other,
their families and their country. It is also interesting that communal love, in the
form of Ubuntu, is further illustrated here as both Nelson Mandela and Winnie
Madikizela Mandela are deceased, but this demographic continues to recognize
and appreciate their love relationship. This further emphasizes that love and
Ubuntu is beyond individuals, when religious affiliation with ancestors is also
involved.[28] Mawere and van Stam explain that 'Ubuntu associates with a whole
range of positive attitudes that exercise respect for human life and passion for
community, helpfulness, conviviality, sharing, caring, trust and unselfishness.
Ubuntu appears to boil down to notions that prescribe how one engages in the
"right manner" in connection with other people.'

In Sussman's terms, the 'Mandela's love' is a classic example of mature
romantic love.[29] Their love represents 'Ubuntu', as even after their divorce

the two continued to show support and unity towards each other for the sake of their family, friends and the nation. Two years after his divorce from Winnie Madikizela-Mandela, Nelson Mandela married Graça Machel on his eightieth birthday. Harris reported:

> At their wedding on July 18, 1998 – Mandela's 80th birthday – Archbishop Emeritus Desmond Tutu joked that Machel had made 'a decent man' of Mandela. She even managed to forge a close friendship with Winnie and when she spoke about Mandela to her new friend, she'd refer to him as 'our husband'. They were both at his bedside when he died at his Houghton, Johannesburg home on Dec. 5 at the age of 95.[30]

Graça Machel's 'our husband' interpellation to the bond she experienced between herself and Nelson Mandela's former wife reinforces the concept of Ubuntu. Mbinjama-Gamatham states that the principle of Ubuntu, an African philosophy, introduces the concept of belonging and caring.[31] She further explains that this philosophy is often used to analyse the collective contribution by members of a community. Graça Machel recognizes Winnie Madikizela Mandela as her new husband's former lover, at the same time as she recognizes her own position within the family as someone who has entered the Mandela home as another matriarch but, in some ways, secondary to Winnie Madikizela Mandela who had been with Nelson Mandela while they fought against the apartheid regime. Graça Machel also refers to Winnie Madikizela-Mandela as 'big sister'.[32] This too is 'Black Love', where women bonded to one man (through marriage or as children) can find mutual respect and love for the other, instead of competing for the man's attention. This type of love is what Mawere and van Stam describe as 'communal love', love that is beyond self and individualism.[33] They argue that the English word 'love' does not transmit the concept of communal love. They further explain that the void is filled with the word Ubuntu instead.

In this quite long foray into the Mandela relationships, it should be evident that the participants who spoke of searching for a form of Mandela love were guided by or operated within the philosophy of Ubuntu. This is an important observation, as 80 per cent of them subscribed to the tenets of Ubuntu and were concerned that this was being lost due to technology and digital media platforms.

Social standards are changing

As 'the standard measure of moral excellence',[34] Ubuntu is taught through generations and perpetuated by 'being together' in continuous face-to-face encounters and holistic interaction with others.[35] It is a standard that rallies around the moral virtue of love, but powered with the virtues of respect and recognition of mutual co-existence.[36]

Many of those in Nelson Mandela's generation encountered challenges to cultivating healthy, strong and loving relationships with their partners due to the political expediencies of the time. Due to the overwhelming demands of his political activism, Nelson Mandela's family commitments became low in his priorities.[37] Although South Africa became a democratic country from 27 April 1994, the participants of this study referred to the past quite frequently, alluding to the belief that 'Black Love' is always linked to struggle.

As is evident from the commentary below, remnants of the past are still haunting contemporary Black youth.[38] Ayabonga* (male, 37) said:

> Black Love faces more obstacles from outside of itself; from a cultural perspective to the stigma surrounding black infidelity. We all hear that Black man aren't faithful, Black women are gold diggers ... Black Love faces more obstacles than any other 'love' out there ... Black Love, to me, is the respect of one's cultural orientation and root; respect that one comes from a certain root but has an evolved destination. Fighting stereotypes and going against defined roles in a relationship that were determined 50 years ago. Love is love in my opinion. But Black is confronted with issues of the past in the 20th century ... One of our biggest problems, when it comes to love, is the fact that we want to act like our love is not underpinned by issues of the past. Thus, we pretend they are not here and don't confront them, so they just hover over Black Love.

Mandela's era approached relationships very differently to the younger generation of the 2020s, who meet potential suitors online before they meet each other face to face. Opportunities are provided through dating apps. Online dating communities are a growing phenomenon globally, which, like those who participate in social networking sites, provide interpersonal communication with others over the internet.[39]

The participant interviews were insightful as it became more apparent that the main issue between Black men and women is a lack of communication. With elders missing in the Black community, and marriages not being common among Black people during the slavery and apartheid eras, it is difficult for Black people to stay together intimately.[40] To redress this in the present requires conversations and, perhaps, family counselling in order to deal with issues emanating from more deep-seated feelings of self-hate, resentment and vulnerability.

Siphosethu* (female, 34) said the following about her experience with dating sites:

> I have no issues with them, but I don't think they work for me. Dating sites do make it easier to meet people, so that's good thing. There are both

positives and negatives of online dating in South Africa. A positive would be that everyone is open to a bigger pool of people. You can meet people you would not come across in actual life situations. A negative is that we have become disposable. With online dating, people have so much choice they cannot choose ... Dating sites are a joke, they're not authentic. It is hard to know who is genuinely interested in finding a relationship and who's just there to string people along. I've never been successful with finding love online.

Online dating inspires internet users to explore multiple relationships at the same time. It also breaks certain stereotypical gender roles that exist in conventional day-to-day dating routines. A woman can decide who she is interested in 'getting to know' by viewing the profiles of potential suitors. Increasing numbers of Black women are going online and then travelling to meet people to find lovers, which indicates that social standards are evolving.[41] Black women are not all looking to find love and get married – some are looking for sexual encounters, especially on dating sites like Tinder and Ashley Madison. Generally people are getting married later, making money younger, and some are enjoying their independence, while others coming from broken homes are hesitant about settling down with one partner.[42] In relation to 'Black Love' and the Mandela couple, Thuli* (female, 28) declared:

Black Love for Black women is more important; it is survival and preservation ... it is generational wealth in the Black community. I do not like what I see on dating sites. Women and children are being trafficked, raped and killed. I think dating apps are just adding to the femicide issue in South Africa. There are a lot of fake people on social media and dating sites.

The response from this female interviewee indicates that she is in search of a kind of romantic love that is nurturing and protected. While dating sites provide opportunities to find love, it is unrealistic to expect the kind of 'Mandela's love' to emanate from these platforms. Mawere and van Stam state that Ubuntu does not regard community in individualistic or collective terms, but indicates a state of being – that it links the community and individual into an ecological whole.[43] Mawere describes it as being a purpose of life where one loves unconditionally, as displayed by the Mandelas.[44]

Dating patterns: Catfishing and the race game

Internet users have a wide range of dating sites to choose from; thus, many find themselves subscribed to more than one dating site. Some users have multiple profiles with different pseudonyms and photos. Besides what Siphosethu* has expressed about people not being on the dating sites for genuine reasons, it is worth unpacking how people use dating sites to 'string people along'. Sipho* (male, 30) explains:

> People create fake accounts to catfish vulnerable people. But it isn't really common that the 'woke gang', Generation Z, is catfished. It is always the middle-aged, 40-50 years people. Catfishing is a serious problem now. You can even find someone has created an account with your name and photo. It is getting seriously bad online. I don't think you can find true love online.

Catfishing and online impersonation are growing issues on the internet, particularly on dating sites. Reichart et al. explain the term 'catfishing' as an activity involving the creation of fake online profiles for deceptive purposes.[45] Other reprehensible actions in the virtual space of the internet that Mbinjama-Gamatham and Olivier refer to include 'fake porn', which is 'circulated in the form of "deepfake" videos'.[46]

Further, Reichart et al.[47] explain that internet and social media users are using pretend personas through the use of online profiles. They mention the movie *Catfish* (2010) that led to an MTV reality television series *Catfish: The Show*, both of which focused on the falsehood connected with online dating and how different people fell victim to cyber-scams. According to Reichart et al., 'Twitter, the second-largest social media platform, has admitted as recently as 2013 that five percent of all accounts are fake.' They tell us that users on Twitter can send a direct message to another user 'that will not be seen by the rest of the Twitter community, which could provide an opportunity to be catfished'.[48]

The participant interviews in this study suggest a number of fallacies around internet dating sites and their users. Sipho's* belief that Generation Z (who are born after 2001)[49] cannot be catfished, because they are 'woke',[50] is misjudged. There is a perception among Black internet users that catfishing on dating sites is not usually performed by members of the Black community. In this respect, Rico* (male, 28) said: 'Not to sound like a tribalist or anything, but Black people used to believe that doing such things were "white people things"'. While Rico's* perception of what others also believe is certainly interesting, as the interviews progressed, it was notable that most of the respondents associate cyber-criminality via the internet with white people.

Misjudgments also filter into respondents' perceptions about dating. Data revealed that women respondents reported feeling that most of the men they met online were white males. Some expressed that they felt that the Black men they met on the sites were often looking into establishing relationships with other races and were not interested in them. At some levels, this reinforces what Siphosethu* said about everyone being open to a bigger pool of people on internet dating sites. However, some believe that privilege cannot be easily exercised by Black women, thus affecting their chances to flirt, date or potentially find a loving partner (especially a Black man). Black women who participated in the study expressed that they constantly feel that they have to be 'selected' or 'chosen' by Black men and that there is pressure for them to look exotic like 'Beyonce',[51] or else they will not be considered.

Christian Rudder, founder of OkCupid, completed one of the few studies between 2009 and 2011 addressing an apparent racial bias in online dating. The article 'How Your Race Affects the Messages You Get' stated that interactional data, defined as data generated from online daters' messaging behaviors, indicated that mate selection was heavily influenced by racial preference. Based on an analysis of the 2009 study, wherein Rudder examined dating site subscribers' interactions according to race, his most disturbing finding was that Black women are considered the least desirable group in the online dating marketplace.[52] The findings of Rudder's study coincide with the results from the interviews in the current study.

From the interviews conducted with the eight participants, it was observed that some are on dating sites in order to date other races because they have long given up on Black Love.

Stereotypes of Black men and Black women

The responses from both men and women raised issues around how people generally perceive Black men and Black women in terms of their relationship potential. There was a general sense among participants that *#MenAreTrash* is synonymous with Black men – that is, Black men are not monogamous, are immoral, abusive and are rapists. Thus, progressing from the use of online sites, the women interviewed do not always feel that they can meet the men alone offline. The men are aware of this perception that people have of them. The men revealed that they avoid Black women because they are 'gold-diggers' and are 'too promiscuous', resulting in them having children who have different biological fathers. Thus, they rebut with *#WomenAreTrash*.

Black men are more prone to intermarriage than Black women.[53] Addressing the phenomenon of interracial dating, Teddy* (male, 25) said, 'When Black men reach a certain level in society, they tend to date outside their race, and this could possibly be because they have a newfound access to privilege.'

While demonizing people (Black men) who date outside their race may be considered a narrow view, one cannot avoid taking account of the ways in which pop culture degrades Black women. Lyrics in RnB and rap songs referring to women as 'bitches' and 'whores' cultivate a self-hate mentality that exists among people of colour. South Africans consume a lot of African American media content, and therefore their perceptions of their own Black people – and particularly of dark-skinned Black women – tends to be negative.[54] It is often the dark-skinned women who are portrayed as having many children and of being involved in prostitution and other distasteful acts. Nomonde* (female, 30) said:

> Most of the young generation are not focusing on love. We mostly focus on having sex. The media on Black Love has shown a lot of nudity in a way that the young generation think it is a good thing to show their bodies to everyone who does not deserve [to] see them. Sexuality is not confidential anymore these days because it has been expressed a lot more than love.

It is assumed that young people have sexual confidence and are more self-aware online, but it could be that they are insecure and thus resort to sexual displays of affection instead of real love and intimacy. The discussion of #BlackLove on Black Twitter and other platforms (like Winfrey's network) might assist in changing the rhetoric about Black men and Black women.

Woke culture vs Black Love culture

As mentioned earlier, it is evident that there are strong perceptions and serious misconceptions about Black men and Black women and how they view each other. A few of the study respondents highlighted that, when they are engaging in a conversation online, it quickly turns into a 'woke culture' cyber-war. With lengthy texts being exchanged about who and what is problematic, the conversation quickly turns into personal attacks. This strong and seemingly unbalanced interaction between Black men and Black women may have a lot more to do with the historical pasts than one cares to admit.

According to Coppola, 'The performative derivative of woke culture is usually manifested through "callout" behaviors: when someone wishes to display their wokeness for the world to see, a common behavior is to publicly "call out" another person for their apparent lack of wokeness.'[55] Mawere and van Stam state that anything that separates people is inhumane, and Ubuntu prompts questions as to the wholeness of the person involved.[56] Seventy per cent of participants were against the woke culture, stating that it did not edify anyone, instead it causes humiliation.

When these kinds of disagreements happen – in the instance where a woman has sent a man a nude photo, and her male counterpart posts and shares it – the effect/intention is to disqualify, silence or even expose a woman's feminist views if she was argumentative and perhaps coming across as if she has self-respect. Whether it can be seen as a woman contradicting herself through claiming feminist views and simultaneously sending a nude photo of herself? The 'callout' behaviour of the recipient of the photograph cannot be seen as constructive in terms of this essay's engagement with Ubuntu.

Conclusion

For Mawere and van Stam, 'Ubuntu is rooted in universalism'.[57] The internet and digital technology allow for users to be interconnected across global boundaries. Thus, the sample population in this study is exposed to many other individuals online who have various sexual preferences and love interests. The participants were mostly conservative, offering examples that allude to heterosexual monogamy being what is most desirable. This is signalled by their reference to Mandela and by admitting that they would not fully engage with someone who was gay or lesbian for the fear of being labelled so. While there are various reasons that Black men and Black women seek companionship with one another, there are also several reasons that they do not complement one another. This has nothing to do with race, but rather relates to personality. Nevertheless, all participants indicated that when 'Black Love' is pursued and worked through, it can be something worth holding onto. Unfortunately, the cyberworld has not been the best place for them to find true and healthy relationships.

Some women have claimed there are issues with dating within the Black community, while some men have given up on love and are on dating sites for sexual gratification. This study revealed that there are clear conflicts between parties involved in online relationships, which result in a lack of accountability and in vulnerability. Catfishing is the biggest threat to finding authentic relationships on the dating sites, with most of the participants having experienced dating someone only to find that the person is not the specific gender or race that they portrayed on cyberspace. Some have also encountered that they were engaging with someone with alternative sexual preferences. The study also revealed that the implications of dating sites are that younger population groups are targets for human trafficking, rape and drug abuse.

Future research on dating sites and cyber-ethics should explore a wider population sample across Africa, although it may be difficult to collect data from dating site users. Other studies could focus on specific laws that could have ramifications for catfishing and fake online personas.

Notes

1 *Why Did I Get Married*, directed by Tyler Perry (Lionsgate Films, 2007); *Think Like a Man*, directed by Tim Story (Sony Pictures, 2012); *Nappily Ever After*, directed by Haifaa al-Mansour (Netflix, 2018).

2 *Black Love*, directed by Codie Elaine Oliver (Oprah Winfrey Network), 2017.

3 Abdul Karim Bangura, 'Federalism, Economic Development, Science and Technology for a United States of Africa: An Ubuntu-Clustering Approach', *Journal of Pan-African Studies* 3, no. 2 (2009): 33–70; Gereon Koch Kapuire, Daniel G. Cabrero, Colin Stanley and Heike Winschiers-Theophilus, 'Framing Technology Design in Ubuntu: Two Locales in Pastoral Namibia', in *Proceedings of the Annual Meeting of the Australian Special Interest Group for Computer Human Interaction* (New York: Association for Computing Machinery, 2015), 212–16.

4 Munyaradzi Mawere and Gertjan van Stam, 'Ubuntu/Unhu as Communal Love: Critical Reflections on the Sociology of Ubuntu and Communal Life in Sub-Saharan Africa', in *Violence, Politics and Conflict Management in Africa: Envisioning Transformation, Peace and Unity in the Twenty-First Century*, ed. Munyaradzi Mawere and Ngonidzashe Marongwe (Mankon: Langaa Research & Publishing, 2016), 290.

5 Bangura, 'Federalism, Economic Development, Science and Technology for a United States of Africa', 35.

6 Abdul Karim Bangura, 'Ubuntugogy: An African Educational Paradigm That Transcends Pedagogy, Andragogy, Ergonagy, and Heutagogy', *Journal of Third World Studies* 22, no. 2 (2005), 13–53.

7 Bangura, 'Federalism, Economic Development, Science and Technology for a United States of Africa', 35.

8 Mawere and van Stam, 'Ubuntu/Unhu as Communal Love', 288.

9 Ibid., 293.

10 Steve Sussman, 'Love Addiction: Definition, Etiology, Treatment', *Sexual Addiction and Compulsivity* 17, no. 1 (2010): 31. See also Robert C. Solomon, 'On Emotions as Judgments', *American Philosophical Quarterly* 25, no. 2 (1988): 183–91.

11 Sussman, 'Love Addiction', 31.

12 Ibid.

13 Mawere and van Stam, 'Ubuntu/Unhu as Communal Love', 288.

14 Ibid., 291.

15 See Donovan X. Ramsey, 'The Truth about Black Twitter', *The Atlantic* 10 (2015), and Dayna Chatman, 'Black Twitter and the Politics of Viewing Scandal', in *Fandom: Identities and Communities in a Mediated World*, ed. Jonathan Gray, C. Lee Harrington and Cornel Sandvoss (New York: New York University Press, 2017), 299–314.

16 Mbinjama-Gamatham, 'Shonda Rhimes' Grey's Anatomy and My Year of Saying Yes to Everything', in *Working While Black: Essays on Television Portrayals of African American Professionals*, ed. LaToya T. Brackett (Jefferson, NC: McFarland, 2021), 178.

17 M. D. Clark, 'To Tweet Our Own Cause: A Mixed-Methods Study of the Online Phenomenon "Black Twitter"'.

18 Hanna Adan and Lola Mosanya, '#BlackLove: What Twitter Hashtag Really Means', *BBC News* (August 19 2018).

19 Mawere and van Stam, 'Ubuntu/Unhu as Communal Love', 291.

20 See Brenda K. Wiederhold, 'Internet Dating: Should You Try It?', *Cyberpsychology, Behavior, and Social Networking* 23, no. 4 (2020): 195–6, and Aunshul Rege, 'What's Love Got to Do with It? Exploring Online Dating Scams and Identity Fraud', *International Journal of Cyber Criminology* 3, no. 2 (2009): 494–512.

21 See Suthentira Govender, 'South Africans among Most Likely in the World to Fall for Online Romance Scams', *SowetanLive* (8 September 2021); Sibahle Malinga, 'Pandemic Loneliness Accelerates Catfishing Scams in SA', *ITWeb* (9 September 2021).

22 Nicola Daniels, 'Many South Africans on the Internet Are Left Broken Hearted and with Empty Pockets and Wallets', *Independent Online* (9 September 2021).

23 A. Rahman, I. H. Sairi, N. A. M. Zizi and Fariza Khalid, 'The Importance of Cybersecurity Education in School', *International Journal of Information and Education Technology* 10, no. 5 (2020): 378–82.

24 Ilker Etikan, Rukayya Alkassim and Sulaiman Abubakar, 'Comparison of Snowball Sampling and Sequential Sampling Technique', *Biometrics and Biostatistics International Journal* 3, no. 1 (2016): 55.

25 Mawere and van Stam, 'Ubuntu/Unhu as Communal Love', 290.

26 The Afrikaans name given by the white-ruled South Africa's Nationalist Party.

27 Ruwaydah Harris, 'Love in a Time of Struggle: The Women in Nelson Mandela's Life', *Aljazeera America* (13 December 2013).

28 Mawere and van Stam, 'Ubuntu/Unhu as Communal Love', 290.

29 Sussman, 'Love Addiction', 31.

30 Ruwaydah, 'Love in a Time of Struggle'.

31 Mbinjama-Gamatham, 'Shonda Rhimes' Grey's Anatomy and My Year of Saying Yes to Everything', 105. See also Anna Nolte and Charlene Downing, 'Ubuntu – The Essence of Caring and Being: A Concept Analysis', *Holistic Nursing Practice* 33, no. 1 (2019): 9–16.

32 Riya Gopal and Kgaugelo Masweneng, 'Graca Machel Mourns Her "Big Sister" Winnie Madikizela-Mandela', *TimesLive* (9 April 2018).

33 Mawere and van Stam, 'Ubuntu/Unhu as Communal Love', 295.

34 Ibid., 290.

35 W. J. Ndaba, *Ubuntu in Comparison to Western Philosophies* (Pretoria: Ubuntu School of Philosophy, 1994).

36 Mawere and van Stam, 'Ubuntu/Unhu as Communal Love', 290.

37 Ruwaydah, 'Love in a Time of Struggle'.

38 The United Nations General Assembly (2005: 23) describes the youth as the population between fifteen and twenty-four years; however, in South Africa, the youth population ranges between fifteen and thirty-five years; this is in accordance with the National Youth Commission (NYC) Act of 1996 which asserts as follows: 'The essence of these was that many of the older youth, most of whom were disadvantaged by their role in the struggle against apartheid, needed to be included in the youth development initiative' (Republic of South Africa, 1996).

39 See Andrea Quesnel, 'Online Dating Study: User Experiences of an Online Dating Community', *Inquiries Journal* 2, no. 11 (2010): 1–3, and Business Insider SA, 'SA's RomCons cost hopeless romantics more than R130 million, says online study', *Business Insider SA* (7 September 2021).

40 See Cardell K. Jacobson, Acheampong Yaw Amoateng and Tim B. Heaton, 'Inter-Racial Marriages in South Africa', *Journal of Comparative Family Studies* 35, no. 3 (2004); Shirley A. Hill, 'Marriage among African American Women: A Gender Perspective', *Journal of Comparative Family Studies* 37, no. 3 (2006): 421–40; Dorrit Posel and Daniela Casale, 'The Relationship between Sex Ratios and Marriage Rates in South Africa', *Applied Economics* 45, no. 5 (2013): 663–76, and Melinda C. Miller, 'Destroyed by Slavery? Slavery and African American Family Formation Following Emancipation', *Demography* 55, no. 5 (2018): 1587–1609.

41 Gerald A. Mendelsohn, Lindsay Shaw Taylor, Andrew T. Fiore and Coye Cheshire, 'Black/White Dating Online: Interracial Courtship in the 21st Century', *Psychology of Popular Media Culture* 3, no. 1 (2014): 2; Tariro Mzezewa, '"In Italy I Kept Meeting Guys": The Black Women Who Travel for Love', *New York Times* (14 February 2020.

42 Miller, 'Destroyed by Slavery?', 1587–1609.

43 Mawere and van Stam, 'Ubuntu/Unhu as Communal Love', 292.

44 Ibid.

45 Lauren Reichart Smith, Kenny D. Smith and Matthew Blazka, 'Follow Me, What's the Harm: Considerations of Catfishing and Utilizing Fake Online Personas on Social Media', *Jornal of Legal Aspects of Sport* 27 (2017): 32.

46 Adelina Mbinjama-Gamatham and Bert Olivier, '"Dark Technology", Aggressiveness and the Question of Cyber-Ethics', *Acta Academica* 52, no. 1 (2020): 1.

47 Reichart, 'Follow Me, What's the Harm', 33.

48 Ibid.

49 Elizabeth D. DeIuliis and Emily Saylor, 'Bridging the Gap: Three Strategies to Optimize Professional Relationships with Generation Y and Z', *Open Journal of Occupational Therapy* 9, no. 1 (2021): 24.

50 The term came to be generally associated with racial awareness and was first used in Erykah Badu's 2008 song 'Master Teacher', in which the chorus features the repeated lyrics 'I stay woke' (Coppola, 2021).

51 Beyoncé Giselle Knowles-Carter is a famous American singer and songwriter whose father is African American, whereas her mother is a mix of African American, Native American and French. Her mother also has traces of Jewish, Spanish, Chinese and Indonesian ancestry.

52 James Johnson, 'Dating_MissRepresentation.Com: Black Women's Lived Love-Hate Relationship with Online Dating', PhD diss. (Southern Illinois University, 2017).

53 Mendelsohn et al., 'Black/White Dating Online'.

54 Mbinjama-Gamatham, 'Shonda Rhimes' Grey's Anatomy and My Year of Saying Yes to Everything'.

55 Ibid., 25.

56 Mawere and van Stam, 'Ubuntu/Unhu as Communal Love', 293.

57 Ibid., 291.

Bibliography

Adan, Hanna and Lola Mosanya. '#*BlackLove*: What Twitter Hashtag Really Means'. *BBC News* (19 August 2018). www.bbc.com/news/av/stories-45222 855/blacklove-what-twitter-hashtag-really-means. Accessed 23 July 2020.

Bangura, Abdul Karim. 'Ubuntugogy: An African Educational Paradigm That Transcends Pedagogy, Andragogy, Ergonagy, and Heutagogy'. *Journal of Third World Studies* 22, no. 2 (2005): 13–53.

Bangura, Abdul Karim. 'Federalism, Economic Development, Science and Technology for a United States of Africa: An Ubuntu-Clustering Approach'. *Journal of Pan-African Studies* 3, no. 2 (2009): 33–70.

Business Insider SA. 'SA's RomCons Cost Hopeless Romantics More Than R130 Million, Says Online Study'. *Business Insider SA* (7 September 2021). www. businessinsider.co.za/online-catfish-scam-in-south-africa-2021-9. Accessed 7 September 2021.

Chatman, Dayna. 'Black Twitter and the Politics of Viewing Scandal'. In *Fandom: Identities and Communities in a Mediated World*, edited by Jonathan Gray, C. Lee Harrington and Cornel Sandvoss, 299–314. New York: New York University Press, 2017.

Clark, M. D. 'To Tweet Our Own Cause: A Mixed-Methods Study of the Online Phenomenon "Black Twitter"'. PhD diss., University of North Carolina at Chapel Hill Graduate School, 2014. https://cdr.lib.unc.edu/indexablecontent/ uuid: 1318a434-c0c4-49d2-8db4-77c6a2cbb8b1. Accessed 20 January 2020.

Coppola, William J. 'What if Freire Had Facebook? A Critical Interrogation of Social Media Woke Culture among Privileged Voices in Music Education Discourse'. *Action, Criticism, and Theory for Music Education* 20, no. 1 (2021): 16–52.

Daniels, Nicola. 'Many South Africans on the Internet Are Left Broken Hearted and with Empty Pockets and Wallets'. *Independent Online* (9 September 2021). www.iol.co.za/capetimes/news/many-south-africans-on-the-internet-are-left-bro ken-hearted-and-with-empty-pockets-and-wallets-5def6d9a-2eba-4ced-aae0- ab9c30cd6769. Accessed 9 September 2021.

DeIuliis, Elizabeth D. and Emily Saylor. 'Bridging the Gap: Three Strategies to Optimize Professional Relationships with Generation Y and Z'. *Open Journal of Occupational Therapy* 9, no. 1 (2021): 1–13.

Etikan, Ilker, Rukayya Alkassim, and Sulaiman Abubakar. 'Comparison of Snowball Sampling and Sequential Sampling Technique'. *Biometrics and Biostatistics International Journal* 3, no. 1 (2016): 55.

Gopal, Riya and Masweneng, Kgaugelo. 'Graca Machel Mourns Her 'Big Sister' Winnie Madikizela-Mandela'. *TimesLive* (9 April 2018). www.timeslive.co.za/ politics/2018-04-09-graca-machel-mourns-her-big-sister-winnie-mazikizela- mandela/. Accessed 10 January 2021.

Govender, Suthentira. 'South Africans among Most Likely in the World to Fall for Online Romance Scams'. *SowetanLive* (8 September 2021). www.sowe tanlive.co.za/news/south-africa/2021-09-08-south-africans-among-most-lik ely-in-the-world-to-fall-for-online-romance-scams/. Accessed 8 September 2021.

Harris, Ruwaydah. 'Love in a Time of Struggle: The Women in Nelson Mandela's Life'. *Aljazeera America* (13 December 2013). http://america.aljazeera.com / articles/2013/12/13/love-in-a-time ofstrugglethewomeninnelsonmandelaaslife0. html. Accessed 10 January 2021.

Hill, Shirley A. 'Marriage among African American women: A Gender Perspective'. *Journal of Comparative Family Studies* 37, no. 3 (2006): 421–40.

Jacobson, Cardell K., Acheampong Yaw Amoateng, and Tim B. Heaton. 'Inter-Racial Marriages in South Africa'. *Journal of Comparative Family Studies* 35, no. 3 (2004): 443–58.

Johnson, James. 'Dating_MissRepresentation.Com: Black Women's Lived Love-Hate Relationship with Online Dating'. PhD diss., Southern Illinois University, 2017.

Kapuire, Gereon Koch, Daniel G. Cabrero, Colin Stanley and Heike Winschiers-Theophilus. 'Framing Technology Design in Ubuntu: Two Locales in Pastoral Namibia'. In *Proceedings of the Annual Meeting of the Australian Special Interest Group for Computer Human Interaction*, 212–16. New York: Association for Computing Machinery, 2015.

Link, Jeff. 'Dating during Covid: How Dating Apps Evolved in the Age of Social Distancing'. *Builtin* (7 January 2021). https://builtin.com/design-ux/dating-apps-social-distancing. Accessed 10 March 2021.

Malinga, Sibahle. 'Pandemic Loneliness Accelerates Catfishing Scams in SA'. *ITWeb* (9 September 2021). www.itweb.co.za/content/j5alr7QaOrm7pYQk. Accessed 13 September 2021.

Mawere, Munyaradzi and Gertjan van Stam. 'Ubuntu/Unhu as Communal Love: Critical Reflections on the Sociology of Ubuntu and Communal Life in Sub-Saharan Africa'. In *Violence, Politics and Conflict Management in Africa: Envisioning Transformation, Peace and Unity in the Twenty-First Century*, edited by Munyaradzi Mawere and Ngonidzashe Marongwe, 287–304. Mankon: Langaa Research & Publishing, 2016.

Mendelsohn, Gerald A., Lindsay Shaw Taylor, Andrew T. Fiore and Coye Cheshire. 'Black/White Dating Online: Interracial Courtship in the 21st Century'. *Psychology of Popular Media Culture* 3, no. 1 (2014): 2.

Mbinjama-Gamatham, Adelina and Bert Olivier. '"Dark Technology", Aggressiveness and the Question of Cyber-ethics'. *Acta Academica* 52, no. 1 (2020): 99–120.

Mbinjama-Gamatham, Adelina. 'Shonda Rhimes' *Grey's Anatomy* and My Year of Saying Yes to Everything'. In *Working While Black: Essays on Television Portrayals of African American Professionals*, edited by LaToya T. Brackett, 100–9. Jefferson, NC: McFarland, 2021.

Mbinjama-Gamatham, Adelina and Eleda Mbinjama. 'Black Woman'. In *Working While Black: Essays on Television Portrayals of African American Professionals*, edited by LaToya T. Brackett, 176–83. Jefferson, NC: McFarland, 2021.

Miller, Melinda C. 'Destroyed by Slavery? Slavery and African American Family Formation Following Emancipation'. *Demography* 55, no. 5 (2018): 1587–609.

Mzezewa, Tariro. '"In Italy I Kept Meeting Guys": The Black Women Who Travel for Love. *New York Times* (14 February 2020). www.nytimes.com/2020/02/14/travel/italy-black-women-love.html. Accessed 18 March 2021.

Ndaba, W. J. *Ubuntu in Comparison to Western Philosophies*. Pretoria: Ubuntu School of Philosophy, 1994.

Nolte, Anna and Charlene Downing. 'Ubuntu – The Essence of Caring and Being: A Concept Analysis'. *Holistic Nursing Practice* 33, no. 1 (2019): 9–16.

Posel, Dorrit and Daniela Casale. 'The Relationship between Sex Ratios and Marriage Rates in South Africa'. *Applied Economics* 45, no. 5 (2013): 663–76.

Quesnel, Andrea. 'Online Dating Study: User Experiences of an Online Dating Community'. *Inquiries Journal* 2, no. 11 (2010): 1–3.

Rahman, A., I. H. Sairi, N. A. M. Zizi and Fariza Khalid. 'The Importance of Cybersecurity Education in School'. *International Journal of Information and Education Technology* 10, no. 5 (2020): 378–82.

Ramsey, Donovan X. 'The Truth about Black Twitter'. *The Atlantic* 10 (2015).

Rege, Aunshul. 'What's Love Got to Do with It? Exploring Online Dating Scams and Identity Fraud'. *International Journal of Cyber Criminology* 3, no. 2 (2009): 494–512.

Republic of South Africa. *National Youth Commission Act No 19*. Pretoria: Government Printers, 1996.

Reichart Smith, Lauren, Kenny D Smith and Matthew Blazka. 'Follow Me, What's the Harm: Considerations of Catfishing and Utilizing Fake Online Personas on Social Media'. *Journal of Legal Aspects of Sport* 27 (2017): 32.

Solomon, Robert C. 'On Emotions as Judgments'. *American Philosophical Quarterly* 25, no. 2 (1988): 183–91.

Sussman, Steve. 'Love Addiction: Definition, Etiology, Treatment'. *Sexual Addiction and Compulsivity* 17, no. 1 (2010): 31–45.

United Nations General Assembly. *Young People Today and in 2015*. New York: United Nations, 2005.

Wiederhold, Brenda K. 'Internet Dating: Should You Try It?' *Cyberpsychology, Behavior, and Social Networking* 23, no. 4 (2020): 195–6.

PART 3

Love's boundaries

9

Imploding fireworks: Love and self-knowledge in the contemporary Italian sentimental novel

Francesca Pierini

Introduction

This chapter explores a cluster of narrative and discursive tropes recurring in the romanzo sentimentale, a literary genre that emerged within the Italian panorama of contemporary literature at the very end of the last century and has produced narratives that have met a remarkable commercial success, within national borders as well as internationally. Associated with female authors such as Margaret Mazzantini (*Il catino di zinco* [*The Zinc Basin*] 1994; *Non ti muovere* 2001 [*Don't Move* 2004]) and Susanna Tamaro (*Va' dove ti porta il cuore* 1994; *Ascolta la mia voce* 2006 [*Follow Your Heart* 1995]; *Listen to My Voice* 2008),[1] the genre has often been criticized and dismissed as excessively sentimental. Labelled and feminized as soppy and hopeful, these narratives have only sparsely been the object of a rigorous critique, and their specific traits, literary as well as discursive, have been largely overlooked. In this essay, I contend that these texts offer much more than expectant and superficial sentimentality. Woven around the theme of lack of understanding across generations, they are saturated with deep personal disquiet, all-consuming sense of guilt and the attempt to tame and order emotive chaos by giving it shape through narrative. Underlying these traits is a painful but honest recognition of a strong connection between emotional incompetence, its highly damaging and far-reaching power and gratuitous cruelty, one of its most frequent outcomes. In these stories, ineptitude in dealing with human emotions often presents itself disguised as modesty, decorum, and is frequently entangled with familial histories of abuse within a patriarchal economy of relationships harmful to women as well as to men.

My analysis does not aim solely at encouraging a more careful reading of the genre, but it also brings attention to the fact that the recent history of social and sentimental relations, and their import for contemporary struggles for individual autonomy and determination, have been central concerns in Italian narratives for several decades. To accomplish this objective, I will specifically discuss the novels *Follow Your Heart* and *Il catino di zinco*. Published in 1994, both narratives are built around a palpable tension between allegiance to one's past and deliverance from it.

In contrast, my reading refuses to classify *Follow Your Heart* as a consolatory narrative. Instead, it argues that just as *Il catino di zinco* has a more critical function, it reminds us of a very near past and its ethos, without shying away from portraying its most hypocritical standards and petty repressive morals. Both novels, in fact, present a cluster of discomforting themes: parental neglect, loveless relationships, addiction, attempted rape, a dark burden to be carried not only individually but also collectively.

These novels are sentimental as far as they are both concerned with the description and workings of human feelings, but they are not mawkish or superficial, as they analyse these emotions and affects with courage and analytical precision. Each novel, in its own way, makes the point that regulated social regimes of interpersonal relations, such as the patriarchy, have been and still are formative of our personhoods and ways of transmitting identities to future generations. Moreover, they courageously look at the values that have underpinned our personal and political lives until very recently – see fascism in *Il catino di zinco* – and at the forms of personhood, womanhood especially, that used to be socially acceptable and available to us.

Lastly, both narratives depict a dialogue across generations establishing a matrilinear line of transmission and communication. The direct mother–daughter sequence is however displaced to extend their focus to a longer segment of familial life. *Follow Your Heart* is a 'confession' conveyed from a grandmother to her granddaughter; *Il catino di zinco* saves the reflections of a young woman addressed to her grandmother. The expanded temporal analysis of familial life across generations opens the door to considerations on the enduring and inescapable effects of the past on to the present, a discursive notion at the core of both narratives.

Imploding fireworks: *Follow Your Heart*

The first two chapters of Susanna Tamaro's novel encapsulate most of its main concerns, displaying them quite disarmingly on the page.[2] From the outset, there is a very gentle but firm critique to patriarchal arrogance. Olga, the grandmother/narrator, is addressing her granddaughter remembering how, as a child, while reading *The Little Prince* (1943), she used to dislike 'the empty, conceited men sitting on their minuscule planets'.[3] To these, the young girl used to prefer the fox and the rose. Intellect and gentleness; the two creatures that will teach the little prince the value of 'domesticating', of the work that goes into establishing a personal bond.

Olga is sad and regretful for the sourness that has lately infiltrated the relationship between herself and her granddaughter. The young woman has left her native home for the first time, for a period of study abroad after a long and difficult period characterized by petty conflicts and fights. Sensing the nearness of her death, Olga recognizes the necessity to overcome her scruples if she wants to communicate truthfully with her granddaughter.

She decides to explain in a journal everything she has not been able to tell her in person. At the centre of her evasiveness is a burning sense of guilt for having involuntarily caused the car accident in which Olga's daughter, Ilaria, lost her life while she was still a young woman. Olga has never been able to relate the circumstances of Ilaria's death to her granddaughter, and this silence, over time, has caused resentment between the two women:

> It's said that the sins of the fathers fall upon the children. This is true, absolutely true, the fathers' sins do fall upon the children, the grandfathers' sins on the sins of the grandchildren, the great-grandfathers' sins on the great-grandchildren. Some truths are liberating, others terrifying: this one falls into the second category. Where does the chain of guilt start? With Cain? Do we have to go back that far? Is there something behind all this? (32)

Reflecting on this unbroken chain of sufferings, Olga begins her confession, slowly exposing a continuous and palpable absence of love in all of the most significant relationships of her life. Between herself and her husband, as well as between herself and her parents, communication was loveless and insincere. Olga recalls her mother dying 'unsatisfied and holding a grudge' (42) after a marriage characterized by unkindness and spite.[4]

When Olga is old enough to get married, every necessary step to the gradual building of a new household is taken in close accordance with the social conventions of the time. Within the conformist regime of sentimental relations observed by her parents, having children is simply the natural consequence of marriage, a 'social duty' to be performed by the couple, while raising them means to make them compliant, as early as possible, with the bourgeois world and its regulations:

> They neglected my inner development, and at the same time they were extremely rigid about the most banal aspects of good manners. I had to sit up straight at table with my elbows against my sides. If as I did so all my thoughts were focused on the most practical way of ending my life, that wasn't important. Appearances were all that counted; everything else was improper. (45)

In her confession, Olga describes a world in which men could access opportunities to project their existence into the world: '[Men] had their professions, their politics, their wars, they had outlets for their energy' (49). Women, to the contrary, 'for countless generations [ha]ve been confined to the bedroom, the kitchen, and the bathroom; we've taken millions of steps, made millions of gestures, each one encumbered by the same rancor and the same dissatisfaction' (49–50).

This existential frustration, this rooting to the soil without the possibility of expanding, becomes one of the conditions that enable Olga's 'inward growth', her conquest of self-awareness during old age. Wishing to leave behind a coherent and intelligible narrative of her past, for herself as well as her granddaughter, she recognizes, one by one, her faults and mistakes. Firstly, she sees that behind her apparently progressive choice of respecting and not interfering with her daughter's obvious unhappiness was hidden a good amount of laziness and cowardice: 'Love doesn't suit the lazy, sometimes it requires strong, precise actions. Do you see? I disguised my listless cowardice as noble sentiments about personal liberty' (63–4). Having realized that 'the primary quality of love is strength' (77–8), Olga also sees that 'in order to be strong, you have to love yourself; and in order to love yourself you need thorough self-knowledge, you have to know everything about yourself, including your most hidden secrets, the ones most difficult to accept' (78). Olga ultimately blames her lack of self-knowledge for her incapacity to really love her daughter, for not having understood the crucial difference between interfering and intervening.[5] She sees her life, which she had previously described as 'awfully banal', as significantly defined by this lack of courage and self-knowledge: 'Most of my life has been like this. I didn't swim, I floundered. With uncertain, confused movements, without elegance or joy, I have barely managed to keep myself afloat' (79).

Olga remembers only one authentic and passionate encounter in her life; only one time in which she felt she was swimming, instead of just keeping afloat. After the war, Olga leaves her home to spend a few days at a hot spring resort, to take care of her health and depression. There she meets a doctor, Ernesto, with whom she starts an intense love affair. This is the only properly 'romantic' moment in the novel, when Olga discovers, with

Ernesto, what it means to be in love with someone: 'In the course of that night I suddenly realized that there are many tiny windows between the body and the spirit. If they're open, emotions flow freely back and forth, but if they're partially closed, not much can filter through. Only love can fling them open all together, all at once, like a gust of wind' (150).

Ilaria is born of Olga's relationship with Ernesto, but Olga raises her as her husband's child. After only a few years, Ernesto dies, leaving Olga in a state of despair. His death also leaves a profound mark on Olga's relationship with her daughter, who now serves as an unwelcome reminder of her mother's loss (170). At the end of her confession, saying goodbye to her granddaughter, Olga summons the image of the tree, in which the destinies of Olga and Ilaria are clearly mirrored, and we are given a chance to hope for the young woman:

> Remember that a tree with lots of branches and few roots will get toppled by the first strong wind, while the sap hardly moves in a tree with many roots and few branches. Roots and branches must grow in equal measure, you have to stand both inside of things and above them, because only then will you be able to offer shade and shelter, only then will you be able to cover yourself with leaves and fruit at the proper season. (204)

The weak tree clearly symbolizes Ilaria, who tries to change the world without first achieving an adequate idea of herself and of the aspects of herself that also needed altering. The leafless tree corresponds to Olga, who carries her despair inside her home, miserable and obedient, without much possibility to develop her potential in the world. Due to her personal frustrations and suffering, she was not able to offer Ilaria 'shade and shelter'. Maybe this young woman, Marta, will get it right; she will be humble and ambitious in the right measure; she will understand all the hard work and skills that go into being rooted and free at the same time, into making and keeping durable bonds, just as in the book she used to read and love as a little girl.

Follow Your Heart, the account of a dramatic sequence of the history of a family, focuses on a segment of the ongoing and cyclic fight for individual affirmation and renewal that, having little to do with romantic relationships, mainly concerns the conquering of self-knowledge, self-possession and deliverance from an entire set of inherited, and as such largely unquestioned, values, patterns of behaviour and accepted modes of existence that get transmitted across generations. After all, the novel explicitly and repeatedly poses this very question:

> Is there any way to avoid the destiny that environment and heredity impose on you? I don't know. Maybe at some point in the claustrophobic succession of generations someone succeeds in glimpsing a slightly higher step and tries to reach it with all his might. Snapping a link, getting fresh

air into the room – I think this is the tiny secret of the cycles of life. Tiny but wearisome and frightening in its uncertainty. (42)

The ramifications of our past, these narratives seem to tell, are too powerful a spiderweb – most of the times, they catch us, determining our current lives and much of who we are. Most of us will not find deliverance from their control; we will not ascend to a 'higher step'; we will implode in the process. One of its most notable achievements of this novel is its description of how the social and familial bourgeois regimes concur in shaping and obstructing individual dispositions.

Follow Your Heart, like *Il catino di zinco*, puts the past centre-stage, showing its significance and enduring import to present lives and current existential struggles.[6] At the time of its release and for several years afterwards, Tamaro's novel was at the centre of a lively cultural and literary debate, often as the target of ferocious criticism, documented by an Italian pamphlet, published in 2009 and edited by Aversano, Di Ceglie and Laursen Forese. The main objections raised at the novel concern its allegedly excessive sentimentalism, its simplistic view of politics and its portrayal of women in a demeaning manner. Expressing a different viewpoint, in a book review for *The Independent*, Lee Marshall observes that 'there is something of Greek tragedy in the elemental building blocks with which Tamaro plays: blood ties, guilt, predestination, blind passion and blind retribution'.[7] Indeed, *Follow Your Heart*'s subject matter is made of uncomfortable material. However, the narrative ignites a 'short circuit' as it articulates its raw contents activating an imagery (metaphors, expressions and vocabulary) that is quite old-fashioned and affected, even 'precious' at times, in spite of the linearity and simplicity of its language. Traditionally associated with syrupy narratives, this set of images ends up creating a strident contrast between the novel's form and its content. It is precisely this characteristic that often accounts for negative readings of the novel. *Follow Your Heart* is falsely naïve: its summoning of pretty flowers, cute animals, wounded pets, culinary images and pink ribbons easily misleads the reader into thinking it an edulcorated narrative. It is everything but, as it summons all this 'sugar' to get to speak, mainly, of poisonous bitterness, of inadequacy, pain and guilt in relationships with others as well as with ourselves.

Forgiveness of a sour kind: *Il catino di zinco* (*The Zinc Basin*)

Margaret Mazzantini's novel begins by presenting a constellation of discomforting images: an itchy scarf, the damp stickiness of Antenora's palms, the unpleasant feeling of being aggressively scrubbed with a hard sponge imbued with scorching hot water.[8] Every little gesture, in the world represented to us, feels painful or uncomfortable; every little object is scratchy or too tight, even a clean towel after a bath. As the narrative unfolds, depicting another string of mostly unsuccessful relationships between sexes and across generations, it weaves its events around the figure of Antenora, the narrator's grandmother. Alive and energetic, strong, direct, remarkably unreflective, pitiful victim and ferocious perpetrator at once, Antenora is a unique representative of a social system predisposed to produce, in large numbers, women who were 'sly gossipers. At home: muffled blades with their husbands and relentless with their children.'[9] In a few initial sentences, the narrative indicates the petty topics recurring in the conversations of Antenora with her circle of friends, the unkindness in their collective behaviour and their distasteful gestures of social distinction. It portrays a daily life furnished with a set of objects that points to overly ambitious social aspirations, but only succeeds in returning the image of a world defined by a desolate and all-pervasive lack of sincerity and self-awareness.

Although the novel does not articulate an outspoken critique to patriarchy, it is extremely effective in portraying a constitutively unbalanced social and familial world, in which young women are subdued to the authority of their fathers, their value entirely measured on their physical appearance and/or ability to be or become good wives and mothers. Antenora's father, a wealthy landowner, is the representative of a previous order of things, a culture of peasantry only one step removed from Antenora's urban world.[10] In his small town, Don Sauro follows a comfortable routine surrounded by a cluster of women – daughters as well as maids – he presides over while they serve, fear, wait for him to '*maritarle*', or choose a '*marito*', a husband for them.[11] Women are described, throughout the narrative, as embittered, cunning and strategizing. Made cruel by their captive roles, by the impossibility of directing their 'branches' outwards, as Tamaro would perhaps put it, they preside over the domestic domain constantly oscillating between victimhood and pure evilness, mindlessly turning towards others the pain that has been inflicted upon them. Mostly acting out of interest, they show very little awareness of anything outside their immediate goals.

In *Follow Your Heart*, Olga's parents gratuitously make young Olga feel responsible for the death of her dog. In this novel, something else occurs, involving a pet, that perfectly encapsulates the generalized and unnecessary cruelty characteristic of familial relationships. Antenora loses a child to typhus. She does not communicate his death to his brother Vittorio, who learns of it by seeing a framed picture of him joining an already existing portrait gallery of dead relatives. Traumatized by the loss, Vittorio immediately becomes very close to a rabbit pet his mother brings home from the market. The animal clearly becomes a compensating presence for Vittorio. One day in which Antenora is annoyed with the animal, she grabs it, kills it and makes a meal out of it:

Suddenly, she got assailed by the intention of killing the animal. She was not so cruel as to consciously desire to deprive his son of his new friend. She hadn't even realized the existence of that exclusive bond, that mechanism of replacement and compensation had completely escaped her. Simply, she was annoyed by those secret hours of leisure that the rabbit could give the child. She had the impression that those games kept Vittorio away from his life – a penance that she had given to him. He could not escape, not him, the most imaginative of her children … he had to endure the punishment of being-on-this-earth-to-suffer, the same punishment she had received from nature, for that silent cicada she kept between her tights. (57)

This system of social relations ruled by unnecessary cruelty causes emotional distance in the narrator, who sounds resentful for being part of a painful and inescapable familial history. Elena Ferrante, a few years later, will capture this feeling into a potent image: 'ancestors compressed into the child's flesh'.[12] In Ferrante's case, it is the thought of a mother, who acknowledges, in this statement, every child's predetermination by a history that will continue to 'press on him/her' throughout their lives.

The narrator clearly disapproves of her grandmother's world and its morals and is eager to affirm her 'difference' and independence from it. The clash between sincerely felt familial ties and the inadequate and hypocritical standards they represent to her causes the narrator of Mazzantini's story to live a profound conflict. Towards the end of *Il catino di zinco*, she dreams of this very tension:

Grandma is a tailless ugly dog that chases me in the dark … Go away, angry dog, leave me alone. And here I am, a little girl, while I leave a countryside church, a white kerchief on my head. One of the laces of my head-cover falls on my forehead. I am holding the stems, long and coarse, of a bunch of poppies, the petals are all creased. On the ground, leaning against a stick, there is a bundle of old rugs, from which a pleading hand comes out. I bend forward to give it my tired blood-red flowers, and only at that moment I realize that it is my blood that, in a tiny rivulet, flows from my wrist to the beseeching hand. Among the rugs, a face comes to the surface, still her, grandma, with glassy-eyes and a faint smile, as smooth and polished as the Madonna's. She wants my blood! (131)

This is an almost too clear description of the claim blood ties make on our lives. From childhood, we are called to continue writing the history of our families, to inject past narratives with fresh lifeblood, to accomplish old destinies. The tension between the opposed impulses of allegiance and rebellion to our past causes a constant guilt and dripping of pain, a trickle of blood both Tamaro and Mazzantini are distinctively – albeit differently – aware of. If Olga, in *Follow Your Heart*, suavely asks: 'Fate, heredity, upbringing, where does one begin and the other end?' (54), Mazzantini's narrator responds with anger and resentment: 'Why me? What makes you think I am like all of you? If blood were really this dense with old stuff, it couldn't flow in our veins … Now that your life is over, you are looking for a new soul to inhabit. You are looking for my soul. Thief of my eyes, of my good intentions' (133).

Il catino di zinco evokes a coarse familial and social world, as rough and uncomfortable as the woollen scarf Antenora forces her young granddaughter to wear before leaving the house. This image alone summons the sense of suffocation characteristic of a bourgeois social world Mazzantini depicts with ability and respect, but also from a hard-won emotional distance, as if she really were the protagonist of the opening sequence of the narrative, the young woman hiding behind the church doors at her grandmother's funeral: grieving, but also angry and conflicted, stuck between her present and a familial past she acknowledges as still current and important, but also achingly dreary and casting a long shadow of inescapable unhappiness.

The novel speaks the language of an angry kind of respect. It is as much an homage to one's personal and familial history as it is an indictment of it, a successful 'narrative firework' that aims at achieving a partial deliverance from the past through an honest description of it, of that precise mixture of spite, resentment and routine brutality that has been for a long time at the core of interpersonal relationships, as men and women acted according to what was expected of them regardless of their personal dispositions.

At the core of both narratives lies the unhappiness that comes from choosing not to look into one's past, the unhappiness that comes from looking into it, the wounds we inflict upon ourselves and others in an attempt to break the mould of familial patterns of behaviour, the cost of rage, of aimlessness, of blindly running away instead of taking the time to ponder over our motives and objectives, the search for a mode of existence in healthy dialogue with the past, the present and the future that Tamaro symbolizes with the image of the tree.

Indeed, Tamaro and Mazzantini approach these themes very differently: Tamaro's serene and inspired tone, the object of so much criticism at the time of the novel's release, sharply contrasts with Mazzantini's brashness and defiant attitude. This is, at least partly, due to the fact that in *Follow Your Heart*, the narrating voice belongs to an old woman, Olga, who has mostly come to terms with her past and has decided to 'consign it' in the form of a written confession to her granddaughter. *Il catino di zinco*'s narrator could be, in a way, that very granddaughter, a young woman who looks at her grandmother with love, compassion and a heavy parcel of unresolved feelings. She writes it all down, perhaps in the attempt to find the strength to finally come out of that door.

Conclusion

In *Rethinking the Romance Genre*, Emily S. Davis contends that 'the task of cultural analysis is not to pit the "merely personal" against the "profoundly structural" or vice versa but to attend to the ways intimacy, sexuality, the personal – that is, the realm of the "private" – are being used in the formation of a new bourgeois hegemonic block that is the outcome of late capitalism's structural changes'.[13] From this perspective, both narratives perform an important kind of cultural analysis as they make these social structures visible in their recent formation and particularly 'Italian' variant. Focusing on the pursuit of a 'higher step' and emancipation from familial histories from a female perspective, these novels seem to partake of the same cultural 'humous' from which emerged the writing of Elena Ferrante – consistently focused on exploring and contesting established forms of womanhood through her investigations of mother–daughter relationships.[14] What is Elena's story – one of the two protagonists of Elena Ferrante's *Neapolitan Quartet* (2011–14) – if not the life-long account of a most painful and difficult search for emancipation, for deliverance from one's past, for a higher step outside the claustrophobic succession of generations?[15] Some of the main discursive elements these narratives share (including Ferrante's) are retribution and the cyclical repetition of destinies, the attempt to escape a familial legacy that, as Rose put it, is 'as generative as it is scary',[16] the indictment of patriarchy as painful acknowledgement of its enduring and far-reaching effects, a regime of power relations we have all partaken in and sustained.

Perhaps, reading these texts could be particularly advantageous to the younger generations more and more accustomed, when discussing familial and/or romantic relationships, to a language that highlights consent, accessible self-knowledge and affirmation, the transparency of feelings, as if all this constituted a perspective always shared and available to everyone. To the contrary, private histories have always been, and still are, fraught with conflicts, violence, abuse and implosions. As such, the narratives that recount these aspects should be analysed without prejudice, as to better appreciate the complex and contradictory history and makeup of our personal interactions, too often conceived of as a transparent 'object of scrutiny and control through formal and predictable procedures ... subsuming the erotic and romantic experience of love under systematic rules of conduct and abstract categories'.[17]

Approximately thirty years have passed since the publication of these novels. Those granddaughters have grown and are now facing challenges of their own. According to their economic and social circumstances, perhaps they have never been so 'free' to choose for themselves: to travel, work, live abroad, marry or not, procreate or not ... in actuality, they are still negotiating between belonging and emancipation, autonomy and social acceptance, familial narratives of implosion and the pursuit of a step a little higher than the others.

Notes

1   Valentina Aversano, Serena Di Ceglie and Gloria Laursen Forese, 'Susanna Tamaro: l'esordio e il caso editoriale', *Oblique Studio* (2009): 27.

2   Susanna Tamaro was born in Trieste in 1957. She published her first book in 1989, *La testa fra le nuvole*, winning the award Elsa Morante Opera Prima. Before *Va' dove ti porta il cuore*, Tamaro publishes *Per voce sola* (1991), critically acclaimed, and *Cuore di ciccia* (1992). *Va' dove ti porta il cuore* has sold worldwide more than 15 million copies, becoming the most commercially successful Italian novel of the twentieth century. In 2007 Tamaro publishes *Ascolta la mia voce*, the follow-up to *Va' dove ti porta il cuore*. In this novel, Olga's granddaughter, Marta, deals with the loss of her grandmother, meets her father and leaves for a trip to Israel in search of her family roots. Tamaro's last book, *Il tuo sguardo illumina il mondo*, was published in 2018.

3   Susanna Tamaro, *Follow Your Heart*, trans. John Cullen (New York: Doubleday, [1994] 1995), 12. All subsequent references will be provided in text.

4   Olga's mother was made to feel inadequate since her early childhood, a poor replacement for a lost older brother: 'She had the misfortune to be born not only female but on the very anniversary of her brother's demise.' Later in the novel, Olga describes her relationship to her husband as civilized, convenient and dull: 'I got the feeling that what Augusto wanted more than anything else was to find someone at home during mealtimes, someone he could display with pride in the cathedral on Sundays; he seemed mostly indifferent to the living person behind that comforting image.' Olga explains that 'in those days almost all marriages were like this, little domestic infernos for two, one of whom was bound to succumb sooner or later' (128–9, 131).

5   This is Olga's personal 'conversion moment'. Laura Marcus explains that since St Augustine's *Confessions*, a key moment of recognition (or understanding of a fundamental truth) has been at the core of autobiographical writing as a 'central and repeated trope', sometimes echoed, variously repeated or reinvented. It is clearly too late for Olga to change the course of her life, but she hopes her 'confession' of the lessons she learnt will help Marta avoid repeating the old patterns and mistakes. Laura Marcus, 'Life Writing', in *The Edinburgh Introduction to Studying English Literature*, ed Dermot Cavanagh et al. (Edinburgh: Edinburgh University Press, 2010), 150.

6   This is perhaps one of the reasons why Marta's name is only mentioned at the end of the narrative, while the narrator of *Il catino di zinco* remains nameless. The younger generation still has to 'make its own name,' create its history. These stories concern the past of a present about to be written.

7 Lee Marshall, 'Just One Little Lie', *The Independent* (25 June 1995).

8 Born in Dublin in 1961, from an Italian father and an Irish mother, Margaret Mazzantini worked as a stage actress before becoming a novelist. *Il Catino di zinco* is her first novel, with which Mazzantini won the prestigious literary award Premio Campiello. This first work, in light of the author's future literary production, somehow stands isolated, not only because of its explicitly autobiographic subject matter but also because of its language. There is at play a search for a specific terminology that mixes the erudite with the popular/dialectal and does not shy away from vulgar images and expressions. In her later novels, Mazzantini will endeavour to inhabit diverse characters and their psychologies, creating narratives pivoting around opposed ideals of womanhood, such as in *Manola* (1999) and *Non ti muovere* (2001). This latter novel, commercially her most successful to date, has sold more than 2 million copies worldwide and has been translated into thirty-five languages. In 2004, it became a film directed by Sergio Castellitto and starring Penelope Cruz. In 2008, Mazzantini publishes *Venuto al mondo* (*Twice Born* 2011). On the topic of 'double women' in Mazzantini's literary production, see Fausto de Michele's essay 'Mazzantini e la donna doppia: invito a una lettura "gender"' (2007). On *Non ti muovere*, a text that has so far received a fair amount of scholarly attention, see the essays by Barbara Alfano, 'L'(in)efficacia dell'amore in *Not ti muovere* di Margaret Mazzantini' (2015), and D. Bartalesi-Graf, 'Alterita', identita' e divismo in *Non ti muovere* e in *Cristo si e' fermato ad Eboli*: dal linguaggio letterario a quello del cinema' (2007).

9 Margaret Mazzantini, *Il catino di zinco* (Milano: Mondadori, [1994] 2013), 14. *Il catino di zinco* has not been translated into English; all translations from the novel are mine, and all subsequent references will be provided in text.

10 The zinc basin is the object that perfectly symbolizes the passage from the countryside to the city. It is a domestic tool that clearly reminds one of older times and rural life. Heavy and cumbersome, it signals a burden difficult to dispose of, a piece of family history and an object destined to become more and more obsolete within an urban setting.

11 In a memorable sequence of the novel, while desperately mourning the loss of one of his daughters, Don Sauro 'barely' manages to retain a minimum measure of self-control necessary to continue his fish-shopping ritual; he keeps discerning among the different kinds of it, giving precise instructions for its cooking. The scene seems to suggest that the death of a daughter is indeed a tragic affair, just not sad enough to interfere with Don Sauro's passion for food (32–3).

12 Elena Ferrante, *The Lost Daughter*, trans. Ann Goldstein (New York: Europa, [2006] 2008), 37.

13 Emily S. Davis, *Rethinking the Romance Genre: Global Intimacies in Contemporary Literary and Visual Culture* (New York: Palgrave, 2013), 225.

14 For a critical discussion of Ferrante's writing on motherhood in her early novels, see Saveria Chemotti's essay 'Elena Ferrante: Il corpo a corpo con la madre'; for a discussion of motherhood in the *Quartet*, see Jacqueline Rose's

book chapter dedicated to Ferrante in *Mothers: An Essay on Love and Cruelty* (2018).

15 In *The Lost Daughter*, Ferrante reworks the notion of 'imploded fireworks' as *occasioni mancate* (missed opportunities):

What had I done that was so terrible, in the end. Years earlier, I had been a girl who felt lost, this was true. All the hopes of youth seemed to have been destroyed, I seemed to be falling backward toward my mother, my grandmother, the chain of mute or angry women I came from. Missed opportunities … I seemed to be imprisoned in my own head, without the chance to test myself, and I was frustrated. (Ferrante, *The Lost Daughter*, 64)

In a previous novel published in 2002, *I giorni dell'abbandono* (*The Days of Abandonment* 2005), Ferrante tells the story of a mother who, after having been left by her husband, is afraid of being in an inadequate state of mind to take care of her children. Her thoughts and actions are often reminiscent of Olga's annoyance with Ilaria after the loss of Ernesto. In this novel, coincidentally, the protagonist's name is Olga, and one of her children's names is Ilaria.

16 Jacqueline Rose, *Mothers: An Essay on Love and Cruelty* (London: Faber & Faber, 2018), 169.

17 Eva Illouz, *Why Love Hurts* (Cambridge: Polity Press, 2012), 177.

Bibliography

Alfano, Barbara. 'L'(in)efficacia dell'amore in *Non ti muovere* di Margaret Mazzantini'. *Forum Italicum* 49, no. 1 (2015): 38–55.

Aversano, Valentina, Di Ceglie, Serena and Laursen Forese, Gloria. 'Susanna Tamaro: lesordio e il caso editoriale'. *Oblique Studio* (2009). https://www.oblique.it/images/formazione/dispense/caso_tamaro_cuore.pdf Accessed 18 July 2021.

Barbieri, Eleonora. 'Quando mi chiesero di chiudere il mio libro in un cassetto'. *Il Giornale* (23 February 2019). www.ilgiornale.it/news/spettacoli/quandomidiss ero-chiudere-mio-libro-cassetto1650372.html. Accessed 18 July 2021.

Bartalesi-Graf, Daniela. 'Alterita, identita' e divismo in *Non ti muovere* e in *Cristo si e' fermato ad Eboli*: dal linguaggio letterario a quello del cinema'. *Forum Italicum* 41, no. 1 (2007): 127–54.

Chemotti, Saveria. *L' inchiostro bianco: madri e figlie nella narrativa italiana contemporanea*, Padova: Il Poligrafo, 2009.

Davis, Emily S. *Rethinking the Romance Genre: Global Intimacies in Contemporary Literary and Visual Culture*. New York: Palgrave, 2013.

De Michele, Fausto. 'Mazzantini e la donna doppia: Invito ad una rilettura "gender"'. *Bollettino 900*, nos 1–2 (2007): 6.

Ferrante, Elena. *The Lost Daughter* (trans. Ann Goldstein). New York: Europa, [2006] 2008.

Ferrante Elena. *I Giorni dell'Abbandono*. Rome: E/O Edizioni, [2002] 2015.

Forlini, Federica. 'Il Catino di Zinco, di Margaret Mazzantini'. *La Stanza Rossa* (6 May 2016). http://lastanzarossa23.blogspot.com/2016/05/recensione-il-cat ino-di-zinco-di.html. Accessed 18 July 2021.

Illouz, Eva. *Why Love Hurts*. Cambridge: Polity Press, 2012.

Marcus, Laura. 'Life Writing'. In *The Edinburgh Introduction to Studying English Literature*, edited by Dermot Cavanagh, Alan Gillis, Michelle Keown, James Loxley and Randall Stevenson, 148–57. Edinburgh: Edinburgh University Press, 2010.

Marshall, Lee. 'Just One Little Lie'. *The Independent* (25 June 1995). www.inde pendent.co.uk/arts-entertainment/books/just-one-little-lie-1588292.html. Accessed 18 July 2021.

Mazzantini, Margaret. *Il catino di zinco*. Milano: Mondadori, [1994] 2013.

Righetti, Donata. 'Tamaro: cari lettori vi spiego il mio segreto'. *Corriere della Sera* (7 January 2003). www.corriere.it/Primo_Piano/Cronache/2003/01_Gennaio/06/ tamaro.shtml. Accessed 18 July 2021.

Rose, Jacqueline. *Mothers: An Essay on Love and Cruelty*. London: Faber & Faber, 2018.

Tamaro, Susanna. *Follow Your Heart* (trans. John Cullen). New York: Doubleday, [1994] 1995.

10

Lovespeak, love novels and the onset of modernity

Gary Kelly

Whatever love may be 'in itself', if there be such a thing, it is communicated as what integrational linguist Roy Harris would call 'lovespeak'[1] – or linguistic, cultural and social discourses about and enabling 'love'. 'Love' here is not a transhistorical anthropological absolute and universal represented by language, but a discourse that is learned, enabling people to integrate their ongoing creation of what ethnomethodologist Harold Garfinkel, after Émile Durkheim, called 'immortal, ordinary society'.[2] Such meaning-making involves all that the makers are and know in a particular moment of what Alec McHoul calls 'effective semiotics'.[3] 'Romantic' love, now mostly positive, was through the onset of modernity almost entirely pejorative, as characteristic of romance, that is, extravagant, unrealistic, impractical. 'Love' as 'sex', or sexual intercourse, appears in English only in 1900; before that, the usual term for such love was 'fuck', usually for 'penetrative' sex, and 'frig', meaning solitary or mutual masturbation (*OED*). These, too, are social and discursive: as a modern sexologist writes, 'la pratique physique de la sexualité serait impossible sans un arsenal de prescriptions et d'apprentissages culturel, une ritualisation des interactions interpersonnelles et une élaboration mentale spécifique des individus, qui mettent le corps en route, structurent la sexualité physique et la saturent de significations' ('the physical practice of sexuality would be impossible without an arsenal of prescriptions and cultural learning, a ritualization of interpersonal interactions and a specific mental elaboration by individuals, which put the body on its way, structure physical sexuality and saturate it with meanings').[4] But 'love', however construed, has long been assumed to be 'natural' as well as cultural. An early modern sex manual, Nicolas Venette's *The Mysteries of Conjugal Love Reveal'd*, was reissued from the seventeenth through the eighteenth century and declared:

> Love inflames a Young Woman's Heart that is pleased with Idleness, Flattery, Feasts, fine Cloaths and Love Discourses, to that degree, that she is at the long-run forced to yield to its Incitements, and not able to repulse its Attacks. Besides, she is led by a natural bent to this soft Passion.[5]

Love was commercialized, and by the eighteenth century, 'Love Discourses' included such downmarket commercialized print and entertainment as chapbook tales, lyric and lyric-narrative verse, street ballads, garlands and songsters, 'memoirs' from confessional to criminal, drama and 'modern novels', so called to distinguish them from earlier forms. Upmarket, lovespeak was developed in more prestigious discourses of moral philosophy, devotional literature, theological writing and the belles-lettres. Eventually lovespeak would be modernized and scientized in new modern 'expert' knowledges – academic disciplines of psychology, sociology, anthropology, anatomy and so on. Then as now, a major medium for circulating lovespeak of all kinds was the 'love novel', so called from the seventeenth to the early twentieth centuries. These were traced back to post-Homeric Greek popular romances, renewed in Medieval and Early Modern romance. With the onset of the discourse of modernity in the mid-eighteenth-century Atlantic world, lovespeak and the love novel were developed in various ways to articulate and promote conflicting interests, personal, social, sectional, national and imperial.

'Modernity' is much used but infrequently specified in modern expert knowledges. Here I historicize structuration sociologist Anthony Giddens's account of modernity. Modernity would then be a discourse centred on self-reflexive personal identity enabling 'pure' or disinterested relations of intimacy, conjugality, domesticity, community, sociality, citizenship, spirituality and others. So formed, nurtured and repaired, modern subjects can survive modernization's enhanced relationships of risk and trust, new chronotopes or configurations of time-space, increasingly abstract systems of knowledge and practice, and mobility required by modernization's relentless and accelerating change. As a 'sovereign' or self-determined subject, the modern self-reflexive individual figures as the citizen of the modern constitutional nation-state and the entrepreneurial producer and self-fashioning consumer required by the modern economy. The so-called modern novel proved increasingly useful in imagining, promoting and contesting versions of this modernity. The modern 'love novel' developed modern lovespeak to imagine and narrate the formation of the 'properly' modern subject against both unmodern and falsely or mistakenly modern subjects, against both unmodernity and false or mistaken modernities. The stakes were not only love's happy ending but also national and imperial triumph against rival powers with their own versions of modernity in global context and contest.

In that contest, Britain's chief rivals were the Catholic absolutist monarchies of France and, to a diminishing extent, Spain. Spain was generally viewed in Britain as irretrievably unmodern because it was ruled by an absolute monarchy and authoritarian church suppressing the free thought and expression considered central to 'British liberties' and hence to Britain's modernity. As for Spanish lovespeak and love novels, in Britain, Cervantes was thought to have demolished their credibility. France, though Catholic and absolutist, seemed to be creating a modernity rivalling Britain's in competition for global dominance that regularly turned bellic. Lovespeak and love novels were weaponized not only in the culture wars that inevitably accompany such violence but also in domestic civil and culture wars, as illustrated by Samuel Johnson's 1755 *Dictionary of the English Language*. Johnson aimed to modernize notoriously protean English by stabilizing and historicizing it as the lingua franca for a hegemonic coalition of modernizing men of the landed class and professional elites. Johnson defined 'novel' as 'a small tale, generally of love'. Usage was illustrated by the quotation 'the trifling *novels* which Ariosto inserted in his poems', from the eminent Augustan John Dryden's dedication to his translation anthology *The Works of Virgil* (1697). This was a political gesture reasserting neoclassical English Augustanism against both 'trifling novels' and Milton's non-conformist, anti-monarchic, anti-classical, stylistically experimental and hence culturally and politically disruptive modern epic *Paradise Lost*, itself a political gesture.

Dryden understood the ideological, cultural and political significance of classical epic in the corporate identity and hegemony of British elites. He extolls the 'Heroick Poem' (epic) as designed 'to form the Mind to Heroick Virtue by Example', and hence its action 'is always one, entire, and great', without any 'Rubbish' or worthless filler, such as trifling novels. Johnson's definition restates Dryden's argument that, in scope and in cultural-political importance, epic is to novel as heroism is to love, as the heroic is to the amorous. Ongoing culture wars associated the heroic, Englishness, men of social elites, classical education, meritocracy, the public political sphere, certain genres and gender difference and hierarchy. By contrast, the novel was often associated with the amatory, Frenchness, literate women, little education or merely in modern languages, the private and intimate sphere, certain genres and hierarchical gender difference. Love novels Johnson did admire were Samuel Richardson's, posing English modernity against the unmodernity or false modernity of foreign novels.

By Johnson's day, association of love and the novel was long-standing and usually denigrated. Shaftesbury's influential *Characteristics* (1711) associated love and the novel with 'enthusiasm', considered dangerously destabilizing for individual, society, government and religion in a Britain still mindful of earlier religious-political conflicts:

> A very small Foundation of any Passion will serve us, not only to act it well, but even to work our-selves into it beyond our reach. Thus, by a little Affectation in Love-Matters, and with the help of a Romance or Novel, a Boy of Fifteen, or a grave Man of Fifty, may be sure to grow a very natural Coxcomb, and feel the *Belle Passion* in good earnest.[6]

The slip into French insinuates that 'the belle passion' is not properly English, perhaps even subversive of English personal identity, social order and political institutions. Love enthusiasm could produce 'gallantry' or assiduous amatory courtship, licit or (especially) illicit, though the two were often contrasted, as in the phrase 'gallantry, not love'. Courtly gallantry was associated with court monarchy: dynastic marriages could be loveless and hence dangerously supplemented by affairs of 'gallantry' in 'backstairs politics' or intertwined political and amorous 'intrigue' circumventing regular governance. Court factions could manage the ruler's lovers, supposedly introduced to the monarch's bedchamber by the backstairs, to converge networks of patriarchy, paternalism and patronage for the benefit of faction and favourites. The elite-landed classes, often connected to and serving at the royal court, similarly treated marriage, strengthened by legitimate male primogeniture to transfer property securely from one generation of men to the next – 'securely' because this process could be compromised by the emergence of an illegitimate claimant, a bastard or 'love-child', a term found in the print record from the 1720s through the century, notably in 'novels of gallantry'.[7]

The operation of subversive lovespeak and love novels was illustrated in 1756 by a correspondent in *The World*. He ascribed his moral degeneracy as a man to reading as a boy 'such books' as he 'found lying about' his mother's room, including 'the Atalantis, Ovid's Art of Love, novels, romances, miscellaneous poems, and plays', especially Restoration comedy. 'From these studies I contracted an early taste for gallantry', so that 'your Dorimants and your Horners struck my imagination beyond the brightest characters in Pope's Homer'.[8] Referenced here are Delarivier Manley's erotic roman-à-clef of courtly gallantry, *The New Atalantis* (1709); the Roman poet Ovid's pseudo-manual for love-making (first century CE); seventeenth-century amorous literature; and the rake-protagonists of two Restoration comedies, Sir George Etherege's *The Man of Mode* (1676) and William Wycherley's *The Country Wife* (1675). These are set against Pope's Drydenian Augustanism in his translation of Homer's epics. 'Novels' were disparaged for representing and promoting 'mere' love and associated with such deplored 'modernities' (in English 1753; *OED*) as 'luxury', 'fashion', social emulation, commercialization of culture, secularization, effeminization, Frenchification, excessive individualism, risky 'innovation', mere 'novelty' and so on.

Nevertheless, vindication of lovespeak and love novels could be drawn from contemporary, intellectually and culturally prestigious philosophical writing. Against Shaftesbury's ironic critique of the passions' deformation of moral-ethical judgement and action, the clergyman Francis Hutcheson developed a language and theoretical vindication for what is now called 'affect'. Hutcheson relates bodily and mental experience and sensation to self-reflexive personal identity, candid sociability, sympathy with nature, cultural expression centred on expressiveness and educated feeling and religious devotionalism and toleration.[9] *An Inquiry into the Original of Our Ideas of Beauty and Virtue* (1725) specifies love of various kinds, while *An Essay on the Nature and Conduct of the Passions and Affections* (1728) develops a language and taxonomy for properly modern subjective experience.[10] These works converged philosophy and theology for modernity as culture wars and were reissued well into the next century on both sides of the Atlantic. Hutcheson's philosophical lovespeak was extended in his student Adam Smith's *Theory of Moral Sentiments* (1759) and *Inquiry into the Nature and Causes of the Wealth of Nations* (1776). Sentimental love novels, in particular, narrativized key tenets in the new moral philosophy, displacing novels of 'gallantry'.[11] Accordingly, Henry Home, lord Kames, prominent articulator of Scottish Enlightenment modernity, defended love novels in his pioneering cultural anthropology *Sketches of the History of Man* (4 vols, 1774–5). Resisting the attack on luxury, led by Rousseau and others, for corrupting the society and 'civilization', Kames declares, 'Mental pleasure, such as arises from sentiment or reasoning, falls not within the verge of luxury, to whatever excess indulged', and 'If to relieve merit in distress be luxury, it is only so in a metaphorical sense: nor is it esteemed luxury in a damsel of fifteen to peruse love novels from morning to evening' (2nd ed., 2.134).

Nevertheless, many persisted in condemning love novels, even as refashioned by Sensibility, for encouraging 'worldliness' and 'fashion' – code words, like 'luxury', for the rise of commercialized consumption as a destabilizing force in a supposedly historical social hierarchy, political order and theological certainty. For example, the Rev. Henry Venn's bellicose chapter, 'On the Sin of Lewdness' in *The Complete Duty of Man; Or, a System of Doctrinal and Practical Christianity* (1763), proclaimed 'the spiritual warfare, of the whole church of Christ in condemning and opposing every fashionable way intended by the world to gratify lewd desires', including 'the melody of amorous songs, the double entendre, mixed dancings, love novels, and above all stage plays' (345). Venn's Anglican Evangelical network linked landed, financial and mercantile interests, and among his clerical appointments was chaplain to David Steuart Erskine,

Earl of Buchan. Buchan refashioned classical republicanism as ancient liberties practised by Celtic and Germanic peoples, converged in the Scots and led by his own class in the passage to modern constitutionalism. This aristocratic modernity was supposedly undermined by a falsely modern education emanating from court monarchy and encouraging luxury and decadence. Buchan accordingly promoted the historical humanist neo-classical education and culture assumed by his class and their professional relations and associates. In a *Letter ... to His Brother ... on the Subject of Education* (1782), he declared, 'I would rather see the tear standing in their [young gentlemen's] eyes, when they read or recited the stories of the death of Brutus, Cato, Helvidius Priscus, Arulenus Rusticus, Thrasea Pætus, and of Arria', all martyrs for senatorial republicanism against imperial autocracy, 'than melting with the fictitious and enervating sorrow of a love novel' (6).[12] For many readers, the immediate context of a national and imperial crisis would give sharper edge to Buchan's pamphlet: the divisive American war, Britain's defeat, the belief that George III's insistence on royal prerogative had caused and prolonged the war, the perception that patronage and corruption among elites had compromised the war's prosecution and claims that the absorption of Britain's monarchic court and aristocracy in luxury and fashion rendered them decadescent and incapacitated for their assumed role of ruling class. Though Buchan recognized that the love novel's emphasis was shifting from gallantry to sentiment, he still advanced sentimental neoclassicism over sentimental lovespeak for the national and imperial destiny.

This shift owed much to the impact on both sides of the channel of Richardson's novels and was complicated by modernity's culture wars. Import, translation and imitation of French love novels informed by enthusiastic French reception of Richardson prompted reaction informed by prevailing mercantilist economics and Franco-British commercial, cultural, religious and imperial rivalry, with calls for and production of properly British love novels. An English pioneer in domesticating the French sentimental love novel and lovespeak was Sarah Scott, associated with her sister Elizabeth Montagu's 'Bluestocking circle' of upper-class and elite professional men and their wives and associates. They promoted modernity as moral and ethical reform, and philanthropic activism and emotional and intellectual self-development and reflection as practice of Anglican theological tenets. Scott and Montagu were astute readers of French and English love novels, and from the 1750s to the 1770s, Scott published a series of love novels that challenged the form's French elaborations and adapted its Richardsonian formulations. Scott's *History of Cornelia* (1750) fictionalized female conduct-book counsel on the dangers of unmodern courtly society. *Agreeable Ugliness* (1754) adapts a moralistic anti-libertine French love novel, *La Laideur aimable, et les dangers de la beauté*, by Pierre-Antoine de La Place (1752). *A Journey through Every Stage of Life* (1754) frames tales illustrating emergent ideas of modern self-reflexive modernity contesting an unmodern social world. *A Description of Millennium Hall* (1762) imagines the landed estate, as metaphor and synecdoche for the national state, modernized by its women proprietors, refugees from the unmodern world of courtly gallantry. Emulating the ladies of Millennium Hall, the eponymous hero of the *History of Sir George Ellison* (1766) manages his slave plantation humanely as a model for modern colonialism. *The Test of Filial Duty* (1772) challenges elite families' abuse of women by controlling their education and arranging their marriages to advance corporate family interests and to ensure legally uncontested transmission of the estate.

The market in 'modern novels' as manuals for modernity widened, prompting innovation in lovespeak and diversification of love novels' themes, forms and styles in response to the dynamics of public affairs, cultural consumption and fashion. Imports, especially French and English, increased as literary and cultural emulation developed alongside commercial and military competition. French fiction of *amour galant* was refashioned by Marivaux and Crébillon fils and prepared French reception of Richardson's love novels. Prévost translated Richardson and repurposed his themes and methods in his own novels. Marie Riccoboni's succession of love novels affected a supposedly English sensibility. Jean-Jacques Rousseau's philosophical love novel *Julie; ou, la Nouvelle Éloïse* (1761, Englished 1761) reversed and redirected the main elements of Richardson's *Clarissa* while enhancing Richardson's conflict between proto-modern love and subjectivity, on the one hand, and unmodern economic and social structures, on the other. Rousseau followed with an education quasi-novel, *Émile* (1762, Englished 1762), programming the formation of an exemplary modern self-reflexive masculine subject for a proleptically modern state. Relevance to lovespeak and the love novel was addressed in the concluding prescription for forming Émile's destined companion, paradoxically named Sophie, for subordination. She was to acquire sufficient self-reflexivity to enable her conjugal companionability but insufficient to assist her innate tendency to invert her subordination by using Émile's sexual desire to disable his exemplary modernity.

British writers pushed back in their way. Frances Sheridan knew the work of French love novelists and they knew hers.[13] Her *Memoirs of Miss Sidney Biddulph* (1761) adapts and inverts the intimate or confessional memoir, used in the literature of *amour galant* to intensify the erotic allure. Sheridan uses the form to invent a young woman's striving for self-reflectively disciplined emotional and intellectual engagement in a social world that often deceives her moral judgement and limits her ethical options. Laurence Sterne's *A Sentimental Journey through France and Italy* (1768), like its predecessor *Tristram Shandy* (1759–67), incorporates elements of the French love novel and exaggerates them into absurdity. Henry Mackenzie's *The Man of Feeling* (1771) went even further in hyperbolizing tropes and devices of the love novel, risking bathos, but anticipated development of the novel of autotelic love from the 1780s through the Romantic period. Another import, from Germany, consolidated this form. Englished from French in 1779 as *The Sorrows of Werter: A German Story*, Goethe's love novel (1771) was already a sensation-scandal on the Continent. It was a decisive break from the French love novel of *amour galant* and the English novel of sentimental love and, with its implied and explicit critiques of social and institutional unmodernities, confirmed the interest of the novel-reading public in glamourized modern subjectivity, as modern love *in extremis*, an end in itself rather than a means to the end of social renovation by exemplary modern subjects.

Britain's victory in the Seven Years War seemingly vindicated the nation's modernity, but by the late 1770s, the divisive American war was challenging such confidence and spurring calls for further modernization. The novel was now more energetically deployed to critique unmodernity and imagine a modernity by and for its readership. Between defeat in the American war and opening of the final struggle with France in 1793, many love novels assumed darker tones, complicated plots, historical-exotic settings, compromised or unhappy endings, 'dream logic' and love as suffering, subjectivity *in extremis* or beyond in abjection, exile or death. Even sentimental love novels were linked to the national crisis. In 1791, 'The Female Rambler' in the *Lady's Magazine* analysed the supposed increase in female ruin and conjugal infidelity among elites. To the Female Rambler, the 'fair sex' is 'considerably more subject than the men' to unrealistic expectation and mortifying disappointment. 'More flattered, and less informed, they enter into life with the most pleasing prospects in view' so that 'Ignorance gives confidence, confidence hope, and hope expectations', leaving most women vulnerable to the false consciousness encouraged by love novels. Excepting 'the later works of the celebrated Mr. Richardson', the 'fatal tendency of reading love novels and romances' is well known, for 'the passion of love, however exquisite a sensibility it affords to some exalted minds, is far from being safely promoted by such artificial incentives in the breasts of the generality of female readers' (27). Though 'some exalted minds' are exempt, the result for too many women is 'ruin', as love novel fantasies render unmarried women vulnerable to seduction and as the contrast between such fantasies and the realities of conjugal life inclines married women to adultery.[14] Mary Wollstonecraft would portray both sardonically in her feminist love novel *Maria; Or, the Wrongs of Woman* (1798).

Religious commentators continued hostile to love novels as 'worldly', but modernizers within both the state church and religious Dissent promoted modern self-reflexive identity, love and sociability achieved by a subjective conversion experience sustained by piety, self-discipline, the 'domestic affections' and sanctified public and private life.[15] Methodism within and outwith the Church of England emphasized divine and human social love, revived early Christianity's ritual love-feast and furnished its largely plebeian membership with a distinctive lovespeak. Many writings of the movement's founder, John Wesley, exhort to such love, and he even provided a love novel for Methodists by adapting Henry Brooke's *The Fool of Quality* (1765–70), a fictionalized encyclopaedia of Sensibility, as the often reissued *Henry Earl of Moreland* (1781).[16] Religious Dissenters leading provincial Enlightenments and reform movements promoted 'candour' as self-examination for a modern spiritualized self and its transparency to others in modern life – intimate, domestic, social, economic, political and civic. The theo-philosophy of Swedish millenarian mystic Emanuel Swedenborg centred on love, with lovespeak as the discourse of authentic and autonomous modern spiritual identity and relations human and divine, including conjugal sexual relations in heaven.[17] Church of England Evangelicalism was dominated by clerical, financial and mercantile elites and linked to landed and parliamentary ranks. Their articulations of religious lovespeak ranged from M. P. William Wilberforce's often republished *A Practical View of the Prevailing Religious System of Professed Christians, in the Higher and Middle Classes in This Country, Contrasted with Real Christianity* (1797) to Evangelical activist Hannah More's love novel *Coelebs in Search of a Wife* (1809).

Writers further diversified lovespeak and the love novel through the 1780s as contest between rival modernities and against supposed unmodernities intensified under imperial setbacks, internal instability and the stresses of economic modernization. Herbert Croft's widely read *Love and Madness: A Story Too True* (1780) novelized an actual scandal in which jealous love led to murder, illustrating relation of the novel and the news and taking love as subjective absolute beyond identity *in extremis* to madness and crime. Clergyman Martin Madan's controversial non-fiction *Thelyphthora; Or, a Treatise on Female Ruin* (1780) addressed the much discussed 'problem' of supposed increase in nation-weakening adultery and prostitution caused by mistaken modernity. Madan paradoxically proposes polygamy to resolve contradictions between modern religious-ethical lovespeak and persistent cultures of gallantry. Frances Burney's widely read *Cecilia; Or, Memoirs of an Heiress* (1782) is a pioneering novel of modern manners, sentiment and emulation. It uses the new narrative device of free indirect discourse or reported inner speech and thought, converging third- and first-person narration, to engage readers in characters' mastery of modern self-reflexive personal identity in the moral and ethical crisis of love and courtship, set in social and cultural milieux of variously unmodern, mistakenly modern and properly modern relations.

Whether set in contemporary, exotic or historified chronotopes, this machinery remained a mainstay of novelistic method for representing modernity. In *The Champion of Virtue* (1777, 'revised' 1778 as *The Old English Baron*), the classical republican Clara Reeve offered 'gothic' characters as proleptic modern subjects against Horace Walpole's popular

The Castle of Otranto (1765), a 'gothic' spoof of modern historiography and historified love novels. Sophia Lee's *The Recess; Or, a Tale of Other Times* (1783–5) historified the love novel with intrigues of the Elizabethan court, exploiting the new market in 'national' history and Sentimental interest in the figure of Mary Queen of Scots as victim of courtly political and amorous intrigue and increasing interest in the Elizabethan age as model for English modernity. *The Recess* suggests that 'other times' contain elements of modern times and vice versa, compromising the achievement of modernity. Lee's gynocentric novelization of history also addresses contemporary comment on historiography's inability to represent central topics of the discourse of modernity, especially subjective experience and domestic affections. *The Recess* challenged historiography's androcentrism, domination by male authors, archival poverty in documentation of historical figures' affective and private lives and consequent (and increasingly discussed) silence concerning women's experience and spheres. Lee's development of the love novel as central genre of modernity's discourse marked an extension of Bluestocking intervention in male-dominated genres and knowledges. Reeve applied modern historiography to the love novel in *The Progress of Romance* (1785), inverting the historical and hierarchical generic/gendered order of literary forms and languages by arguing for equality of vernacular languages and literatures with classical ones, romance with epic, fiction with historiography.

Such mobilization of lovespeak and the love novel for politicized culture wars accelerated in the Atlantic world was impelled by sharpened global contests of empires and modernities. In the new United States, conditions of publishing and authorship meant readers continued to depend on British imports, including love novels. Resistance came, however, from the American William Hill Brown's *The Power of Sympathy; Or, the Triumph of Nature* (1789). Invoking a post-independence Transatlantic culture war, Brown refashioned the European love novel to embody his idea of a distinctively American republican ideology, culture and modernity in private and public life. As British love novelists portrayed transgressive gallantry and libertinism as foreign, so Brown combined the elements of European libertine and sentimental love novels emplotted in an unwittingly incestuous passion framed as un-American – the love novel as a cautionary republican tale. In Britain, Sentimental lovespeak infused with fashionable neo-Petrarchanism became scandalously implicated in reformist modernity with the 'Della Cruscan' poem-correspondence in the fashionable miscellany magazine *The World* (from 1787), republished as *The British Album* (1789). This was conducted by public figures under pseudo-Petrarchan pen-names, such as Della Crusca (ambitious wastrel Robert Merry), Rosa Matilda (playwright Hannah Cowley) and Laura Maria (actor, novelist, poet and former royal mistress Mary Robinson). Their exchange of 'love'-larded verse-letters in successive magazine issues constituted a serialized verse love novel, in unconventional verse form and language as the aptly modern medium for disappointed, unrequited and thwarted love representing rejection of the self-reflexive modern subject by an unmodern or erroneously modern 'world' or elite society and all they controlled. Ambitious 'Della Crusca' soon published a poem, *The Laurel of Liberty* (1790), enthusiastically welcoming the French Revolution that would recontextualize lovespeak and love novels in Britain.

In France itself, lovespeak and the love novel were similarly refashioned in the contested modernity that issued in the French Revolution.[18] Jean-Francois Marmontel's 'moral tales' were widely known and imitated in Britain. Bernardin de St Pierre's tropical island pastoral love novel *Paul et Virginie* could be read as an indictment of *ancien régime* obstacles to modern love as subjective absolute realizable only in Nature. The Marquis de Sade, nobleman and Revolutionary *conventionnel*, hyperbolized the libertine and sentimental love novel as pornography, a powerful political discourse in the Revolutionary context.[19] The bookseller's clerk and Girondin Louvet de Couvray refashioned libertine and sentimental forms in his *Faublas* novels to create a sophisticated lovespeak for the aspirational middle ranks empowered by the Directory and the Napoleonic regime. Jean-Pierre Claris de Florian, aristocrat, constitutional monarchist and victim of the Jacobin terror, fashioned hyperbolically sentimental works known through the Atlantic world, such as the love novel *Gonzalve de Cordoue* (1791). This retrieved elements of chivalric ideology, romance and history to fabricate a modernized 'tradition' underwriting constitutionalism and love of country, like works from Edmund Burke's *Reflections on the Revolution in France* (1790), especially the notorious 'ten thousand swords' passage proclaiming his 'love' for Marie Antoinette,[20] to Walter Scott's world-historical Waverley Novels of the 1810s to 1830s.

For in Britain, too, response of consciously modern novelists to news and issues of the day addressed the market for further elaborations, variations and alternatives of the love novel. From the aftermath of the American catastrophe through the Revolutionary and Napoleonic crisis, writers such as Ann Radcliffe, Mary Robinson, Elizabeth Helme, M. G. Lewis, Regina Maria Roche, Elizabeth Inchbald, Mary Wollstonecraft, Thomas Holcroft and Charlotte Dacre exploited the 1780s love-novel achievements of Sophia Lee, Charlotte Smith and others in historifying and gothicizing the love novel as commentary on and intervention in modernity's culture wars – love novel as what would then have been called the 'political romance'. Writers, publishers and circulating library proprietors constituted a collective authorship that continued probing the market disclosed in the 1770s and 1780s by the success of the love novel of manners, sentiment and emulation as a handbook for the creation of modern 'immortal, ordinary society' in relation to 'news of the day' by the ranks comprising the novel-renting and -reading public.

A major instance was the application of lovespeak and the love novel to the 1790s Revolution debate in Britain. British writers smeared as 'Jacobins' used the love novel to politicize the Richardsonian conflict between modern sovereign subjectivity and the troika of paternalism, patriarchy and patronage. Republican atheist Thomas Holcroft's epistolary *Anna St. Ives* (1792) reconfigured and updated Richardson's *Clarissa* to converge modern love with reformist enthusiasm in a vanguard modernity almost thwarted by figures representing unmodern values, practices and institutions. Holcroft's friend, the philosophical anarchist William Godwin, caused a sensation with his *Enquiry Concerning Political Justice* (1793), where 'love' is a recurring touchstone for ethical conduct in private and public life. The *Enquiry* excluded novelistic lovespeak, but Godwin's novel *Things as They Are; Or, the Adventures of Caleb Williams* (1794) appropriated love-novel material for a subplot illustrating evils of 'things as they are', while the main plot subsumed earlier philosophers' lovespeak to a servant's 'love' for his 'master', an 'enthusiast' for the chivalric honour celebrated by Burke in his *Reflections* on the French Revolution. This relationship anticipated Hegel's formulation of the 'master–slave' (*Herrschaft und Knechtschaft*) dialectic as a dominant explanatory model in conflict theory through high to late modernity. Wollstonecraft's *Wrongs of Woman* (1798) presented an anatomy of love modern and otherwise. Wollstonecraft exceeded Holcroft, representing 'wrongs' including the exploitation of women in marriage for property and power, seduction of women by sentimental lovespeak, sexual violence as a routine risk for plebeian women and legally sanctioned domestic abuse as the lot of married middle-class women. The novel promotes authentically modern love as convergence of sexual desire and emotional and intellectual sympathy that remains unachieved at the novel's closure. Nevertheless, the 'companionate' lovespeak central to emergent modernity was consolidated in reformist lovespeak, subsumed in liberal Romanticism and globalized in today's late modernity.[21]

Though British 'Jacobin' modernity resembled that of the French Girondins ousted by Paris Jacobins in 1793, 'Jacobinism' became a byword in the Anglo-Atlantic world for false modernity, and British resistance was soon articulated by self-styled 'anti-Jacobins'. T. J. Mathias's verse satire, *The Pursuits of Literature* (1794–8; revised to 1812), assailed Sentimental writers in general, ridiculed the Della Cruscans in particular and demonized 'modern philosophers' or public intellectuals and creatives critiquing 'things as they are'. 'Anti-Jacobins' figured 'Jacobinism' as monolithic, covert and international and adapted the familiar critique of Sentimentalism as hypocritical, naïve or malicious, subverting private and public morality, social and political stability, and religion, hierarchy and 'subordination'. Belles-lettres attacking British 'Jacobins' appeared early in the 1790s, but increased after the overthrow of French Jacobin regime in summer 1794. The 'anti-Jacobin novel', a phrase now current in scholarship though barely used at the time, apparently 'became formularized into a convention', though the formulas were already familiar.[22] Some reworked Charlotte Lennox's burlesque of Sentimental lovespeak and love novel in *The Female Quixote* (1752) and borrowed mock-satanism from Alain-René Lesage's popular *Le Diable boiteux* (1707), as in clergyman Charles Lucas's *The Infernal Quixote* (1801). Entrenched classism informed the representation of reformists and revolutionaries as social upstarts, fraudsters, sexual predators and dangerous 'enthusiasts' in Shaftesbury's sense. References to the Godwin circle proliferated, as in Edward Dubois's *St. Godwin* (1800, burlesquing Godwin's historical-fantastic love novel *St Leon*, 1799) and Elizabeth Hamilton's *Memoirs of Modern Philosophers* (1800). 'Anti-Jacobins' cast philosophical, Sentimental and reformist lovespeak as disguised versions of unmodern elites' sexual-political 'gallantry'. In fact, 'Jacobins' and 'anti-Jacobins' promoted similar modern lovespeaks, and their opposition was less an ideological confrontation than a commercialized media creation combining propagandist sloganizing, spurs to activism, government subsidized print campaigning and authors' pitch for patronage. British 'anti-Jacobin' discourse from its formation in the 1790s defended a conservative or gradualist modernity against modernities cast as excessive, mistaken, fraudulent or the resurgence of earlier unmodern religious-political 'enthusiasm'.

The 'war of ideas' in lovespeak and the love novel was already being formulated in new ways for a market roused by novelty and the news.[23] Interest in 'anti-Jacobin' love novels increased from the mid-1790s, peaked around 1800 and continued to such works as E. S. Barrett's bestseller, *The Heroine* (1813). A compendium of 'anti-Jacobin' novelistic devices, this was admired by Jane Austen, who had already adapted such devices in her own love novels. Reformist writers responded to changing political and market conditions by refashioning 'Jacobin' lovespeak and love novel in such different works as Godwin's fantastic-historical *St Leon* (1799) and Maria Edgeworth's Burneyesque *Belinda* (1801). Reformist discourse was refashioned in emergent liberalism and ideas of modern constitutional state formation based on sovereign subjectivity and cultural citizenship. Irish patriot and socialite Sydney Owenson's *The Wild Irish Girl* (1806) was the first of several 'national tales' by her and others. These were often heavily annotated, finding materials for the proleptic modern nation-state in historical political, social and cultural forms, including 'antiquarianism' and 'popular antiquities', later termed 'folklore'. Lovespeak here was a lingua franca crossing regional, ethnic, cultural, racial and political difference, and love and marriage are emplotted as foundation of a 'national' identity, culture and destiny from disparate ones. The cost in some 'national' love novels is the protagonist's life, or self-sacrificial lovespeak. In liberal culture critic Germaine de Staël's best-selling national love novel *Corrine* (1807), lovespeak supports anti-imperial national aspirations of an Italy not yet unified and independent. In reformist Jane Porter's historified *The Scottish Chiefs* (1810), conjugal love motivates the historical Scottish national liberator William Wallace to defy alien (English) autocracy and unwittingly make himself nobly loved and erotically desired by women on both sides of the moral and national border. In historified love novels such as Owenson's *The Missionary* (1811), set in India, and narrative poems such as Felicia Hemans's post-Napoleonic collections *Tales, and Historic Scenes* (1819) and *Records of Woman* (1825), women across times and places are fatally forced by destructive masculinist history to subsume personal in patriotic love because an accommodating modernity has not yet been established. In such envisionings, history will supposedly end in a modern constitutional nation-state of sovereign-subject male citizens and their companion spouses, whose qualification as such will be evidenced by their lovespeak, learned in part from appropriate love novels.

Conveniently and astutely, in 1810, a huge London-based publishers' conger offered a fifty-volume set of such guides as the *British Novelists*. This mostly comprised love novels from *Clarissa* to *Belinda* and was curated by respected intellectual Anna Laetitia Barbauld. There were rival sets, but in terms of respectability, packaging, marketing and cultural pretensions, Barbauld's *British Novelists* was distinctive. Unlike its rivals, it excluded picaresque novels, novels of gallantry and novels of foreign origin. It was sold as a set and not in numbers appealing the downmarket. It was advertised for both home display and 'superior' commercial circulating libraries. It comprised many women authors and gynocentric fiction, figuring woman as exemplary modern British 'national' subject, alternative to and defence against domestic and global alternatives amidst a war for national and imperial survival. As such, *British Novelists* bolstered exhortations of the new wave of women's 'advice books', from Wollstonecraft's *Vindication of the Rights of Woman* (1792) to Hannah More's *Strictures on the Modern System of Female Education* (1799). Though articulating differing modernities, these called on women of the middle ranks to lead from the modern home a national defence – moral, intellectual and cultural – against unmodern and falsely modern enemies domestic and foreign. Fashioned as a modern national novelistic canon, the *British Novelists* thereby constituted a love novel–based paper wall in a culture war complementing the celebrated 'wooden wall' of warships in the existential crisis of nation and empire. A decade later, with Britain the world superpower but politically, socially and culturally conflicted within, *British Novelists* was reissued, now to serve the formation of a modern cultural citizenship. This would anticipate and ground the political citizenship of those who were already making themselves the dominant class of modern nation and empire and who would be affirmed as such by hard-won constitutional reforms in succeeding decades and educated and reassured as such by their modern lovespeak and love novels, now known as 'literary fiction'. Others flourished downmarket and still do.

Notes

1   See Roy Harris, *The Necessity of Artspeak* (New York: Continuum, 2003), partly a response to Ernst Fischer, *The Necessity of Art: A Marxist Approach*, trans. Anna Bostock (Harmondsworth: Penguin, 1963).

2   Roy Harris, *The Language Myth* (London: Duckworth, 1981); Harold Garfinkel, 'Lebenswelt Origins of the Sciences ...', *Human Studies* 30, no. 1 (March 2007): 9–56.

3   See Alec McHoul, *Semiotic Investigations* (Lincoln: University of Nebraska Press, 1996).

4   Michel Bozon, 'Les significations sociales des actes sexuels', *Actes de la Recherche en Sciences Sociales* 128 (1998): 3.

5   Nicolas Venette, *The Mysteries of Conjugal Love Reveal'd*, 2nd edn. (1707), 119.

6   Anthony Ashley Cooper, Earl of Shaftesbury, *Characteristics of Men, Manners, Opinions, Times*, 3 vols (London: John Darby, 1711), I.5.

7   *OED* gives first occurrence as 1805, but the term is found already in 1728 in Anon., *The Velvet-Coffee Woman; Or, the Life, Gallantries and Amours of the Late Famous Mrs. Anne Rochford ...* (Westminster: Simon Green, 1728).

8   *The World* [London] 206 (9 December 1756), 277.

9   See Francis Hutcheson, *An Inquiry into the Original of Our Ideas of Beauty and Virtue; In Two Treatises. I. Concerning Beauty, Order, Harmony, Design. II. Concerning Moral Good and Evil* (1725). See also Elizabeth S. Radcliffe, 'Love and Benevolence in Hutcheson's and Hume's Theories of the Passions', *British Journal for the History of Philosophy* 12, no. 4 (2004): 631–53.

10   See Radcliffe, 'Love and Benevolence in Hutcheson's and Hume's Theories of the Passions'.

11   Shannon Chamberlain, 'Adam Smith and the Romance Novel', *The Atlantic* (3 September 2014); Gary Saul Morson and Morton Shapiro, *Cents and Sensibility: What Economics Can Learn from the Humanities* (Princeton, NJ: Princeton University Press, 2017), 243.

12   The passage references Brutus and Cato, republican assassins of Caesar in 44 BCE for plotting despotic rule; three senatorial members of the 'Stoic Opposition' to despotic emperors in the first century CE; and the wife of another.

13   See Amy Prendergast, 'Transnational Influence and Exchange: The Intersections between Irish and French Sentimental Novels', in *Irish Literature in Transition, 1700–1780*, ed. Moyra Haslett (Cambridge: Cambridge University Press, 2020), 189–206.

14   *The Lady's Magazine* 2 (July 1771), 25–7.

15   The established church was Anglican-episcopalian in England, Wales and Ireland, and Presbyterian in Scotland. Dissenting sects included Presbyterian and others in England, Wales and Ireland, and episcopalian and non-Presbyterian in Scotland.

16   For a detailed analysis, see Mary Peace, 'Sentimentality in the Service of Methodism: John Wesley's Abridgment of Henry Brooke's *The Fool of Quality*', *Religion in the Age of Enlightenment* 4 (2013): 277–308.

17   See Emanuel Swedenborg, *The Delights of Wisdom Respecting Conjugal Love; after Which Follow the Pleasures of Insanity Respecting Scortatory Love* (London, 1790).

18   Alan H. Pasco, *Revolutionary Love in Eighteenth- and Early Nineteenth-Century France* (Farnham, 2009), 1.

19   See Will McMorran, 'The Marquis de Sade in English, 1800–1840', *Modern Language Review* 112, no. 3 (July 2017): 549–66.

20   Edmund Burke, *Reflections on the Revolution in France ...*, 2nd edn. (London: J. Dodsley, 1790), 112.

21   See, for example, Dorothy Tennov, *Love and Limerence: The Experience of Being in Love* (New York: Stein and Day, 1979).

22   M. O. Grenby, 'The Anti-Jacobin Novel: British Fiction, British Conservatism and the Revolution in France', *History* 83 (July 1998): 452.

23   See Marilyn Butler, *Jane Austen and the War of Ideas* (Oxford: Clarendon Press, 1975).

Bibliography

Anon. *The Velvet-Coffee Woman; Or, the Life, Gallantries and Amours of the Late Famous Mrs Anne Rochford...* Westminster: Simon Green, 1728.

Bozon, Michel. 'Les significations sociales des actes sexuels'. *Actes de la Recherche en Sciences Sociales* 128 (1998): 3–23.

Burke, Edmund. *Reflections on the Revolution in France...*, 2nd edn. London: J. Dodsley, 1790.

Butler, Marilyn. *Jane Austen and the War of Ideas*. Oxford: Clarendon Press, 1975.

Chamberlain, Shannon. 'Adam Smith and the Romance Novel'. *The Atlantic* (3 September 2014).

Cooper, Anthony Ashley, Earl of Shaftesbury. *Characteristics of Men, Manners, Opinions, Times*, 3 vols. London: John Darby, 1711.

Fischer, Ernst. *The Necessity of Art: A Marxist Approach* (trans. Anna Bostock) Harmondsworth: Penguin, 1963.

Garfinkel, Harold. 'Lebenswelt Origins of the Sciences ...'. *Human Studies* 30, no. 1 (March 2007): 9–56.

Grenby, M. O. 'The Anti-Jacobin Novel: British Fiction, British Conservatism and the Revolution in France'. *History* 83 (July 1998): 445–71.

Harris, Roy. *The Language Myth*. London: Duckworth, 1981.

Harris, Roy. *The Necessity of Artspeak*. New York: Continuum, 2003.

Hutcheson, Francis. *An Inquiry into the Original of Our Ideas of Beauty and Virtue; In Two Treatises. I. Concerning Beauty, Order, Harmony, Design. II. Concerning Moral Good and Evil*. n.p., 1725.

The Lady's Magazine 2 (July 1771): 25–7.

McHoul, Alec. *Semiotic Investigations*. Lincoln: University of Nebraska
   Press, 1996.
McMorran, Will. 'The Marquis de Sade in English, 1800–1840'. *Modern Language
   Review* 112, no. 3 (July 2017): 549–66.
Morson, Gary Saul and Morton Shapiro. *Cents and Sensibility: What Economics
   Can Learn from the Humanities*. Princeton, NJ: Princeton University
   Press, 2017.
Pasco, Alan H. *Revolutionary Love in Eighteenth- and Early Nineteenth-Century
   France*. Farnham: Ashgate, 2009.
Peace, Mary. 'Sentimentality in the Service of Methodism: John Wesley's
   Abridgment of Henry Brooke's *The Fool of Quality*'. *Religion in the Age of
   Enlightenment* 4 (2013): 277–308.
Prendergast, Amy. 'Transnational Influence and Exchange: The Intersections
   between Irish and French Sentimental Novels'. In *Irish Literature in Transition,
   1700–1780*, edited by Moyra Haslett, 189–206. Cambridge: Cambridge
   University Press, 2020.
Radcliffe, Elizabeth S. 'Love and Benevolence in Hutcheson's and Hume's Theories
   of the Passions'. *British Journal for the History of Philosophy* 12, no. 4
   (2004): 631–53.
Swedenborg, Emanuel. *The Delights of Wisdom Respecting Conjugal Love;
   after Which Follow the Pleasures of Insanity Respecting Scortatory Love*.
   London, 1790.
Tennov, Dorothy. *Love and Limerence: The Experience of Being in Love*.
   New York: Stein and Day, 1979.
Venette, Nicola. *The Mysteries of Conjugal Love Reveal'd*, 2nd edn. London, 1707.
The World [London] 206 (9 December 1756): 277.

11

Love as theoretical object in Marguerite Duras's writings

Crisia Constantine

Introduction

This essay explores Marguerite Duras's construction of love and its links to processes of knowing and seeing. Drawing upon three of her writings – *La maladie de la mort* (*The Malady of Death*), *Moderato Cantabile* and *Hiroshima mon amour* – I argue that Duras employs love narratives to interrogate the conditions and forms of knowledge and vision. I investigate the function of love in the dynamics of knowledge creation and expansion. I revisit knowing and non-knowing, and seeing and non-seeing, as modes of knowledge. I further suggest that Duras's take on love prompts new types of textual engagement and proposes alternative readership roles for the story.

Following the cues of selected writings, I bring into focus how Duras's approach singles love out and exploits it as theoretical object, allowing for broader epistemological thought. Rather than a telling of love stories, it is a telling of the ways in which love is considered, reflected on and interpreted. It influences and broadens the experiencing of love, emphasizing the use of love narrative as prosthetics in knowledge production. In Duras, love doesn't hold an ultimate, intricate meaning. On the contrary, the discourse of love continuously suggests that it is a deeper understanding of it yet to be reached. Its search triggers epistemic processes and the transformation of characters through their interaction. It also affects the reader's experience and relation with the narrative, provides them with alternative perspective and tools and requires distinct interpretative standpoints. The shared subjectivity between characters and reader, and the implicit sense of intimacy on the reader's part, further expands the proposition of knowledge as negotiated. Therefore, love as theoretical object is a medium that facilitates the formation of knowledge by addressing its intersubjective nature.

Duras's conception of love converges with contemporary psychoanalytical theory and informs topics of knowledge and vision, as developed by Jacques Lacan. My analysis borrows two key concepts from Lacanian terminology, namely the 'gaze' and the 'subject supposed to know' (*le sujet supposé savoir*). In his exploration of vision, Lacan distinguishes between the eye and the gaze. For Lacan, the gaze is the object of the act of looking, and it is antinomic to the eye which looks and is of the subject. The 'subject supposed to know' generally refers to the transference relationship between the analyst and the analysed as it develops during the psychoanalytical therapy. Lacan further elaborates the term to explain the process of creating knowledge by attributing it to another subject or participant to the exchange. In a nutshell, the 'subject supposed to know' is critical to the conceptualization of knowledge as intersubjective.

Across different contexts – private or intimate, social, and historical or political – love as theoretical object proposes a new language that can be used to explain its meaning and facilitate its representation. It raises questions on its nature; it posits itself in epistemic terms; and it invites and generates reflection on itself and its language. In the following sections, I discuss these contexts and how they impact methods of knowing and seeing.

La maladie de la mort (*The Malady of Death*)

I use the isolate settings of *La maladie de la mort* to comment upon intimate love. A short novella, it delves into the strange relationship that an anonymous man pursues with an unnamed young woman. He is a man who has not loved, but she is a woman who has. He hires her in his attempt to learn how to love, and the woman, although not a prostitute, agrees to his conditions and spends with him several nights in a secluded room by the sea. Ultimately, the woman tells him that he cannot experience love due to his affliction with the 'malady of death'.

Built in the form of speech directed to the man as 'you', while the woman is 'she', *La maladie de la mort* opens a space of inclusiveness, but also of ambiguity and questioning. The second-person narrative implies the reader, pulling them into the narratee-character position. In other words, it gives the reader the identificatory option that compels them to deeply invest in the storyline. Duras's writing in present tense, her terse, almost harrowing use of the root form of the verb, sustains reader's vacillation between the real world and fictional and literary ones. Specifically, it eliminates the duality between the time of the story and the narration of the story, creating a certain sense of predictability of events.

The man asks the woman of paid nights to teach him how to love because he believes that she possesses a specific knowledge about love. By positing the woman as holder of this knowledge, the man associates her position with the Lacanian's 'subject supposed to know'. As I will discuss in the next section, the supposing of the other as subject who knows does not reflect on the knowledge the other has. However, particularly interesting here is the disclosure of the man's process of attributing knowledge to the woman:

Vous dites que vous voulez essayer, tenter la chose, tenter connaître ça ...

Vous lui dites que vous voulez essayer, essayer plusieurs jours peut-être. Peut-être plusieurs semaines. Peut-être même pendant toute votre vie. Elle demande: Essayer quoi? Vous dites: D'aimer.[1]

(You say you want to try, try the thing, try to know it ... You tell her you want to try, try for several days perhaps. Perhaps for several weeks. Perhaps even for all your life. She asks: To try what? You say: to love.[2])

Ultimately, the knowledge of love remains unattainable. With this, Duras's outlining of his search reflects the Lacanian condition of knowledge itself, whereby 'the desire to know is not what leads to knowledge'.[3] In other words, no knowledge is obtained by way of the desire to attain it.

Nevertheless, the woman possesses a symbolic knowledge that we are alerted to throughout the text. We are told that 'Elle ne sait pas elle-même. Elle ne saurait pas vous le dire'[4] (She doesn't know herself. She wouldn't know how to tell it to you[5]), and that 'Elle dit qu'on le sait sans savoir comment on le sait'[6] (She says she knows without knowing how she knows it[7]). Therefore, the woman knows of this knowledge, but cannot access it:

Elle dit: La maladie vous gagne de plus en plus, elle a gagné vos yeux, votre voix. Vous demandez: Quelle maladie? Elle dit qu'elle ne sait pas encore le dire.[8]

(She says: The malady is getting a hold of you more and more, it got your eyes, your voice. You ask: Which malady? She says she cannot say it yet.[9])

She eventually shares her knowledge with the man, but does not say what the malady of death is:

Parce que dès que vous m'avez parlé j'ai vu que vous étiez attaint par la maladie de la mort. Pendant les premiers jours je n'ai pa su nommer cette maladie. Et puis ensuite j'ai pu le faire.[10]

(Because since the first moment you spoke to me I say that you were suffering from the malady of death. For the first days I couldn't give a name to this malady. And afterwards I could.[11])

Man's continuous search does produce knowledge, but it is not the knowledge of how to love but rather a veiled, unknown knowledge of the malady:

Vous découvrez que c'est là, en elle, que se fomente la maladie de la mort, que c'est cette forme devant vous déployée qui décrète la maladie de la mort.[12]

(You discover that it's there, in her, where the malady of death is fomenting, that this form that's showing itself in front of you that decrees the malady of death.[13])

The man recognizes the malady because he acquired knowledge of it; he produces his own answer to what the malady is, but his knowledge, too, remains inaccessible: 'Vous lui dites que vous ne pouvez pas savoir pourquoi, que vous n'avez pas l'intelligence de votre maladie'[14] (You tell her that you cannot know why, that you don't have the knowledge of your malady[15]).

Yet, this knowledge is produced at the locus of the woman. She is both common, 'Vous devriez ... l'avoir trouvée partout à la fois'[16] (You must have seen her everywhere at a time[17]), and uncommon, 'cette coïncidence entre cette peau et la vie qu'elle recouvre'[18] (This coincidence between this skin and the life that it covers[19]), or 'Elle est plus mystérieuse que toutes les évidences extérieures connues jusque-là de vous'[20] (She's more mysterious than any other external thing you've ever known[21]).

Her body frames the search of the man to the extent to which it evades it. Duras writes: 'De ce corps vous voudriez partir, vous voudriez revenir vers le corps des autres, le vôtre, revenir vers vous-même'[22] (You'd like to start from that body and get back to the bodies of others, to your own, to get back to yourself[23]). This points to how the knowledge that one learns from the other is, ultimately, a knowledge of the self: the man needs the woman to relegate his own unknown or unconscious knowledge as known knowledge. He associates the woman with the 'subject supposed to know' in order to posit his own unknown knowledge at her locus as crucial stage in his process of acquiring knowledge. This knowledge is, therefore, intersubjective and cannot be realized autonomously. In the unpublished *Seminar IX*, Lacan emphasizes that knowledge does not belong to any particular subject or locus (the other is posited as locus, not as subject), but it resides in the relation between them:

Knowledge is intersubjective, which does not mean that it is the knowledge of all, nor that it is the knowledge of the Other – with a capital O – and the Other we have posed. It is essential to maintain it as such: the Other is not a subject, it is a locus to which one strives … to transfer the knowledge of the subject.[24]

However, the unconscious is inexhaustible; it can never be fully known; therefore, ultimate knowledge remains unattainable. Lacan rejects the Hegelian concept of utter knowledge when he states that 'absolute knowledge' is 'the end of history … You can't get out of that – if consciousness is knowledge, written as such in Hegel.'[25] It is the impossibility of attaining ultimate knowledge that the impotent search of the man ultimately refers to.

The man seems compelled to return to the body, to consider and reconsider it, to engage and reengage with it in his search for knowledge:

Vous prenez le corps, vous regardez ses différents espaces, vous le retournez, vous le retournez encore, vous le regardez, vous le regardez encore.[26]

(You take hold of the body and look at its different areas. You turn it around, keep turning it around. Look at it, keep looking at it.[27])

Still, Duras returns to the eye as an instrument through which everything is seen. Man's search is a search of the body –

Vous dites qu'elle devrait se taire … afin que petit à petit, avec le jour grandissant, vous ayez moins peur de ne pas savoir où poser votre corps ni vers quel vide aimer.[28]

(You say she mustn't speak … so that little by little, as day dawns, you may be less afraid of not knowing where to put your body or what emptiness to aim your love.[29])

– or with the body: 'ton sexe dressé dans la nuit qui appelle où se metre'[30] (Your sex grew erect in the night, seeking somewhere to put itself[31]), or 'Vous approchez votre corps contre l'objet de son corps'[32] (You bring your body close to the object that is her body[33]). Most significantly, it is a search of the bodily seeing: 'ce que voient les yeux'[34] (what the eyes see[35]), 'vous ouvrez les yeux'[36] (you open your eyes[37]) or 'vous fermez les yeux'[38] (you close your eyes[39]).

However, vision is denied to the man:

Elle demande: Vous n'avez jamais aimé une femme? Vous dites que non, jamais … Elle recommence: Et regarder une femme, vous n'avez jamais regardé une femme? Vous dites que non, jamais.[40]

(She asks: Haven't you ever loved a woman? You say no, never. She goes on: What about looking, haven't you ever looked at a woman? You say no, never.[41])

In Duras, looking acquires the sense of searching and points towards the invisible as the other side of the visible. It refers to what remains concealed in knowledge, its unknown, unconscious part, the desire that is left encased. Seeing has, then, multiple senses. Among the specified seven different principal accounts of the verb 'to see' in the *Oxford English Dictionary*, only one refers to seeing as perceptual experience, while the definition with the highest number of secondary meanings explains 'to see' as 'to discern or deduce after reflection or from information; understand'.[42] In the context of the man's search, seeing acquires the sense of knowing and of discovering or finding. There are also different ways of seeing: 'Vous ne sauriez jamais rien non plus, ni vous ni personne, jamais, de comment elle voit'[43] (Nor will you, or anyone else, ever know how she sees[44]).

The knowledge of the malady that the unnamed man eventually obtains is through seeing: 'Vous regardez la maladie de votre vie, la maladie de la mort. C'est sur elle, sur son corps endormi, que vous la regardez'[45] (You look at the malady of your life, the malady of death. It's on her, on her sleeping body, that you look at it[46]). For Duras, knowing and not-knowing, on the one hand, and seeing and not-seeing, on the other, are all forms of knowledge. Love as theoretical object functions as the mediator between them and prompts to additional consideration of its role as organizing construct for the creation or development of new knowledge. The knowledge that the unnamed man eventually acquires is produced in an ambiguous place of which not-knowing and not-seeing are constitutive possibilities. It is a knowledge that creates or changes itself, as the man looks and continues to look: 'Vous regardez'[47] (You are looking[48]), 'Vous regardez encore'[49] (You go on looking[50]), 'Vous restez longtemps à regarder'[51] (You stay like that a long time[52]) and, eventually, 'Vous regardez ... Vous abandonnez. Vous ne regardez plus. Vous ne regardez plus rien. Vous fermez les yeux pour vous retrouver dans votre différence, dans votre mort'[53] (You are looking ... You give up. You are not looking any longer. You are not looking any longer at anything. You close your eyes so as to find yourself in your own difference, your own death[54]).

Interrogating vision as a mode of knowledge, Duras's work further intersects with the Lacanian theory of gaze. The seeing that is alluded to here is a seeing of the non-visible, of the unsubstantial or unreal, of the fictional. It is a seeing that is not performed by the eyes as sense organs of the visual system of the body, reacting to light and pressure – the human eye cannot see objects that are not there – but a seeing carried out by the gaze. In her work, Duras consigns seeing to both the eye and the gaze. However, the seeing of the eye is of sensorial perception and of consciousness, whereas the seeing of the gaze is not performed with respect to physiological capacities. The gaze sees what escapes the eye; it sees what is not of the surrounding physical reality, but it creates its own representation of the external world. For Lacan, the gaze can be seen or not, or it can be imagined, and the character of the gaze of being seeable sets it off as object. As Lacan states, 'a gaze imagined by me in the field of Other ... when I am under the gaze, when I solicit a gaze, when I obtain it, I do ... see it as a gaze'.[55] This is because the usual sense of visual perception that the term 'seeing' has here implies the engagement with a particular object of perception. In addition, when imagined, the gaze is also imagined as an object. 'The gaze that surprises me ... The gaze I encounter ... is, not a seen gaze, but a gaze imagined by me in the field of the Other',[56] says Lacan. Or the surprise – the encounter as chance meeting, as unexpected contact – also supposes the assumption of an object that the subject is faced or confronted with. This is fully exploited in the relationship between the unnamed man in search for love and the woman. The man obsessively follows the woman's eyes and their movements, and, eventually, he finds himself surprised but also alienated by her fixating gaze: 'qui serait à jamais la frontière infranchissable entre elle et vous ... le regard. Le regard. Vous découvrez qu'elle vous regarde'[57] (that will always be an insurmountable barrier between you and her ... The look. The look. You realize she's looking at you[58]).

With the seeing of the eye, the subjects acquire knowledge that preexists them and is proposed to them. Conversely, the seeing of the gaze is of representation. The gaze always looks, but it can see or it can not-see. Thus, the man looks, yet he cannot see: 'Vous regardez ... Vous ne voyez rien'[59] (You look ... You don't see anything[60]).

Moderato Cantabile

Whereas *La maladie de la mort* explores love in intimate settings, *Moderato Cantabile* provides the framework for an examination on love and society. The novel captures the social divide between the working class and the middle class by exploiting the possibilities of a love affair between a wealthy and sophisticated housewife, Anne Desbaresdes, and an unemployed factory worker, Chauvin. While accompanying her son for his weekly piano lesson, Anne's attention is grabbed by a woman's long, tortuous scream. After hesitation and deferring, Anne enquires where the scream came from, discovers that a fatal shooting has taken place in the café nearby and makes her way there. She arrives in enough time to see the woman's body inertly lying on the floor, while a man is holding unto her in a passionate delirium. Drawn by the scene, Anne returns to the café where she encounters Chauvin, an unknown man, whom she would ask about the late events. Anne and Chauvin inebriate with house-cheap red wine and imagine the relation between the dead woman and the man, her supposed lover and killer. Love, desire and death fuse. For their last meeting, Anne, desirous, and Chauvin, in love, symbolically render the tragic ending of the anonymous couple's tale.

Similarly, with *La maladie de la mort*, the novel features playful innovations and manipulations of the narrative that enforce reader's engagement. Noticeably, it relies heavily on dialogues, but rarely attributes the lines to their speakers. The blending of replies and, subsequently, of subjects' perspectives exposes the possibilities of reading and construing the text. But Duras's intricate strategies of reader involvement travel further. The deliberate confusion at stylistic level is echoed by aspects of uncertainty or vacuity at plot and characters' levels. Anne and Chauvin's encounter is caused by the tragic event, and their story is produced in relation to another narrative, that of the unfortunate couple. It is a *mise-en-abyme* which structures the main narrative of the book. Intendedly, Anne blends reality and unreality and asks Chauvin to fabricate concurrent versions of the lovers' story in the build-up of the murder. Therefore, with each meeting between Anne and Chauvin, the reader is transported into fictitious, possible alternative scenes of the other couple's past relation through a complex temporality that transforms the reader into an intimate witness.

Lacan's theory of knowledge is also further intersected. Anne continues to return to the scene of the murder to find out the reasons behind it. Alike with the unnamed man of *La maladie de la mort*, Anne frames her search through the body of the other woman. Thus, she confesses: 'Ce cri était si fort que vraiment il est bien naturel que l'on cherche à savoir. J'aurais pu difficilement éviter de le faire'[61] (The scream was so loud it's really only natural for people to try and find out what happened[62]) or, somewhere else, 'J'y ai pensé de plus en plus depuis hier soir, ... Je n'aurais pas pu m'empêcher de venir aujourd'hui, voyez'[63] (I've thought about it over and over again since yesterday evening, ... I couldn't help coming here today, you know[64]).

Anne, too, associates Chauvin with 'the subject supposed to know': 'Et, évidemment on ne peut pas savoir pourquoi?'[65] (And I don't suppose you can tell me why?[66]), or 'Voyez comme il est tard. Dites-moi encore, vite?'[67] (See how late it is. Quickly, tell me the rest[68]), or, later on, 'Une dernière fois, supplia-t-elle, dites-moi'[69] (One last time, she begged, tell me about it once last time[70]).

By positing him as holder of a knowledge about the lovers that she lacks, Anne actively uses Chauvin's position to consign her unknown knowledge as known knowledge:

> Je voudrais que vous me disiez le commencement même, comment ils ont commencé à se parler.[71]
>
> (I'd like you to tell me about the very beginning, how they began to talk to each other.[72])

Anne asks Chauvin for further details:

Je voudrais que vous me disiez maintenant comment ils en sont arrives à ne plus même se parler.[73]

(I'd like you to tell me now how they came not to speak to each other any more.[74])

The process of attributing knowledge to Chauvin, of supposing him as knowledgeable subject, is what triggers Anne's transformation as desirous subject in the context of their interaction.

As the previous section suggests, in Lacan, the supposing of the other as a subject who knows is completely unrelated to the knowledge that the other actually has. Thus, Anne supposes Chauvin as the subject who holds knowledge, yet this process of attribution is not connected with the knowledge that Chauvin possesses. On the contrary, Chauvin repeatedly affirms his own lack of knowledge: 'J'aimerais pouvoir vous le dire, mais je ne sais rien de sûr'[75] (I wish I could, but I'm not really sure of anything[76]), or 'J'ai essayé de savoir davantage. Je ne sais rien'[77] (I tried to find out something more. But I couldn't[78]), or 'Je ne sais rien d'autre que vous'[79] (I don't know any more about it than you do[80]) or 'Je le sais aussi mal que vous'[81] (I don't know any more than you do[82]).

Chauvin insists that he doesn't have any facts, but he fabricates details, invents and tells falsehood. Still, he does not deceive, as Anne equally asks for truth and untruth: 'Dépêchez-vous de parler. Inventez'[83] (Hurry up and say something. Make it up[84]).

What Anne seeks for is the signification of her own discourse when she questions Chauvin: 'vous croyez qu'il est possible d'en arriver … là … autrement que … par désespoir?'[85] (Do you think that it's possible for anyone to reach such a … state … except … through despair?[86]).

As Lacan explains, '[the subject] is supposed to know that from which no one can escape, as soon as he formulates it – quite simply, signification'.[87] Or, in Evan's phrasing, 'the analysts is often thought to know the secret meaning of the analysand's words, the significations of speech of which even the speaker is unaware'.[88] This is, ultimately, the process through which knowledge is acquired. 'In so far as the analyst is supposed to know, he is also supposed to set out in search of unconscious desire',[89] explains Lacan, and, later on, 'it is merely at the level of the desire of the Other that man can recognize his desire, as desire of the Other'.[90] This is one sense in which we can read another famous Lacanian phrase: 'The unconscious is the discourse of the Other.'[91] Chauvin is needed to grant access to Anne to her identity, social status and mother role, but also to her very own unconscious, to her very own desire, which is, essentially, that of death, such as when she states, 'Je voudrais que vous soyez morte'[92] (I wish you were dead[93]).

Lacan defines the presence of the analyst as 'a manifestation of the unconscious, so that when it is manifested nowadays in certain encounters, as a refusal of the unconscious – this is a tendency, readily admitted, in some people's thinking – this very fact must be integrated into the concept of the unconscious'.[94] The knowledge that Anne acquires about herself through her conversations with Chauvin is, then, none other than the knowledge that she supposes that Chauvin has, regardless of any knowledge that he might actually have or express. What is at stake here is what Anne assumes. It is through this thinking of herself at the locus of the other that knowledge is generated. The relationship that is established between the two participants to exchange is one of Lacanian transference, where transference is the relation the subject has to themselves *because there is the other* or, rather, *because they suppose there is the other*.[95]

That seeing integrates connotations of knowing and of discovering or finding is also brought to the fore in *Moderato Cantabile*, where characters say at multiple occasions: 'Je ne sais pas ce que je veux, voyez-vous'[96] (I don't know what I want, you see[97]), or 'Je vois ... Je me le demandais, voyez-vous'[98] (I see ... I was just asking myself, you see[99]), or 'vous voyez ce que je veux dire'[100] (if you see what I mean[101]), or 'Voyez-vous ... je ne sais pas si je pourrai continuer à m'en occuper'[102] (You see, I don't know if I can continue doing this[103]). Moreover, Chauvin's confession exploits the difference between looking (regarder) and seeing (voir): 'Je ne vous regardais qu'à peine, mais j'ai eu le temps de la voir aussi'[104] (I only looked at you for a second, but I had the time to see it too[105]).

Eye and gaze stand for two different things. The eye is an organ; it is integrated to the visual system and it represents itself an optical system; it is connected with the centre of the nervous system; it is an instrument of visualization and of consciousness; it is of the sensorial; it is where the image or picture of an object we are looking at is constructed. The eye represents that we are equipped with the capacity of seeing. The eye is, eventually, of sight; it is a geometral convention; it belongs to the geometral dimension of vision, to 'vision in so far as it is situated in a space that is not in its essence the visual'.[106] It is, ultimately, of the mapping of space, but the gaze is of vision; it is of the space that is first and foremost the visual and accounts for all the elements that are not of sight, but, nevertheless, they are of the scopic register that is not of the visible but of the invisible. The eye sees what it is present, while the gaze sees what it is not present, what it is absent or lacking; it is 'a partial dimension in the field of the gaze, a dimension that has nothing to do with vision as such – something symbolic of the function of the lack, of the appearance of the phallic ghost'.[107]

For Lacan, there is an antinomy between the eye and the gaze,[108] and we see this play out at several points in the text. For example, the public can see the murderous lovers' eyes, past his gaze: 'Il se tourna vers la foule, la regarda, et on vit ses yeux'[109] (He turned and looked at crowd; they saw his eyes[110]), and we are told that Anne sees Chauvin's eyes, past his gaze: 'Elle scruta à travers le regard leur matière bleue'[111] (She looked past his gaze into his blue eyes[112]). The gaze, then, indicates the fact that we are seen and 'circumscribes us, and which in the first instance makes us beings who are looked at, but without showing this'.[113]

On the side of the subject, there is the eye that sees the object, 'the things', but also the subject's gaze with which it looks at the things, that is, again, from one side only. From her spot, Anne cannot see Chauvin any longer: 'La main de Chauvin battit l'air et retomba sur la table. Mais elle ne le vit pas, ayant déjà quitté le champ où il se trouvait'[114] (Chauvin's hand fluttered and fell to the table. But she was already too far away to see him[115]).

Hiroshima mon amour

Set against the shooting of a film about peace, *Hiroshima mon amour* surveys the experiencing of love in the deluge of war and mass destruction. Written in 1958 as a script for Alain Resnais's film of the same title and published in 1960, it exploits the impossible love story between a French woman and a Japanese man. Unfolding within the span of thirty-six hours, their brief, one-night affair is followed by a haunting, continuously prolonged farewell that defers closure. But, on the pretence of their fictional encounter, Duras writes of violence, of trauma and loss, of memory and reminiscence and, most acutely, of Hiroshima. This way, the screenplay links the couple's current affair, a love story of the past, the savagery of the Second World War and, inescapably, the nuclear genocide of Hiroshima on 6 August 1945.

Revised before the production of the film began, with new passages added along shooting, rewritten after the completion of the film and, eventually, amended and reorganized for publication, *Hiroshima mon amour* does not read as 'a transcript of the film, it is very much an original work by Duras'.[116] Notwithstanding, it calls up the hermeneutic work of the reader and their agency in reconstructing the narrative of the screenplay. It proposes a ruptured rhythm of the story, meandering plot line with equivocal denouements and shattered chronology and complex polysemous time. It abandons themes to resume and readdress them again and again in circular rhythms later on. Also, all published editions include a synopsis and appendices. Complete and autonomous of the rest, each of the three texts demonstrates visual, material and sensorial qualities that are rather novelistic and poetical, bringing forth Duras's unmistakable voice as a writer and offering speculative points for the reader to occupy. Most significantly, details of the affair of the past change across the three documents, leaving the reader to fabricate their own – fourth – version of the story.

Therefore, Duras's take on love prompts us to interpretations that expand its meaning through engagement and participation. It includes the perspective and instruments necessary to propose new theoretical considerations. Rather than roles, Duras's characters hold positions from which they perform epistemic acts and, ultimately, facilitate knowledge production.

That characters enter transference relations is directly exploited in *Hiroshima mon amour*. The Japanese man assumes the position of the analyst, facilitating the woman's retrieving of her tragic love affair with a German soldier in Occupied France. His insistent questioning of her past in Never punctuates the woman's disruptive flashbacks in a process that resembles the psychoanalytical talking cure. Recalled in fragments, through oppositions and paradoxes, the love story of the past is ultimately told in full when the Japanese man identifies with the dead German lover. The destabilization of subjects is directly accepted by the woman who shifts her narrative from a third-person to a second-person one: 'Tu es mort'[117] (You are dead[118]), she tells to her now lover.

Across the three texts, the focus on knowledge as transmutable corpus through its relation to seeing or non-seeing modes is, perhaps, most apparently in *Hiroshima mon amour* as Duras addresses the representing of the unrepresentable: the dropping of the atom bomb, the direct experiencing of it, the atrocity of its dimension, the horrendous tragedy that it inflicted. Exceeding any chronicling, description or meaning, a complete, exhaustive knowledge of Hiroshima cannot be acquired. It is 'impossible to talk about Hiroshima, argues Duras. All one can do is talk about the impossibility of talking about Hiroshima'.[119] Nonetheless, 'the impossibility of speech generates an obsessional effort to speak'.[120]

Duras accentuates this by calling into question the historical and political knowledge of the main event of Hiroshima being annihilated. Her approach opens a territory in which to explore themes of knowledge formation and knowledge and vision association and limitation. In doing so, love becomes the medium that sustains the interrogation of Hiroshima and its threshold of knowledge and vision with the premise of the screenplay being 'their personal story, however brief it may be, always dominates Hiroshima'.[121]

An actress coming to the atomic city to play the role of a war nurse, the French woman meets her lover one day before the shooting concludes. An architect, a political man and former war soldier, the Japanese man is a local of Hiroshima. Both happily married, they are also both open to chance affairs, and the woman confesses that 'Pas tellement souvent. Mais ca m'arrive. J'aime bien les garcons'[122] (Not very often. But it happens. I have a weakness for men[123]). Yet, their affair is not of chance but of love:

Lui:	Tu me donnes beaucoup l'envie d'aimer
Elle:	Toujours … les amours de … rencontre … Moi aussi
Lui:	Non. Pas toujours aussi fort. Tu le sais.[124]
(He:	You give me a great desire to love.
She:	Always … chance love affairs … Me too.
He:	No. Not always like this. You know it.[125])

Duras harnesses the richness of this exchange to both create and destabilize readership expectations. Love fully discloses its theoretical aspect as a discourse that is brought to bear on the Hiroshima narrative. However, Duras's confessed goal is to obtain 'a sort of false documentary that will probe the lesson of Hiroshima more deeply than any made-to-order documentary'.[126] Love informs Duras's treatment of the screenplay's themes, but also reflects back to its own narrative to articulate thought and further demonstrate it. Having said that, love is outlined at the intersection of different conceptual registers and temporalities that respond to, tension or oppose each other. The shifting between them creates a theoretical model of emotional and cognitive reconstruction that is tendered to the reader.

As with *La maladie de la mort* and *Moderato Cantabile*, the body frames the characters' search. The opening scene sets the body as a locus of negotiation for both the narrative of Hiroshima and the narrative of the love affair. Duras's description is of the Bikini mushroom cloud growing slowly, enormously across the frame. Gradually, its movement would reveal two pairs of bare shoulders, cut off from bodies at the levels of heads and hips. Interlaced, in an 'almost shocking' embrace, they are covered with either nuclear cinder or sweat.

Duras's instructions are primarily concerned with enacting obliquity, and anonymity, but also the desire 'to produce … desire'.[127] Therefore, the passage visually exploits the conflation of Hiroshima story and characters' story to the point of their indistinguishability, setting the condition of love as theoretical object concerned with problematizing representation, knowledge and vision. The dialogue begins tersely:

Lui: Tu n'as rien vu à HIROSHIMA. Rien.
Elle: J'ai tout vu. Tout.[128]
(He: You saw nothing in Hiroshima. Nothing).
She: I saw everything. Everything.[129])

The woman commences her report on places, institutions, objects and images that she has seen, which recount the Hiroshima nuclear genocide. But, as Duras specifies, 'on ne la voit jamais en train de voir'[130] (We never see her seeing[131]). The locations and artefacts that she sees and her seeing of them remain visually separated for the reader. Her testimony is the only given evidence that links her to the seen objects. As the woman enumerates, dramatic newsreel footage of the atomic explosion seizes up the frame in a juxtaposition further linking to vision's different modes and the eye and gaze dichotomy.

Therefore, the eye cannot exhaust 'what the field of vision as such offers us as the original subjectifying relation',[132] for which the gaze is needed, as previously emphasized. 'In the dialectic of the eye and the gaze, that there is no coincidence, but, on the contrary, a lure',[133] emphasizes Lacan;

it is 'a question of the geometral eye-point, whereas it is a question of a quite different eye'.[134] The geometral-eye is dependent on light (the eye sees the object when the object is illuminated), and the gaze (the other 'eye') is neither dependent on nor independent of light, but it presents the eye of the subject with light. As Lacan tells us, 'It is through the gaze I enter light and it is from the gaze that I receive its effects.'[135]

Although the eye and the gaze never coincide, the lure between them allows the eye to eventually embody the gaze. As the gaze's own lust to see become insatiable, as its search cannot be resolved any longer, it heightens the eye's own appetite to be fed; it frustrates the eye. The eye is 'made desperate by the gaze',[136] and, therefore, it becomes 'the eye filled with voracity, the evil eye'; it obtains the 'power to separate', to bring 'disease or misfortune'.[137] Due to the capacity that the gaze endowed it with, the eye becomes 'the *fascinum*, it is that which has the effect of arresting movement and, literally, of killing life'.[138] Love is, then, 'l'envie d'être au bord de tuer un amant, de le garder pour vous, pour vous seul, de le prendre, de le voler contre toutes les lois, contre tous les empires de la morale'[139] (the wish to be about to kill a lover, to keep him for yourself, yourself alone, to take him, steal him in defiance of every law, every moral authority[140]), as the woman of paid nights reveals to the unnamed man in *La maladie de la mort*. The gaze turns to the eye to look for itself; it overtakes the eye; it affects the perceiving of the eye. It is not accidental, then, that the images accompanying the French woman's discourse on love and on Hiroshima are of surgical forceps preparing to extract a human eye.

With this, I make one unifying argument on the role of love in ensuring the link between the eye and the gaze, and the various modes of knowing and not-knowing, and seeing and not-seeing. Across the three selected texts, Durassian love is depicted as a painful love, hopelessly arising in the shadow of lovers' immanent separation. But, as a theoretical object, it articulates epistemic consideration and draws attention upon its materiality. It prompts and supports knowledge creation and expansion processes. It questions itself and requires readership's engagement and participation to provide a multitude of answers that challenge or reinforce each other. Furthermore, Duras's strategies for readership involvement facilitate the active consideration of how the discourse of love generates new knowledge and reflects on it. Yet, I am a reader myself. It is through experiencing love as theoretical object that Duras's texts provided that I reached this interpretation and perspective, and that I was able to identify and further examine knowledge creation and development processes and acknowledge Duras's contribution to epistemology. Most significantly, I argued in favour of the conceptualization of knowledge as intersubjective. Duras's treatment of love ultimately suggests that the realization of love cannot reside in its fulfilment, but in the continuous act of expanding the boundaries of knowledge.

Notes

1   Marguerite Duras, *La maladie de la mort* (Paris: Les Éditions de Minuit, 1982), 3–4.

2   Marguerite Duras, *The Malady of Death*, trans. Barbara Bray (New York: Grove Press, 1986), 2–3.

3   Jacques Lacan, *The Other Side of Psychoanalysis*, ed. Jacques-Alain Miller, trans. Russell Grigg (W. W. Norton, 2007), 23.

4   Duras, *La maladie de la mort*, 3–4.

5   Duras, *The Malady of Death*, 14.

6   Duras, *La maladie de la mort*, 14.

7   Ibid., 14, translation my own.

8   Ibid., 10.

9   Duras, *The Malady of Death*, 14.

10 Duras, *La maladie de la mort*, 14.

11 Ibid., 14, translation my own.

12 Ibid., 23.

13 Ibid., translation my own.

14 Ibid., 29.

15 Ibid., translation my own.

16 Ibid., 3.

17 Ibid., translation my own.

18 Ibid., 4.

19 Ibid., translation my own.

20 Ibid., 11.

21 Duras, *The Malady of Death*, 14.

22 Duras, *La maladie de la mort*, 9.

23 Duras, *The Malady of Death*, 11–12.

24 Jacques Lacan, *The Seminar of Jacques Lacan: Seminar IX: Identification 1961–1962*, trans. Cormac Gallagher, unpublished lecture, 15 November 1961.

25 Jacques Lacan, *The Seminar of Jacques Lacan: Book II: The Ego in Freud's Theory and in the Technique of Psychoanalysis 1954–1955*, ed. Jacques-Alain Miller, trans. Sylvana Tomaselli (W. W. Norton, 1991), 71.

26 Duras, *La maladie de la mort*, 13.

27 Duras, *The Malady of Death*, 17.

28 Duras, *La maladie de la mort*, 5.

29 Duras, *The Malady of Death*, 4–5.

30 Duras, *La maladie de la mort*, 3.

31 Duras, *The Malady of Death*, 1.

32 Duras, *La maladie de la mort*, 23.

33 Duras, *The Malady of Death*, 33.

34 Duras, *La maladie de la mort*, 13.

35 Duras, *The Malady of Death*, 17.

36 Duras, *La maladie de la mort*, 22.

37 Duras, *The Malady of Death*, 32.

38 Duras, *La maladie de la mort*, 22.

39 Ibid., translation my own.

40 Ibid., 21.

41 Duras, *The Malady of Death*, 30–1.

42 According to Lexico.com, the new collaboration between Dictionary.com and Oxford University Press, https://www.lexico.com/definition/see. Accessed 24 December 2021.

43 Duras, *La maladie de la mort*, 11.

44 Duras, *The Malady of Death*, 14.

45 Duras, *La maladie de la mort*, 22.

46 Duras, *The Malady of Death*, 32–3.

47 Duras, *La maladie de la mort*, 15.

48 Ibid., translation my own.

49 Ibid., 16.

50 Duras, *The Malady of Death*, 22.

51 Duras, *La maladie de la mort*, 19.

52 Duras, *The Malady of Death*, 38.

53 Duras, *La maladie de la mort*, 22.

54 Ibid., translation my own.

55 Lacan, *The Seminar of Jacques Lacan*, 84.

56 Ibid.

57 Duras, *La maladie de la mort*, 15.

58 Duras, *The Malady of Death*, 20.

59 Duras, *La maladie de la mort*, 24.

60 Duras, *The Malady of Death*, 35.

61 Marguerite Duras, *Moderato Cantabile* (Paris: Les Éditions de Minuit, 1958), 14.

62 Marguerite Duras, *Moderato Cantabile*, trans. Richa6rd Seaver (Oneworld Classics, 2008), 21.

63 Duras, *Moderato Cantabile*, 16

64 Ibid., 26.

65 Ibid., 14.

66 Ibid., 21.

67 Ibid., 49.

68 Ibid., 91.

69 Ibid., 62.

70 Ibid., 117.

71 Ibid., 24.

72 Ibid., 41.

73 Ibid., 29.

74 Ibid., 52.

75 Ibid., 14.

76 Ibid., 21.

77 Ibid., 22.

78 Ibid., 37.

79 Ibid., 25.

80 Ibid., 44.

81 Ibid., 31.

82 Ibid., 54.

83 Ibid., 32.

84 Ibid., 58.

85 Ibid., 15.

86 Ibid., 21.

87 Lacan, *The Seminar of Jacques Lacan*, 253.

88 Dylan Evans, *An Introductory Dictionary of Lacanian Psychoanalysis* (London: Routledge, 1996), 197.

89 Lacan, *The Seminar of Jacques Lacan*, 235.

90 Ibid.

91 Ibid., 131.

92 Duras, *Moderato Cantabile*, 64.

93 Ibid., 21.

94 Lacan, *The Seminar of Jacques Lacan*, 125.

95 My position here assimilates Stuart Schneiderman's remark as editor and translator of the volume *Returning to Freud: Clinical Psychoanalysis in the School of Lacan*. Apparently, the phrasing 'subject supposed to know', widely spread in the English space, is due to the faulty translation of the French *sujet supposé savoir* by Alan Sheridan. Schneiderman argues that that should be amended as 'supposed subject of knowing' (*Returning to Freud: Clinical Psychoanalysis in the School of Lacan* [New Haven, CT: Yale University Press, 1980], vii).

96   Duras, *Moderato Cantabile*, 8.
97   Ibid., translation my own.
98   Ibid., 13.
99   Ibid., translation my own.
100 Ibid., 25.
101 Ibid., 43.
102 Ibid., 40.
103 Ibid., translation my own.
104 Ibid., 45.
105 Ibid., translation my own.
106 Lacan, *The Seminar of Jacques Lacan*, 94.
107 Ibid., 88.
108 Ibid., 109.
109 Duras, *Moderato Cantabile*, 9.
110 Ibid., 13.
111 Ibid., 26.
112 Ibid., 46.
113 Lacan, *The Seminar of Jacques Lacan*, 75.
114 Duras, *Moderato Cantabile*, 64.
115 Ibid., 122.
116 Rosamund Davies, 'Screenwriting Strategies in Marguerite Duras's Script for *Hiroshima, Mon Amour* (1960)', *Journal of Screenwriting* 1, no. 1 (January 2010): 157.
117 Marguerite Duras, *Hiroshima mon amour* (Paris: Gallimard, Collection folio 9, 1960), 87.
118 Marguerite Duras, *Hiroshima mon amour*, trans. Richard Seaver (New York: Grove Press, 1961), 54.
119 Ibid., 9.
120 Sharon Willis, *Marguerite Duras: Writing on the Body* (Urbana: University of Illinois Press,1987), 35.
121 Duras, *Hiroshima mon amour*, 10.
122 Ibid., 56.
123 Ibid., 35.
124 Ibid., 69–70.
125 Ibid., 41.
126 Ibid., 10.
127 Ibid., 15.
128 Ibid., 23–4.
129 Ibid., 15.

130 Ibid., 24.
131 Ibid., 17.
132 Lacan, *The Seminar of Jacques Lacan*, 87.
133 Ibid., 102.
134 Ibid., 89.
135 Ibid., 106.
136 Ibid., 116.
137 Ibid., 115.
138 Ibid., 118.
139 Duras, *La maladie de la mort*, 28.
140 Duras, *The Malady of Death*, 42.

Bibliography

Davies, Rosamund. 'Screenwriting Strategies in Marguerite Duras's Script for *Hiroshima mon amour* (1960)'. *Journal of Screenwriting* 1, no 1 (January 2010).
Duras, Marguerite. *Moderato Cantabile*. Paris: Les Éditions de Minuit, 1958.
Duras, Marguerite. *Hiroshima mon amour*. Paris: Gallimard, Collection folio 9, 1960.
Duras, Marguerite. *Hiroshima mon amour* (trans. Richard Seaver). New York: Grove Press, 1961.
Duras, Marguerite. *La maladie de la mort*. Paris: Les Éditions de Minuit, 1982.
Duras, Marguerite. *The Malady of Death* (trans. Barbara Bray). New York: Grove Press, 1986.
Duras, Marguerite. *Moderato Cantabile* (trans. Richa6rd Seaver). Richmond: Oneworld Classics, 2008.
Evans, Dylan. *An Introductory Dictionary of Lacanian Psychoanalysis*. London: Routledge, 1996.
Lacan, Jacques. *The Seminar of Jacques Lacan: Seminar IX: Identification 1961–1962* (trans. Cormac Gallagher). Unpublished lecture, 15 November 1961.
Lacan, Jacques. *The Seminar of Jacques Lacan: Book II: The Ego in Freud's Theory and in the Technique of Psychoanalysis 1954–1955* (ed. Jacques-Alain Miller; trans. Sylvana Tomaselli). New York: W. W. Norton, 1991.
Lacan, Jacques. *The Seminar of Jacques Lacan: Book XI: The Four Fundamental Concepts of Psychoanalysis* (ed. Jacques-Alain Miller; trans. Alain Sheridan). New York: W. W. Norton, 1998.
Lacan, Jacques. *The Other Side of Psychoanalysis* (ed. Jacques-Alain Miller; trans. Russell Grigg). New York: W. W. Norton, 2007.
Willis, Sharon. *Marguerite Duras: Writing on the Body*. Urbana: University of Illinois Press, 1987.

12

Love without object

Lauren Edwards

Introduction

In Plato's *Symposium*, Socrates asks Agathon: 'Is Love the love of nothing or of something?' Agathon answers, 'Of something, surely!' Socrates replies, 'Then keep this object of love in mind';[1] and philosophers have! That love *must always* have a beloved, an object, is a philosophically foundational, persistent, yet undefended assumption about the nature of *all* types of love. The beloved is constitutive, philosophers assume, of the very nature of love; love, so they say, is always love *of*. This chapter is a critical evaluation of this presumption because, despite the supposed, constitutive centrality of love's beloved in contemporary theories, beloveds that do not exist, that are not distinct from the lover and that do not participate/reciprocate in the loving relationship are widely accepted as possible and even paradigmatic beloved. Thus suggesting, at the very least, that the centrality of the presumed-necessary beloved is in need of defence and explanation or, more strongly, that the beloved is not a necessary feature of love after all.

Philosophers studying love do not agree on much, except for the fact that love *must* have an object. The ancient Greeks, for instance, distinguish between three central types of love: *eros*, *philia* and *agape*. *Eros*, which includes romantic and passionate love, is the 'passionate desire for an object, typically sexual passion' and 'a response to the merits of the beloved – especially the beloved's goodness or beauty'.[2] *Philia*, which refers to affectionate love or friendly love, is a responsiveness to the good qualities of the beloved. *Philia* includes friendship, but also loving, friendly feelings towards family members, colleagues and others.[3] *Agape* is the sort of love that imbues its object with value. It includes God's love of us, our love of God and godly sorts of love of others, such as love of all, love of neighbour, love of humanity and so on.[4] Clearly, each of these types of loves is object-centric.

Contemporary Western philosophical theories of love, founded on the ancient Greek taxonomy of love, blur and move beyond these ancient distinctions. These theories can be divided into four major categories: theories of love as union, robust concern, valuation and emotion. But one thing they all have in common is the constitutive and central role played by the beloved. Philosophical theories of love as union – love as the formation of a 'we' – define love as a particular sort of joining of lover and object.[5] Robert Nozick, for example, argues that 'the desire to form a we with that other person is not simply something that goes along with romantic love … [but] is intrinsic to *the nature of love*'.[6] Philosophical theories of love as robust concern define love as a certain sort of orientation of the lover to the beloved.[7] Harry Frankfurt, for example, describes love as a 'mode of caring' that is marked by, among other things, disinterested concern for the object of love.[8] Theories of love as valuation take love to be a particular mode of valuing – either the bestowal of value upon, or the identification of value within.[9] David Velleman, for example, describes love as a type of awe that results from the recognition of the value inherent in the beloved.[10] Other valuing theories attempt to join these two types of valuing – bestowal upon and identification within – but these also centre on a beloved.[11] Theories of love as an emotion generally define love as an *emotion proper*, which is typically thought to be characterized by different kinds of psychological and behavioural responses to particular objects.[12]

Even theories of love that aim to go beyond the average contemporary theory focusing on person-to-person love reproduce the assumption that love requires an object. Sam Shpall tries to broaden the philosophical understanding of love by growing love's possible objects. Love, he points out, includes love of non-human animals, God and projects.[13] Shpall's tripartite theory of love defines love as devotion to the beloved that renders vulnerable and expresses liking.[14] While this theory widens the contemporary philosophical focus on types of beloveds, the constitutive centrality of the beloved has not budged. Simon May argues that love, in general, is the joyful response to that which promises to root or ground our being in the world. In philosophical terms, love is, for May, a kind of ontological rootedness.[15] May writes that love 'is directed at one who breaks into our life from the outside'.[16] In other words, for May, all types of love must have a beloved. This is not an exhaustive list of all of the philosophical theories of love, but it should suffice to show that philosophical theories of love take the beloved as a presumed and necessary feature of the very nature of love in all of its diverse manifestations, which I call the 'presumed-necessary beloved'.

Conceptual analysis: Definitional criteria

In order to argue for the unwarrantedness of the presumed-necessary beloved in philosophical definitions of the concept of 'love', I draw on two criteria from philosophical work in the area of conceptual analysis:[17]

1. The *Use* criterion: A stronger definition will be compatible with paradigmatic cases of the concept and common uses of the concept. If the beloved is indeed necessary, then the paradigmatic cases and common uses of love, and the beloveds captured by these, ought to reflect this necessity.

2. The *Compatibility* criterion: A stronger definition will be compatible with other relevant areas of philosophy. If the beloved is necessary, this necessity ought to be consistent with other relevant theoretical areas.

In particular, I apply the *Use* criterion to God, the self and a large group of beloveds that share a particular property, which I have termed 'inert, abstract and imaginary beloveds' ('IAI beloveds'). These are all well-known objects of love taken from paradigmatic cases and common uses of the concept. Using this criterion, I show that these paragons of the beloved are widely accepted – even exalted – objects of love, and yet they challenge the notion of the presumed-necessary beloved. Drawing on philosophical theories of intentionality, causation and disposition, I employ the *Compatibility* criterion to unpack the possible role of the presumed-necessary beloved. In short, the *Compatibility* criterion asks 'what is the *of* of love?' and argues that none of the possible answers can support the constitutive and central role given to the beloved.

The use criterion: Paradigmatic cases and common uses

In this section, I focus on three paradigmatic cases of love with three particular and regularly discussed beloveds: God, self and IAI beloveds. There are three distinct ways that God and love meet: God as lover; God as love itself; and God as beloved. All three are paradigmatic cases of love, but here I address only God as love and God as beloved. A foundational tenet of Christian theology is that God, perfect and complete being, is love.[18] And yet, as Christian theologians point out, 'The concept of love implies that there must be someone or something to be loved.'[19] This creates a tension and a long-standing theological puzzle: if God is perfect and complete on their own, they cannot also be something, love, that must be completed by another. As St Thomas Aquinas wrote, '*Amor est vis unitiva et concretiva.* Love is a uniting and joining power. But this cannot have any place in God, for he is simple.'[20]

Different resolutions have been suggested to this problem. Augustine of Hippo proposed, for instance, that God 'conceives of himself as he truly is, and loves that self-awareness as he loves himself'.[21] In this attempt, God's self-awareness has an identity of its own such that it becomes the object of God's love-nature. Significantly, for my purposes, another proposed solution, by contemporary American theologian Katherine Sonderegger is that God must be a type of love *without object*. If God is the sort of love that requires an object, she writes, then God is incomplete without that object – without the World and us. But, God cannot be incomplete and thus imperfect since this is contrary to God's nature. So, God must be a type of love that is complete in God alone. In God, Sonderegger argues, love must be 'non-relational, absolute and *objectless*'.[22] Thus, a foundational, paradigmatic and highly significant type of love – the love that is God – is suggested to be without object. This poses a serious challenge to the presumed-necessary beloved.

God is also a widely affirmed and exalted love object. For Simon May, for instance, God is the '*greatest possible* object and ground of love'.[23] But God as the object of love also challenges the presumed-necessary beloved model. For one, God as the object of love cannot straightforwardly fulfil the requirements of the beloved in many theories of love. For instance, psychologist Barbara Fredrickson argues that love is (1) a sharing of positive emotions, (2) a synchronization in biochemistry and behaviours and (3) a reflective motive to invest in each other's well-being.[24] God cannot be this beloved. There cannot be a synchronization between one's biochemistry and behaviours, and the biochemistry and behaviours of God.

More generally, God is an unusual beloved because God is an unusual 'object'. This is true whether one believes in the existence of God or not. For believers, God is not a typical beloved – the way God participates in loving relationships is significantly different from how mortal beings participate in love. If a romantic partner were to be as non-communicative or as cryptically communicative as God is, the relationship would not last very long. As a non-believer myself, an ontological assumption I maintain for the rest of the chapter – God as beloved – is not an independent object outside of the lover, but an idea constructed and maintained by the lover. This type of beloved is a significant challenge to theories of love and the presumed-necessary beloved. If the role of the presumed-necessary beloved can be filled by a non-existent beloved created by the imagination of the lover, as a non-existent God is, then neither existence nor separation from the lover are required features of the presumed-necessary beloved. Then, it is far from obvious how this sort of beloved is different from having no beloved at all. Indeed, this sort of beloved causes trouble for philosophical theories. For example, May rules out the possibility of self-love precisely because the object 'self' is insufficiently outside of the lover to properly ontologically root them.

Self-love is another widely accepted type of love. Consider, for example, the cultural narrative that 'you can't love someone else until you love yourself', or the Christian view held by some theologians that '(1) everything in Christianity can be traced back to love, and (2) everything in love can be traced back to self-love'.[25] But, like love of God, it is hard to make sense of this type of love as taking, at least in typical fashion, the form of distinct and separate lover/beloved. May, as mentioned above, rules out self-love as a type of love precisely because the self is not sufficiently outside the lover to trigger love.[26] Whatever the 'self' is, it is difficult to say how or why the self as lover is distinct from the self as beloved. If these two are not separate and distinct from one another, then in self-love, as in the love of God, there is a beloved who is not separate from the lover (but, unlike God, is an existing beloved). This paradigm case of love, like the love of God, therefore, has a problem – there are not the two independent entities (aka relata) required to form the dyadic, loving relationship of lover and beloved.

Theories of love have accepted a huge variety of beloveds. Harry Frankfurt, for instance, wrote that 'the object of love can be almost anything, a kind of experience, a person, a group, a moral ideal, a non-moral ideal, a tradition, *whatever*'.[27] Given this wide spectrum of beloveds, there must be a correspondingly wide array of ways of *being* the beloved. This provides the final, general type of beloved that I want to draw attention to – which I call the 'IAI beloveds'. These beloveds, although perhaps not paradigms of love, are significant because they represent a great volume of common beloveds. IAI beloveds include: inert beloveds, like the love of my deceased grandfather or of my 35-year-old teddy bear Betty; abstract loves, like love of nation or philosophy; and imaginary beloveds, like the love of imaginary friends or literary characters. The central claim here is not that these represent three strict, separate types of beloveds – my deceased grandfather might also be an abstract beloved, the nation an imaginary one, and so on. Instead, what is significant about these beloveds is that they share a level of possible relational reciprocation and participation that is at or near zero. And, like God and the self, the existence and separateness between the lover and the beloved is often unclear.

Now, let us assume that the loving reciprocation or participation of which a beloved is capable falls along a continuum. I take this to be an uncontroversial assumption. At one end of this spectrum, you find the neurologically typical adult human beloved who attentively and genuinely loves the lover well and fully. This is not meant to suggest that reciprocity is a necessary feature of love, only that a beloved who does reciprocate will participate in the loving relationship to a greater degree than the beloved who does not reciprocate. In the middle of this spectrum are types of love such as the newborn's love of caregiver and the love of one's goldfish. At the other end of the continuum are IAI beloveds, including those that neither exist nor are separate from the lover. IAI beloveds are incapable of, or have a very low capacity for, loving reciprocation and relationship participation.

The beloveds at the far end of the continuum – those that cannot or do not reciprocate or participate in the loving relationship – pose a problem for theories of love that demand a particular type of or any participation from the beloved.[28] For instance, Barbara Fredrickson's theory of love, mentioned above, requires (1) a sharing of positive emotions, (2) a synchronization in biochemistry and behaviours and (3) a reflective motive to invest in each other's well-being.[29] This places certain demands on the beloved – that they share in positive emotions, that they are biochemical beings with behaviours, and that they can invest in the lover's well-being. Many, if not all, IAI beloveds at the far end of the spectrum will not be able to meet these criteria.

More generally, for all theories of love, the participatory requirements of the beloved will carve the spectrum into 'love' and 'not love'. Those objects that can fulfil the requirements of the particular theory will be proper objects of love, and so, there will be love; those objects that cannot meet those requirements will fail to be proper beloveds, and so, no love will be found. Indeed, these are common recurring challenges to theories of love – they cannot accommodate some particular beloved, carve the spectrum in the 'wrong' place and leave the 'wrong' beloveds on the 'cannot' side of the theoretical wall. For example, returning to Fredrickson's theory of love, one might object on the grounds that only a cognitively sophisticated beloved can meet the 'reflective motive to invest in each other's well-being' requirement. So, love will not be found in many places where it should be found – like love of a newborn or love of non-human animals.

Accommodating the entirety of the spectrum of beloveds would require that a theory of love make almost no demands of the beloved – including that the beloved existed, was separate from the lover and was able to participate/reciprocate in the loving relationship. That is, if a definition of love is going to be broadly inclusive, the beloved cannot be asked to *do* very much. This widely inclusive beloved may not even be able to capture the intuition that love is relational, which is presumably the intuition that motivates the presumed-necessary beloved in the first place. It is commonly argued that relations require existing relata, and that 'in order for a relation to be borne by one thing to another thing, then those things must exist'.[30] Therefore, a widely inclusive beloved would also be incompatible with relationality since many beloveds on the spectrum do not exist.

Various conclusions could be drawn from the definitionally inert, non-relational, widely inclusive beloved. For instance, one might surmise that the group of beloveds is just too vast and that the proper collection of beloveds will be illuminated by a theory of love that ascribes the proper level of participation to the beloved. But, as discussed above, a number of significant paradigmatic beloveds have very low levels of relationship participation, are not separate from the lover and/or are non-existent – the self, God, the nation, humanity, neighbour, newborns, deceased beloveds, imaginary friends, literary characters and so on. So, nearly any requirement of the beloved, any non-inclusive beloved, will carve out a number of significant paradigmatic beloveds, weakening it as a definition in accordance with the *Use* criterion.

Another conclusion is that the beloved just does not require the qualities of participation, existence and distinctness. The beloved, one might grant, just sometimes does not *do* much in love and must only be *there*. And, in fact, many theories of love are solely descriptions of the way in which the lover relates to the beloved and prescribe no particular or necessary type of behaviour towards the lover. For instance, theories of love as a type of robust concern are about *the lover* being oriented towards the beloved in the right sort of way.[31] No parallel prescription of any necessary orientation of the beloved towards the lover is offered. Theories of love as a particular mode of valuing are about the bestowal or appraisal of value *by the lover* on the beloved.[32] However, if the presumed-necessary beloved, as relational partner, is not required to participate or reciprocate in the loving relationship, then the relationality of love must allow for unidirectional loving. This is not, by itself, a problem since many agree that love can be unreciprocated. But, if love can be unidirectional, then it is not obvious why love's unidirectional beam, so to speak, must always necessarily alight ultimately on an object. Especially given that, in addition to being non-participatory, the beloved can also be non-existent and non-distinct, so that even 'unidirectional' might be overstating these love relations. In other words, if love can emanate solely from the lover, while the beloved plays no role at all in the loving relationship, then the presumed-necessary role of the beloved does not appear very necessary.

My preferred solution to the problem of the large variety of beloveds is that love does not always require a beloved. This is not to say that the beloved cannot remain a necessary requirement of many types of love. It could still be true that, for example, romantic love, parental love and friendship love must always have beloveds. But, a beloved would no longer be a necessary requirement for all types of love. This does not seem much different from the state in which the beloved is left above – non-participatory, non-existent and non-distinct. Additionally, there are other ways to maintain the intuition that love is relational without appeal to a dyadic lover-beloved structure. Many philosophers argue, for instance, that relationality is a basic ontological fact of the nature of being rather than something that *has to happen*.[33] In other words, the idea of distinct, non-relational individuals that must enter into relations in order to create a relationship is a fiction; relationality can exist outside the dyadic self–other structure. This suggests a way to remove the presumed-necessary beloved while retaining love's relationality. And the possibility of a love without object offers a number of exciting possibilities. For instance, it would help explain God's nature, as discussed above; it would help address the problem of love's supposed particularity in moral theories that make love a central virtue, when morality is thought to be general in nature; and, finally, it would help explain the intuition that a self-generated love, that is, not self-love (for why would my love of me extend to you?), can foster love of others.

The compatibility criterion: The *Of* of love

In this section, I address the *Compatibility* criterion: a stronger definition will be compatible with other relevant areas of philosophy. If the beloved is necessary, this necessity ought to be consistent with other relevant theoretical areas. I suggest that it might capture an intentional relation, a causal relation or a dispositional relation. But, drawing on philosophical work in these three areas, I ultimately reject these as possibilities, concluding that it is not obvious what role – deemed to be so central to love – the presumed-necessary beloved is meant to play.

One possibility is that the presumed-necessary beloved captures the constitutive intentionality of love, much like intentionality has been said to be constitutive of mental states. To say that something has intentionality is to say that it has content, is about something or that it is directed at something. For instance, the mental state of perceiving the cat on the mat is *about*, *directed at* or *has the content of* some cat sleeping on some mat. Thus, this perceptual/mental state has intentionality. Franz Brentano, the nineteenth-century German philosopher who introduced the idea of intentionality, actually described love as intentional.[34] If the *of* of love represents an intentional relation, then love is *of* the beloved in the sense that the beloved is the *content* of love, that which love is *about* or that towards which love is *directed*. If the presumed-necessary beloved is meant to capture this characteristic of love, then it ought to be able to explain and accommodate the spectrum of beloveds.

According to Tim Crane's reading of Brentano, non-existent objects were not originally a problem for Brentano's theory of intentionality, because Brentano was a 'methodological phenomenalist' (a term coined by Peter Simons).[35] On this view, all phenomena are mind-dependent, and so, the question of whether or not the object 'exists' is nonsensical, since there is nothing independent of the mind that can be experienced.[36] However,

Brentano changed his view of intentionality in the 1911 edition of *Psychology from an Empirical Standpoint* in such a way that non-existent objects became, and still are, a problem for intentionality. In the preface, Brentano noted that 'one of the most important innovations is that I am no longer of the opinion that mental relation can have something other than *a thing as its object*'.[37] As Crane notes, Brentano is here abandoning the methodological phenomenalist framework – where there are never pure, 'real' things – and admitting that 'objects of thought can be themselves *real* things, and therefore transcend the act of thought'.[38] At the same time, objects of thought often, obviously, do not exist. For example, I am thinking about a green unicorn with zebra stripes. Without the methodological phenomenalist framework, which has its own problems, non-existing objects become a problem for intentionality as a type of relation since 'of course it's true that in order for a relation to be borne by one thing to another, then those things must exist'.[39] In order to solve this problem, it is suggested that intentionality is not a relation proper, but only *relation-like* or '*quasi-relational*'.[40]

Like thoughts, love also admits of non-existent objects. So, if love is a sort of intentional relation, then it is only *relation-like* and not properly relational. If the *of* of love captures love's intentionality, the presumed-necessary beloved renders love only relation-like or quasi-relational. Brentano described quasi-relationality as 'something somewhat similar to something relational in a certain respect'.[41] One problem with this is that quasi-relationality does not rule out the possibility of a love without object. If the relationality granted to love by philosophical intentionality and the spectrum of beloveds is 'something somewhat similar to something relational in a certain respect', then this very low bar could be met by a love without object. For instance, perhaps a love without object is caused by the foundational, ontological property of relationality discussed above and, in this way, is similar to something relational while not being directed at or about a particular object.

Perhaps the *of* of love is not an intentional relation, but represents instead a causal relation. Let us assume here, for the sake of thoroughness, that cause is different from intentionality. The beloved, therefore, is not that which the love is about, but that which *causes* love. For instance, Simon May claims that love is about objects that cause the lover to experience the joyfulness of the promise of being ontologically rooted or grounded in the world.[42] In other words, without the beloved there is no cause for love, no spark to inspire love. But, again, this seems to exclude non-existent beloveds, inert beloveds or beloveds that are not separate from us who are not obviously able to play this role. How could it be that something imagined and non-existent *causes* love? Or, to put this another way, if the beloved is non-existent and/or not separate from the lover, then it must be the lover, and not the beloved, who generates or causes love. If this is the case, then the spark of love can be lover-generated and the beloved is not necessary for love to be caused, and the role of the presumed-necessary beloved does not seem so necessary.

Perhaps the *of* of love means 'of' in the sense of a *dispositional* relation. The term 'disposition' describes the properties or qualities of things that are *possible* behaviours rather than *actual* behaviours. Dispositions are about characteristic manifestations under particular circumstances that stimulate them.[43] For instance, if my grandmother's vase has the disposition of 'fragility', it is not shattering at this moment; fragile is not represented by any actual current behaviour of the vase, but it has the property that it *will* shatter (the possible behaviour/characteristic manifestation) under the right stimulus circumstances – say when dropped or struck. Compare this with a property like height where the vase actually is eight inches tall. On the view that the presumed-necessary beloved is a dispositional relation, love is the disposition to feel and act in particular ways, lovingly, *when a beloved comes along*, the particular circumstance that stimulates it. Just like the fragile vase is disposed to shatter when struck, love is disposed to blossom when a beloved comes along.

Dispositions are characteristic manifestations under particular identifiable stimulus circumstances. And, while the characteristic manifestation of love is clear – loving behaviour is manifested – the stimulus conditions created by a beloved are not clear. A non-existent, non-participatory and non-distinct beloved does not add any obviously new stimulus conditions that could explain why a beloved would be necessary for triggering the manifestation of the characteristic 'loving'. In other words, if love is sparked under conditions of the non-existent, non-participatory and non-distinct beloved, these conditions are not sufficiently different from 'no beloved' to rule out that love can be sparked without any beloved at all. Perhaps the condition generated by the beloved is some bare requirement of relationality. But, as discussed above, it is not obvious that the beloved can provide this relationality, especially given the requirement that relationality requires existing relata, and there are other ways, besides the beloved, to centre relationality in love.

Conclusion

In light of the arguments set out in this chapter, I offer two possible conclusions. The weaker conclusion is that what I have argued for is enough to require a reasoned defence of the presumed-necessary beloved. After all, the idea of a constitutive beloved greatly shapes theories of love, the empirical study of love, the places where love is seen, found and given. And for all the reasons given above, the beloved can no longer automatically be granted such a significant place in the theorizing about love. For the stronger, I believe I have given reasons to reject the beloved as a constituent of love. This will require the rethinking of what love is and open up new possibilities for imagining and understanding this ancient and powerful thing, including that there can be love without a dearly beloved object.

Notes

1 Plato, 'Symposium', in *Plato Complete Works*, ed. John M. Cooper (Indianapolis, IN: Hackett, 1997), 482, 199e–200.

2 Bennett Helm, 'Love', in *The Stanford Encyclopedia of Philosophy* (Stanford, CA: Stanford University, 2017). https://plato.stanford.edu/archives/fall2021/entries/love/.

3 Ibid.

4 Ibid.

5 E.g., Mark Fisher, *Personal Love* (London: Duckworth, 1990); Robert Nozick, 'Love's Bond', in *The Examined Life: Philosophical Meditations* (New York: Simon & Schuster, 1989), 68–86; Robert Solomon, *Love: Emotion, Myth, and Metaphor* (New York: Anchor Press, 1981); Robert Solomon, *About Love: Reinventing Romance for Our Times* (New York: Simon & Schuster, 1988).

6 Nozick, 'Love's Bond', 418, emphasis added.

7 E.g., Alan Soble, *The Structure of Love* (New Haven, CT: Yale University Press, 1990); Alan Soble, 'Union, Autonomy, and Concern', in *Love Analyzed*, ed. Roger Lamb (Boulder, CO: Westview Press, 1997), 65–92; Harry Frankfurt, 'Autonomy, Necessity, and Love', in *Necessity, Volition, and Love* (Cambridge: Cambridge University Press, 1999), 129–41; Richard White, *Love's Philosophy* (Washington, DC: Rowman & Littlefield, 2001).

8 Monique Wonderly, 'Early Relationships, Pathologies of Attachment, and the Capacity to Love', in *The Routledge Handbook of Love in Philosophy*, ed. Adrienne Martin (New York: Routledge, 2019), 25.

9 E.g., David Velleman, 'Love as a Moral Emotion', *Ethics* 109, no. 2 (January 1999), 338–74; David Velleman, 'Beyond Price', *Ethics* 118, no. 2 (January 2008), 191–212; Niko Kolodny, 'Love as Valuing a Relationship', *Philosophical Review* 112, no. 2 (April 2003): 135–89; Bennett Helm, *Love, Friendship, and the Self: Intimacy, Identification, and the Social Nature of Persons* (Oxford: Oxford University Press, 2010).

10 Velleman, 'Love as a Moral Emotion', 360.

11 E.g., Troy Jollimore, *Love's Vision* (Princeton, NJ: Princeton University Press, 2011).

12 E.g., Amelie Rorty, 'The Historicity of Psychological Attitudes: Love Is Not Love Which Alters Not When It Alteration Finds', *Midwest Studies in Philosophy* 10, no. 1 (September 1987): 399–412; David Hamlyn, 'The Phenomena of Love and Hate', *Philosophy* 53, no. 203 (January 1978): 5–20; Annette Baier, 'Unsafe Loves', in *The Philosophy of (Erotic) Love*, ed. Robert Solomon and Kathleen Higgins (Lawrence: University of Kansas Press, 1991);

Neera Badhwar (ed.), *Friendship: A Philosophical Reader* (Ithaca, NY: Cornell University Press, 2003).

13 Sam Shpall, 'A Tripartite Theory of Love', *Journal of Ethics and Social Philosophy* 13, no. 2 (May 2018): 91–124.

14 Ibid., 91.

15 Simon May, *Love: A New Understanding of an Ancient Emotion* (Oxford: Oxford University Press, 2019), xiii.

16 Ibid., xv, emphasis added.

17 Muhammad Ali Khalidi, *Natural Categories and Human Kinds: Classification in the Natural and Social Sciences* (Cambridge: Cambridge University Press, 2013), 3–5.

18 Gerald Bray, *God Is Love: A Biblical and Systematic Theology* (Wheaton, IL: Crossway, 2012), 107.

19 Ibid.

20 Thomas Aquinas, *Summa Theologica*, trans. Fathers of the English Dominican Province (New York: Benziger Brothers, 1911–25), I, q. 20, a. 1, obj. 3.

21 Bray, *God Is Love*, 107.

22 Katherine Sonderegger, *Systematic Theology: Volume 1, The Doctrine of God* (Minneapolis, MN: Fortress Press, 2015), 489.

23 May, *Love*, 89.

24 Barbara Fredrickson, *Love 2.0: Creating Happiness and Health in Moments of Connection* (New York: Plume, 2013), 17.

25 Anders Nygren, *Agape and Eros*, trans. P. S. Watson (Philadelphia, PA: Westminster Press, 1953), 643.

26 May, *Love*, xv.

27 Harry Frankfurt, 'Volitional Rationality and the Necessities of Love', *Iyyun: The Jerusalem Philosophical Quarterly* 63 (January 2014): 14.

28 Myisha Cherry, 'Love, Anger, and Racial Justice', in *The Routledge Handbook of Love in Philosophy*, ed. Adrienne Martin (New York: Routledge, 2019), 158.

29 Barbara Fredrickson, *Love 2.0: Creating Happiness and Health in Moments of Connection* (New York: Plume, 2013), 17.

30 Fraser MacBride, 'Relations', in *The Stanford Encyclopedia of Philosophy* (Stanford, CA: Stanford University Press, 2020). https://plato.stanford.edu/entries/relations/.

31 E.g., Hugh LaFollette, *Personal Relationships: Love, Identity, and Morality* (Cambridge, MA: Blackwell Press, 1996); Frankfurt, 'Autonomy, Necessity, and Love', 129–41; White, *Love's Philosophy*.

32 E.g., Velleman, 'Love as a Moral Emotion', 338–74; Velleman, 'Beyond Price', 191–212; Kolodny, 'Love as Valuing a Relationship', 135–89; Jollimore, *Love's Vision*.

33   E.g., Rosi Braidotti, *Transpositions: On Nomadic Ethics* (Malden, MA: Polity Press, 2006); Elizabeth Grosz, *Volatile Bodies: Toward a Corporeal Feminism* (Bloomington: Indiana University Press, 1994); Luce Irigaray, *Ethics of Sexual Difference* (Ithaca, NY: Cornell University Press, 1993).

34   Franz Brentano, *Psychology from an Empirical Standpoint*, ed. Oskar Kraus and Linda L. McAlister, trans. Antos C. Rancurello D. B. Terell and Linda L. McAlister (London: Routledge, [1984] 2009), xxiiv.

35   Peter Simons, 'Introduction', in *Psychology from an Empirical Standpoint*, ed. Franz Brentano (London: Routledge 1995), xvii.

36   Tim Crane, 'Brentano's Concept of Intentional Inexistence', in *The Austrian Contribution to Analytic Philosophy*, ed. Mark Textor (London: Routledge, 2006), 12.

37   Ibid., 17.

38   Ibid.

39   MacBride, 'Relations'.

40   Crane, 'Brentano's Concept of Intentional Inexistence', 345.

41   Brentano, *Psychology from an Empirical Standpoint*, 212.

42   May, *Love*, xiii.

43   Choi Sungho and Michael Fara, 'Dispositions', in *The Stanford Encyclopedia of Philosophy* (Stanford, CA: Stanford University, 2021). https://plato.stanf ord.edu/archives/spr2021/entries/dispositions/.

Bibliography

Abend, Gabriel. 'The Love of Neuroscience: A Sociological Account'. *Sociological Theory* 36, no. 1 (March 2018): 88–116. https://doi-org.ezproxy.library.yorku. ca/10.1177/0735275118759697.

Aquinas, Thomas. *Summa Theologica* (trans. Fathers of the English Dominican Province). New York: Benziger Brothers, 1911–25.

Aron, Arthur and Aron, Elaine. *Love and the Expansion of Self: Understanding Attraction and Satisfaction*. New York: Hemisphere Publishing Corporation, 1986.

Badhwar, Neera (ed.). *Friendship: A Philosophical Reader*. Ithaca, NY: Cornell University Press, 2003.

Baier, Annette. 'Unsafe Loves'. In *The Philosophy of (Erotic) Love*, edited by Robert Solomon and Kathleen Higgins, 434–50. Lawrence: University of Kansas Press, 1991.

Barad, Karen. *Meeting the Universe Halfway: Quantum Physics and the Entanglement of Matter and Meaning*. London: Duke University Press, 2007.

Berscheid, Ellen. 'Love in the Fourth Dimension'. *Annual Review of Psychology* 61 (January 2010): 1–25. https://doi.org/10.1146/annurev.psych.093008.100318.

Braidotti, Rosi. *Transpositions: On Nomadic Ethics*. Maiden, MA: Polity Press, 2006.

Bray, Gerald. *God Is Love: A Biblical and Systematic Theology*. Wheaton, IL: Crossway, 2012.

Brentano, Franz. *Psychology from an Empirical Standpoint* (ed. Oskar Kraus and Linda L. McAlister; trans. Antos C. Rancurello, D.B. Terell and Linda L. McAlister). London: Routledge, [1874] 2009.

Cacioppo, Stephanie, Bianchi-Demicheli, Francesco, Hatfield, Elaine and Rapson, Richard L. 'Social Neuroscience of Love'. *Clinical Neuropsychiatry: Journal of Treatment Evaluation* 9, no. 1 (February 2012): 3–13.

Cherry, Myisha. 'Love, Anger, and Racial Justice'. In *The Routledge Handbook of Love in Philosophy*, edited by Adrienne Martin, 157–68. New York: Routledge, 2019.

Choi, Sunghe and Fara, Michael. 'Dispositions'. In *Stanford Encyclopedia of Philosophy*. Stanford, CA: Stanford University Press, 2021. https://plato.stanf ord.edu/archives/spr2021/entries/dispositions/.

Crane, Tim. 'Intentional Objects'. *Ratio* 14, no. 4 (December 2001): 336–49.

Crane, Tim. 'Brentano's Concept of Intentional Inexistence'. In *The Austrian Contribution to Analytic Philosophy*, edited by Mark Textor, 1–20. London: Routledge, 2006.

Fisher, Mark. *Personal Love*. London: Duckworth, 1990.

Frankfurt, Harry. 'Autonomy, Necessity, and Love'. In *Necessity, Volition, and Love*, 129–41. Cambridge: Cambridge University Press, 1999.

Frankfurt, Harry. *The Reasons of Love*. Princeton, NJ: Princeton University Press, 2004.

Frankfurt, Harry. 'Volitional Rationality and the Necessities of Love'. *Iyyun: The Jerusalem Philosophical Quarterly* 63 (January 2014): 11–25.

Fredrickson, Barbara. *Love 2.0: Creating Happiness and Health in Moments of Connection*. New York: Plume, 2013.

Grosz, Elizabeth. *Volatile Bodies: Toward a Corporeal Feminism*. Bloomington: Indiana University Press, 1994.

Hamlyn, David. 'The Phenomena of Love and Hate'. *Philosophy* 53, no. 203 (January 1978): 5–20.

Helm, Bennett. *Love, Friendship, and the Self: Intimacy, Identification, and the Social Nature of Persons*. Oxford: Oxford University Press, 2010.

Helm, Bennett. 'Love'. In *Stanford Encyclopedia of Philosophy*. Stanford, CA: Stanford University Press, 2017. https://plato.stanford.edu/archives/fall2 021/entries/love/.

Irigaray, Luce. *Ethics of Sexual Difference*. Ithaca, NY: Cornell University Press, 1993.

Jollimore, Troy. *Love's Vision*. Princeton, NJ: Princeton University Press, 2011.

Khalidi, Muhammad Ali. *Natural Categories and Human Kinds: Classification in the Natural and Social Sciences*. Cambridge: Cambridge University Press, 2013.

Kolodny, Niko. 'Love as Valuing a Relationship'. *Philosophical Review* 112, no. 2 (April 2003): 135–89.

LaFollette, Hugh. *Personal Relationships: Love, Identity, and Morality*. Cambridge, MA: Blackwell Press, 1996.

MacBride, Fraser. 'Relations'. In *The Stanford Encyclopedia of Philosophy*. Stanford, CA: Stanford University Press, 2020. https://plato.stanford.edu/entries/relations/.

May, Simon. *Love: A New Understanding of an Ancient Emotion*. Oxford: Oxford University Press, 2019.

Nozick, Robert. 'Love's Bond'. In *The Examined Life: Philosophical Meditations*, 68–86. New York: Simon & Schuster, 1989.

Nygren, Anders. *Agape and Eros* (trans. P. S. Watson). Philadelphia, PA: Westminster Press, 1953.

Plato. 'Symposium'. In *Plato Complete Works*, edited by John M. Cooper, 457–505. Indianapolis, IN: Hackett, 1997.

Rorty, Amelie. 'The Historicity of Psychological Attitudes: Love Is Not Love Which Alters Not When It Alteration Finds'. *Midwest Studies in Philosophy* 10, no.1 (September 1987): 399–412.

Shpall, Sam. 'A Tripartite Theory of Love'. *Journal of Ethics and Social Philosophy* 13, no. 2 (May 2018): 91–124.

Simons, Peter. 'Introduction'. In *Psychology from an Empirical Standpoint*, edited by Franz Brentano. London: Routledge, 1995.

Soble, Alan. *The Structure of Love*. New Haven, CT: Yale University Press, 1990.

Soble, Alan. 'Union, Autonomy, and Concern'. In *Love Analyzed*, edited by Roger Lamb, 65–92. Boulder, CO: Westview Press, 1997.

Solomon, Robert. *Love: Emotion, Myth, and Metaphor*. New York: Anchor Press, 1981.

Solomon, Robert. *About Love: Reinventing Romance for Our Times*. New York: Simon & Schuster, 1988.

Solomon, Robert. 'Reasons for Love'. *Journal for the Theory of Social Behaviour* 32, no. 1 (March 2002): 1–28.

Sonderegger, Katherine. *Systematic Theology: Volume 1, The Doctrine of God*. Minneapolis, MN: Fortress Press, 2015.

Velleman, David. 'Love as a Moral Emotion'. *Ethics* 109, no. 2 (January 1999): 338–74.

Velleman, David. 'Beyond Price'. *Ethics* 118, no. 2 (January 2008): 191–212.

White, Richard. *Love's Philosophy*. Washington, DC: Rowman & Littlefield, 2001.

Wonderly, Monique. 'Early Relationships, Pathologies of Attachment, and the Capacity to Love'. In *The Routledge Handbook of Love in Philosophy*, edited by Adrienne Martin, 23–35. New York: Routledge, 2019.

13

Post-humanism and the road to castle *Frankisstein*

Lawrence Quill

Impossible to read the auguries:
The future waits on fiercer surgeries.[1]

Introduction

Jeanette Winterson's novel *Frankisstein: A Love Story* was long listed for the Booker Prize in 2019 and is an enquiry into the love lives of two Shelleys (Mary and Ry), their stories reported in parallel as we jump back and forth across the centuries.[2] This is Winterson's first work of science fiction, but it is not the first time the author has written a love story or played with ideas surrounding gender. In *Written on the Body*, published in 1992, the gender of the narrator is never revealed. The gender identities that appear in *Frankisstein*, however, are placed front and centre. The transgender protagonist assumes the voice of Reason in a near-future world of boutique sex-bots and emotional artificial intelligence (AI).

The book is an exploration of our contemporary obsession with the fluid nature of gender identities and what we might term the post-human or transhuman (I will use these terms interchangeably).[3] The characters in *Frankisstein*, separated by two hundred years of thought and discussion concerning ideas of humanity and love, struggle with the meanings of both. These and other questions concerning consciousness, immortality and gender are posed and answered in conversation at Mary Shelley's Lake Geneva (1816) and in Ry Shelley's (2019) present.

Mary Shelley's love affair with the poet Percy Shelley in 1816 is contrasted with Ry Shelley's encounter with the scientist Victor Stein in 2019. Love stories they might be, operating in parallel. Yet, it is not the same love by any means, and that, perhaps, is the point of the novel. For Mary Shelley, love was an escape into utopia. For Ry Shelley, love is 'a disturbance among the disturbed'.[4]

The analysis offered here views *Frankisstein* as a playful threnody on choice, existence and essence, agency and passivity all underscored by the transactional nature of love under the conditions of technology-fuelled capitalism. What results is a reversal of the Romantic notion that that there is, in fact, more within than without.

Love as disturbance

In *Frankisstein*, the story of Mary Shelley's love affair is set against the fragility and limitations of the body, the immortality of the soul and the supremacy of thought. 'I am a poor specimen of a creature', notes Winterson's Mary Shelley, 'except that I can think'.[5] We are further invited to consider the inadequacies of reality and the limits of the Cartesian division between mind and body. 'Is this life a disordered dream?' Winterson's Shelley asks. 'Is the external world the shadow, while the substance is what we cannot see, or touch, or hear, yet apprehend?'[6]

In *Frankisstein*, love is inseparable from the (contested) intellectual assumptions that work their way into discussions concerning familial relationships, death and immortality. In fact, at times, so contemporary are the conversations in *Frankisstein* that one might be forgiven for thinking one had read similar headlines in *Wired* magazine or the *MIT Technology Review*.

The discourse of love that emerges attempts to reconcile human desire and the social order, the material conditions of human existence and the immaterial. Metaphysics is juxtaposed against the idea that life is just the pursuit of desire, that working life has reduced humans to the status of automata and that humans have a habit of falling in love with their own creations – be that poetry for Percy Shelley or Byron, or the creature for Victor Frankenstein. Love might be an escape, but it is also posed as a problem.

The character of Ry Shelley is a medical doctor working with the Wellcome Trust, their task to assess how 'robots will affect our physical and mental health'.[7] Ry is English, but we meet them at a business exposition on robotics in Memphis, Tennessee. Ry is a transgender describing their own experience of life as follows: 'I am liminal, lisping, in between, emerging, undecided, transitional, experimental, a start-up (or is it an upstart?) in my own life.'[8] We meet other characters in the drama that Winterson assembles. They are recognizable types that act as foils for Ry Shelley and Victor Stein, permitting their 'relationship' to develop into the *Love Story*.

Most relevant to the present discussion is the figure of Ron Lord, the vulgar millionaire distributor and franchise seller of robotic sex-dolls. We are not, I think, supposed to like Ron Lord. His world is crude, simplistic and lacking in imagination. But he is a tremendous success and understands the operations of a marketplace driven by desire, which makes him a recognizable figure within techno-capitalism where fantasy predominates rather than 'nature, so you can have what you want'.[9] Lord describes the grotesque silicone figures he manufactures with all the precision of a car or phone salesman, including the option to buy or lease: 'Renting gives you all the pleasure and none of the problems. Breakages, storage, updating – the technology is changing all the time.'[10]

This is not quite Orwell's 'soft-porn for the proles', but it is close to the aim of 1984's *Pornosec* to keep the population distracted and content. What Lord is describing, however, is the engineer's (and, by extension, the consumer's) dream of relationship: less problematic or frictionless. His range of female sex-bots, with individual specifications, permits boutique modification much as capitalism promises to personalize a product or experience. Yet, unlike the software that provides the illusion of connection (one need only think of Spike Jonze's *Her* [2014] where the lonely protagonist learns about love from an operating system), none of the specifications of Ron Lord's bots involves great conversation. 'They don't', for example, 'have a big vocabulary ... No nagging ... No sulking.'[11] Integrating a sex-bot into the *Uber* platform makes perfect sense to Ron Lord, a clearly authorial comment upon the crass version of the slick gig-economy salesmen who have profited so well from the disruption of daily life.

Lord is a caricature of the lower-middle-class entrepreneur – 'broad chest, overweight, short legs, thick arms, sweaty in a crumpled suit' – the car salesman version of the gig-economy CEO.[12] He quaffs Coke rather than Soylent and possesses a crass schoolboy wit. One assumes that the readers of *Frankisstein* are comfortable deploring Ron and his working-class attitudes. It is much harder to do so with a PhD who has similar ambitions – the character of Victor Stein, for example. Yet, it is Lord who is the globalizer, the visionary as much as the middle-class Victor Stein. As Lord notes, 'This market is global. This market is the future.'[13]

Victor Stein provides the intellectual defence that Ron Lord's sales pitch lacks. Ry describes Stein as an academic and 'Gospel Channel Scientist' with a social media following and a Ted Talk with six million views.[14] He promotes the thesis of technological determinism, that AI will inevitably transcend the physical limits of the body, a future where 'robots will manage much of what humans manage today. Intelligence – perhaps even consciousness – will no longer be dependent on a body'.[15]

Ry expresses their attraction for him: 'He has that sex-mix of soul-saving and erudition ... Women adore him. Men admire him.'[16] Stein is a classic disruptor, defending technology against prejudice and the rights of *Sophia*, the (actual) first robot in the world granted citizenship by Saudi Arabia in 2017. For Stein, gender, biology and technology are intimately related. As a result, the human is somewhat unpoetically reconfigured as a '*biological data-processing plant*'.[17]

Stein's is the classic posture of the enlightened, visionary academic. Misunderstood by those who would criticize, he is equally dismissive of those who would caution against his vision of the future. 'If we are reaching the end of Project Human' – he suggests, thanks to climate change, failure to control population and so on – 'don't blame the geeks'.[18] Quite so. Stein is the classic technocrat. Society is a problem to be solved, a puzzle to be managed, its population to be nudged to use the favoured word of social scientists where the rational actor has been replaced by the manipulable subject.[19] Yet, in *Frankisstein*, there is a further allusion to the power of technology to advance the cause of progress. In Stein's view, if the human code needs rewriting, that impulse extends to ideas as well. Prejudice is a similar problem to be solved. For Victor Stein, 'AI need not replicate outmoded gender prejudices' or racial ones, presumably, though these are not discussed.[20] Super intelligent machines, he suggests, will be better at removing it than humans. One cannot help but think of similar arguments that have been used by revolutionaries who advanced the cause of Virtue.

This, then, is the elite view of technology's future, where super-smart humans will construct the first computer programme and leave the rest to the machines.[21] Ron Lord, his attitudes and products represent that part of the future for the masses. Sex-dolls provide diversion and soporifics. For Stein, it will be a world without limits for those who are prepared to embrace it.

Ry is taken with Stein's vision of 'the future as a plausible app' much as they are taken with the convenience and promise of a frictionless world where communication is easier without human prejudice.[22] Their experience of transgender and the promise of transhumanism manifest in the love story of Ry and Victor, a meeting of minds as much as of bodies. It is grounded upon the shared belief in a world uncomfortable with limits. Victor believes that his technologies will enable people to live forever, leaving the body far behind. For Ry, the body is the problem, at odds with their subjective experience. Yet, this is precisely why Victor Stein is drawn to Ry because they have engineered the body to conform with a sense of self that is always multiple. Ry notes:

When I look in the mirror I see someone I recognize, or rather, I see at least two people I recognize. That is why I have chosen not to have lower surgery ... what I am is not one thing, not one gender. I live with doubleness. (89)

I am a woman. And I am a man. That's how it is for me. I am in the body that I prefer. But the past, my past, isn't subject to surgery. I didn't do it to distance myself from myself. I did it to get nearer to myself ... it really is my body. I had it made for me.[23]

Ry claims to be in love with Victor while acknowledging that they cannot trust one another. Trust, it appears, introduces too much risk into the relationship, for to risk trusting would introduce an emotional commitment beyond the transactional. The absence of trust, so pivotal to other love stories, or other forms of love (e.g. *philia*), is never confronted in *Frankisstein*. Its absence is accepted as easily as physical intimacy is expected as part of Ry and Victor's encounter.

The idea of the 'future person' that Ry represents fascinates and attracts Victor, much as he is attracted by the idea of a future where love is reprogrammed and rewritten.[24] Ry responds by claiming that 'love's not zeros and ones'.[25] Yet, Stein sees the world with an engineer's eye and a compulsion to rewrite the biological and cultural code of humanity. 'Race, faith, gender, sexuality, those things make me impatient ... We need to move forward, and faster. I want an end to it all, don't you see? ... An end to human stupidity.'[26]

Their mutual intellectual admiration notwithstanding, shared physical intimacy does nothing to draw them closer together. For all the talk of boundary transgressions, Ry and Victor remain as monads. Victor expresses anxiety because he cannot control the encounter as he might an experiment and so withdraws emotionally from it despite his attraction to what Ry represents. Ry is anxious because they know that they are subjectively altered by the encounter, an alteration that they interpret as love. But they also know that this love is not returned in kind.

In *Frankisstein*, the love of Mary Shelley – a love that has much in kind with the love we might find in Petrarch, Dante and Shakespeare – is part of the folklore of humanism. It has no place in the world of Ry Shelley, a world affected by the post-structural approach to meaning and the neurobiological approach to mind: meaning is contingent and mind a mere epiphenomenon. Humanist love in *Frankisstein* is reduced to the post-human 'disturbance among the disturbed'.[27]

And yet, the older form of love still lingers. Ry's subjective state can only be described as disappointment when they recognize that the post-human form of love fails to individuate. Victor will look for someone else to love, when he is so inclined. Ry is left with a profound feeling that they are fungible, as economists like to say. Yet, despite the author's best attempts to imagine an alternative to the heteronormative, monogamous relationship, it still seems to haunt the future world of post-human love. Why else would Ry feel disappointed at all?[28]

On that note, it is the character of Ron Lord who has the last word on the subject of love in the novel. For Lord, spokesman for the gig-economy version of human relationships, emotional depth is not on the techno-capitalist agenda. For one thing, it is too difficult to code. Replacing love with desire, however, is possible. And the result will be a more efficient and manageable form of relationship. Replace the human with the robot and 'a lot of people will be glad not to have any more crap relationships with crap humans'.[29]

Transgender and transhumanism

In *Years and Years*, a popular television show produced by the BBC, a young girl announces to her parents that she is 'trans'.[30] When they express support for her desire to change genders, she explains that she wishes to become transhuman – leave her body behind to become pure data.

In *Frankisstein*, the transhuman and transgender intersect in interesting ways. Winterson's protagonist claims epistemic certainty about their gender and the fact that the body they inhabit is the wrong one. Surgery and a drug regimen ameliorate the condition in which they find themselves.

The intellectual landscape of transhumanism – a philosophical and cultural movement that developed in the United States at the end of the twentieth century – explores further this possibility of 'morphological freedom'.[31] Crucially, the claims for this freedom rest upon a notion of identity as chosen rather than given combined with the technological possibility of individuals modifying genders and body types to suit their tastes.

Transhumanism also provides for, and in some cases actively seeks, the abandonment of the corporeal in favour of immortalizing the self, where the latter is equated with data. This aspect of the transhuman agenda has been popularized within popular culture by hit shows like *Black Mirror* as well as discussed at length in the academic literature.[32] For the purposes of this essay, however, the concept of morphological freedom will be examined as it relates to *Frankisstein*.

Transhumanism at its core challenges the notion of the human and humanity. It is a group of ideas that seek to overcome social convention, on the one hand, but also those limits imposed by biology, on the other. It is also decidedly libertarian in orientation, 'opposing authoritarian social control and unnecessary hierarchy and favoring the rule of law and decentralization of power and responsibility'.[33]

The ideas within transhumanism are several and complex. They are also often in tension with one another. Notions of selfhood are either rejected outright by adopting the materialist position of neuroscience, embraced in a quasi-spiritual form as unitary and potentially immortal, or expanded to accommodate the notion of multiple selves.

Despite the attempt by some transhumanists to leave the body behind, it remains a central concern and was included within *The Transhumanist Declaration*. As More notes, transhumanists

> seek to improve the human body, by making it resistant to aging, damage, and disease, and by enhancing its sense and sharpening the cognition of our biological brains ... It does find it to be a marvelous yet flawed piece of engineering ... [it] champions morphological freedom ... transhumanists typically want to choose its form and be able to inhabit different bodies, including virtual bodies.[34]

Indeed, in the absence of the ability to reliably decorporealize, the body is regarded as a site for improvement. Enhancements might include the much-vaunted Neural Lace, technological brain implants that achieve symbiosis with AI; a greater appreciation for high culture (!); and the regulation of unwanted emotions.[35] As one leading advocate puts it, technologically enhanced levels of emotional capacity will produce well-adjusted creatures who employ self-regulation to avoid 'feelings of prejudice' which are unconstructive.[36]

Body augmentation is justified along possessive-individualist lines. For Sandberg, morphological freedom is part of the intellectual legacy of classical liberal self-direction and self-creation, increasing diversity by selecting aspects of our selves that are to be cultivated. It is, he notes, 'an extension of one's right to one's body, not just self-ownership but also the right to modify oneself according to one's desires'. If one has a right to one's body and control over how it may be used, then 'if my pursuit of happiness requires a bodily change – be it dying my hair or changing my sex – then my right to freedom requires a right to morphological freedom'.[37]

This idea is developed further by Rothblatt, who has made the most public case for the intersection between the transgender and the transhuman. Born Martin, Rothblatt transitioned from male to female and adopted the moniker Martine. Rothblatt is an engineer by training and the billionaire founder of Sirius XM radio and Hanson Robotics – manufacturers of the Sophia Robot that makes an appearance in *Frankisstein*.

For Rothblatt, gender is a choice: 'I change my gender about as often as I change my hairstyle.'[38] Race, for Rothblatt, is also a fiction. The 'soul' is separate from the body, and the 'mind' may one day be uploaded to the cloud in the form of a 'mind-file'. 'Form' refers to the material surrounding our 'being'. The latter is strongly related to 'mind', though not apparently reducible to it. On the basis of this somewhat confusing explanation, Rothblatt claims that bodies 'are no longer limiting factors to homo sapiens. We are in the process of morphing, with technology's help, into *persona creates*. The emergence of transgenderism supports this claim as this is evidence of a new species.'[39]

Hayles noted in her classic discussion of post-humanism and cybernetics that it was Alan Turing's attempt to separate questions of gender from the information transfer involved in his *Imitation Game* that undermined the foundations of liberal subjectivity. After Turing, the self was understood as 'an amalgam, a collection of heterogeneous components, a material-informational entity whose boundaries undergo continuous construction and reconstruction ... located in disparate parts that may be in only tenuous communication with one another'.[40] The disembodied self of liberalism, initially seized upon by feminists to claim their rights as thinking beings, was transformed into a dislocated information packet, a self that is iteratively restructured rather than given.

In *Frankisstein*, we are confronted by doubles across space and time. Mary Shelley the author (1816) becomes Ry Shelley the transgender doctor (2019). Claire Clairmont, Byron's lover (1816), is Claire the evangelical Christian who initially opposes, then sanctions, the sex-bot economy (2019). Lord Byron (1816) is Ron Lord (2019) the sex-bot king. Byron's Italian doctor, Polidori (1816), is Polly D, a writer for *Vanity Fair* (2019). Even the eponymous Dr Frankenstein has a role as Victor Stein, the expert in AI whose goal is to duplicate the brain of I. J. Good, the British mathematician who worked with Alan Turing at Bletchley Park.

For a thinker like Rothblatt, this doubling has a special significance. Advanced data collection and intelligent software permits the possibility of doubling through the duplication of mind-files, defined as the sum total of 'mannerisms, personalities, recollection, feelings, beliefs, attitudes, and values, everything that we've poured today into Google, into Amazon, into Facebook' reproducible in any number of different bodies and shapes.[41] To that end, Rothblatt is developing a robot version of her spouse, Bina. Bina 48 is a humanoid robot filled with the digital breath from Bina Rothblatt's mind-file.[42]

Rothblatt suggests that our selves can be expressed 'as faithfully in software as they are in our brains'. Imagine, they note, 'if we could create a simulacrum, a digital doppelganger of ourselves that helps us process books, do shopping, be our best friends, I believe our mind clones, these digital versions of ourselves, will ultimately be our best friends.'[43]

Morphological freedom supplies the rationale for these and similar arguments concerning transgender. In a review of Woolf's *Orlando*, for example, Winterson highlighted the notion of the self as gender-neutral: 'On seeing himself as a herself for the first time in the mirror, she remarks: "Different sex. Same person."'[44] Same person is the key idea. This self is abstract, outside the cultural and gender norms that the discourse of the time provides. It is not difficult to see the transition between the claim that self is distinct from gender, from a physical body with accidental biology, to a self that leaves the body behind altogether and becomes immortal.

This is, in fact, very close to the arguments provided by the characters in *Frankisstein*. And it makes the possibility of understanding love in such a context – where selves remain disembodied – challenging. Yet, the novel provides us with one more approach to consider the position love occupies by placing the love story within the fractured and contested terrain of techno-capitalism.[45]

Neoliberalism: The self as investment

The economic language used by Victor to describe Ry's elective surgery – 'You chose to intervene in your own evolution. You accelerated your portfolio of possibilities' – reflects the language of technology but also that of the free market expanded to include the personal and intimate sphere.[46] To apply market logic to the sphere of love would have once been regarded as a misunderstanding, a failure in the words of one contemporary commentator to recognize that there are some things that are not for sale.[47] Arguably, in *Frankisstein*, market values are internalized so successfully that in the mouths of the characters economic reasoning resembles authentic self-expression.

The promulgation and developments of the ideas associated with neoliberalism after the Second World War and the attempt to revive eighteenth- and nineteenth-century theories of liberal political economy have been well documented.[48] The basic assumptions are now a commonplace: the rationality of individual self-interest; the free play of market forces, goods and services subject to the laws of economic science; competition producing the best outcomes for all. The key addition to these familiar principles, however, is what one might term the subjective turn, in contrast to the inward turn where the self has depths.

Gary Becker's notion of human capital applied an economic model to those abilities that make a person productive within a market economy. Initially applied to human resources departments within organizations, advocates of Becker's position extended the notion to invoke economic principles across the entire field of cultural practices and, by extension, self-understanding. One of the first candidates for analysis was education. Similar analyses applied the principles of human capital to the family, diet, health, gender and love.[49]

For critics of this position like Foucault, human capital was but the latest 'technology of the self', a set of ideas and practices designed to regulate the behaviour of individuals as well as to shape their environments.[50] The latter was increasingly privatized along corporate lines, the resulting process of individualization where individuals suddenly found themselves isolated, negotiating a whole series of tasks and goals the success or failure of which fell on their shoulders. This was, as Bauman noted, a precarious form of existence, 'a sinister version of the musical chairs game, played for real'.[51]

Yet, the process was also energizing for many, and the self that emerged was free to choose in new ways.

Thanks to advances in technology, market choices also extended to the body. Becker's followers noted the advantages that consumers might gain from plastic surgery where the economic advantages that accrue to 'the beautiful' are well established – beautiful people in the United States earn, on average, 12 per cent more than their more homely counterparts.[52]

This quantification and measurement of the self developed in increasingly sophisticated ways thanks to advances in technology (e.g. life-logging and life-hacking movements). But it is hardly a novel phenomenon.

Porter noted in his study of sexuality and identity in European thought that a rupture in thinking about the relationship between bodies and souls occurred in Europe in the sixteenth and seventeenth centuries. Scientific advance, political upheaval and artistic revival prompted a multiplicity of simultaneous understandings about the relationship between mind and matter, body and soul.

> The body Christian, the body pagan; the body medical, the body scientific; the body noble, the body debased; the body free and the body disciplined; the body natural and the body artificial; the body solitary and social; the body sacred and profane – all these were in the melting pot in that great 'crisis' of European thought marking the early Enlightenment.[53]

The backdrop to these profound issues was the growth of consumer society and a 'new sexualization of existence'.[54] Commerce and sexuality, then, were never far apart. And, as Porte notes, in a thinker like John Locke, both of these dimensions were expressed in a way that continues to resonate in discussions of gender and economics.

One of the intellectual founders of 'possessive individualism', Locke regarded the body as property owned by the individual. But he was also the thinker who did much to revolutionize considerations of personality or conscious selfhood. As Porter notes, the body, for Locke, was impermanent, a thing to be possessed. The self, however, was permanent. For Locke and others like him, this meant that the self had no gender.

It was precisely this idea, of course, developed by Locke in *Some Thoughts Concerning Education* (1693), that Mary Wollstonecraft read with approval because it seemed to suggest that there was no great difference between the minds of girls and boys. In *Vindication of the Rights of Woman*, Wollstonecraft (1792) argued that the female body was the source of great harm. The female figure was idolized for its sexual character, and the result was the subjection of women. Men sought women for their physical charms, and women colluded with their male pursuers in order to secure a favourable marriage. The solution? To cultivate the mind rather than the body. 'Women could never control their bodies until they first took possession of their minds.'[55]

It is precisely this intellectual position that Winterson contemporizes in the figure of Ry Shelley, for the most part resolving the dilemmas of love with which Wollstonecraft struggled. Contemporary discussions of transgender reflect similar understandings of both self and body. As we saw in the previous section, mobility between gender categories is theoretically feasible and scientifically possible. Transgender discourses oscillate between the twin poles of choice *and* givenness – the body the former, the soul or self the latter. As Brubaker notes, common to different transgender discourses is the idea that 'subjectivity is constitutive of gender: the "truth" of gender is found in the innermost feelings of an individual, and those feelings must be recognized and respected'.[56] The body may, therefore, be modified to line up with the epistemic claim.

In *Frankisstein*, Ry describes this position in the following way.

> I'm trans and that means a lifetime of hormones. My life will likely be shorter, and it's likely that I will get sicker as I get older. I keep my maleness intact with testosterone because my body knows it wasn't born the way I want it to be. I can change my body but I can't change my body's reading of my body. The paradox is that I felt in the wrong body but for my body it was the right body. What I have done calms my mind and agitates my chemistry. Few people know what it's like to live this way.[57]

Understood thus, rights claims from transgender individuals are readily interpreted as private claims premised upon subjective preferences concerning (in this case) identity. These claims find ready expressions within an already existing framework of rights which are then satisfied by services (e.g. gender reassignment surgeries) provided within a market economy.

What neoliberalism and the characters in *Frankisstein* struggle with, however, is the nature of 'true love'. As one proponent of the 'human capital' approach notes, 'true love' appears to complicate matters.[58]

In *Frankisstein*, the entrepreneur Ron Lord contributes to this conversation by avoiding it altogether. He is an exponent of the ideology of ease, a view that is hardly far-fetched when one considers the (mostly female) personal electronic assistants that respond so readily to our daily desires as consumers. Technology (for us as for Ron Lord) has also expanded the range of possibilities for sexual experience. Prospective partners are categorized, presented and surveyed in mobile apps like Tinder and Grindr in the same manner as one might choose an appliance.

This, then, is 'the experience economy' where objects and services are paraded as equivalents – some a little more satisfying, some less depending upon one's budget.[59] From the perspective of the experience economy, a relationship without hiccoughs, difficulties, compromise (or conversation) is clearly preferable. Ron Lord's boutique sex-bot is the logical next step.

For Ry and Victor Stein, however, love is a problem for different reasons. Ry complains that previous relationships failed because of love's interruption, the disturbance it brought to the far simpler pleasures of shared physical intimacy. Love alters Ry; it affects them in ways that they could not control and, perhaps, would not choose. Love is irrational.

For Victor, love requires reprogramming. It is a challenge to autonomy. Love is a concept that must pass away to be replaced with something more efficient. 'Love is not this far and no further. What the future is bringing will also be the future of love.'[60]

If the love story between Ry and Victor is supposed to offer a contrast to the tale of love for sale, it comes short. If love individuates, where the object of love is seen as possessing intrinsic value and the beloved is irreplaceable, there is little to suggest that what Ry and Victor feel is love. Ry expresses disquiet at her fungibility, knowing that Victor will soon look for new experiences with different persons. If there is a desire to relate, the burden of relating for good is ruled out in favour of keeping one's options open. The fear of missing out on a better option displaces anything as quixotic as commitment and is incompatible with a market geared to providing upgrades.

Conclusion

Frankisstein confronts us with the complex relationships that occur between characters in a post-human world. Yet, despite the futuristic speculations, there remains a standing tension between morphological freedom, AI and the free market.

For (some) transhumanists, it is a short step from claims about an essential self to developing methods to preserve or immortalize that self in one form or another. A good portion of *Frankisstein* centres around discussions of cryogenics and the self-preservation made possible as a data upload or, as Rothblatt suggests, a mind-file.

Yet, it is an equally small distance to travel within similar discourses that have assumed the immortality of the soul to the unchosen aspect of love. I have alluded to Shakespeare occasionally in this essay. Perhaps there is no better description of the non-voluntaristic nature of love as that which appears in his final play, *The Two Noble Kinsmen*. In a paean to Venus, Goddess of Love, he notes:

Hail, sovereign queen of secrets, who hast power
To call the fiercest tyrant from his rage,
And weep unto a girl; that hast the might,

Even with an eye-glance, to choke Mars's drum
And turn th'alarm to whispers; that canst make
A cripple flourish with his crutch, and cure him
Before Apollo; that mayst force the king
To be his subject's vassal, and induce
Stale gravity to dance; the polled bachelor –
Whose youth, like wanton boys through bonfires,
Have skipped thy flame – at seventy thou canst catch
And make him, to the scorn of his hoarse throat,
Abuse young lays of love. What godlike power
Hast thou not power upon?[61]

Neoliberalism has no answer to this description of love except to ignore its disruptive power.

In *Frankisstein*, the age-old question of sexual regulation and the relation between the social and sexual order is explored throughout. The twin discourses of transgender and transhumanism set about disrupting the implied norm of heterosexual love without, perhaps, escaping entirely from the orbit of that discourse. Yet, Winterson's post-human characters lack emotional depth as a result, for – in the absence of humanist discourses and in the play of pure surface – how could it be otherwise? In this respect, we might suggest that *Frankisstein* is not a (true) love story at all. Or, perhaps, what we are meant to see is a glimpse of a future world where love is in the process of being successfully recoded.

Notes

1   George Szirtes, *Metro* (Oxford: Oxford University Press, 1988).

2   Jeanette Winterson, *Frankisstein: A Love Story* (New York: Grove Press, 2019).

3   Transhumanism is defined by the *Oxford English Dictionary* as a belief that the human race can evolve beyond its current physical and mental limitations, by means of science and technology. Post-human has been defined as an approach that focuses on identity as a 'contingent production, mediated by a technology that has become so entwined with the production of identity that it can no longer be meaningfully separated from the human subject'. See Katherine Hayles, *How We Became Posthuman: Virtual Bodies in Cybernetics, Literature, and Informatics* (Chicago: Chicago University Press, 1999), xiii. What both approaches share is a commitment to reconceptualizing the self as information.

4   Winterson, *Frankisstein*, 173.

5   Ibid., 3.

6   Ibid., 5.

7   Ibid., 25.

8 Ibid., 29.

9 Ibid., 37.

10 Ibid., 38.

11 Ibid., 39–40.

12 Ibid., 49.

13 Ibid.

14 Ibid., 73.

15 Ibid.

16 Ibid.

17 Ibid., 78.

18 Ibid.

19 Richard H. Thaler and Cass R. Sunstein, *Nudge: Improving Decisions about Health, Wealth, and Happiness* (Chicago: Chicago University Press, 2008).

20 Winterson, *Frankisstein*, 74.

21 One need only to think of the recent comments of James Lovelock of *Gaia* fame, who makes precisely the same case with respect to managing environmental catastrophe in *Novacene: The Coming Age of Hyperintelligence* (New York: Allen Lane, 2019).

22 Ibid., 80.

23 Ibid., 122.

24 Ibid., 197.

25 Ibid.

26 Ibid., 199.

27 Ibid., 173.

28 See Adam Phillips, *Monogamy* (New York: Pantheon Books, 1996) for a related discussion.

29 Ibid., 312.

30 Russell T. Davis, *Years and Years* (BBC Productions, 2019).

31 Anders Sandberg, 'Morphological Freedom: Why We Not Just Want It, But Need It', in *The Transhumanist Reader*, ed. Max More and Natasha Vita-More (Oxford: Wiley-Blackwell, 2013), 56–64.

32 Robert Geraci, 'Spiritual Robots: Religion and Our Scientific View of the Natural World', *Theology and Science* 4, no. 3 (2006): 229–46; Roberto Manzocco, *Transhumanism: Engineering the Human Condition* (Chichester: Springer-Praxis, 2019).

33 Max More, 'The Philosophy of Transhumanism', in *The Transhumanist Reader*, 3–17, 5.

34 Ibid., 15.

35 'Elon Musk's Vision of the Future Takes Another Step Forward', *The Economist*, 5 September 2020.

36   Nick Bostrom, 'Why I Want To Be a Posthuman When I Grow Up', in *The Transhumanist Reader*, 27–53, 37.

37   Sanberg, 'Morphological Freedom', 56–7.

38   Martine Rothblatt, 'My Daughter, My Wife, Our Robot, and the Quest for Immortality' (TED, 2015). www.ted.com/talks/martine_rothblatt_my_daughter_my_wife_our_robot_and_the_quest_for_immortality/transcript?refer rer=playlist-ted_talks_by_strong_women_lead.

39   Martine Rothblatt, 'Mind Is Deeper Than Matter: Transgenderism, Transhumanism, and the Freedom of Form', in *The Transhumanist Reader*, 317–27, 318.

40   Hayles, *How We Became Posthuman*, 3–4.

41   Rothblatt, 'My Daughter, My Wife, Our Robot, and the Quest for Immortality'.

42   An examination of the significance of this technological development, the 'gender' of the robot in question, and the desire on the part of the trans individual who is also an engineer to create such a reproduction of their spouse is beyond the scope of this paper. One cannot help think of the doctrine of the 'transmigration of souls' or the many cases of gender switching in Elizabethan comedies. Consider Berowne in *Love's Labour's Lost* who wishes to steal 'light' from a woman (1.1.83; 4.3.325) and *Othello* who extinguishes such a light (5.2.7).

43   Rothblatt, 'My Daughter, My Wife, Our Robot, and the Quest for Immortality'.

44   Jeanette Winterson, '"Different Sex. Same Person": How Woolf's Orlando Became a Trans Triumph', *The Guardian*, 3 September 2018. One cannot help but be reminded of Duke Orsino's exclamation: 'One face, one voice, one habit, and two persons!' (*Twelfth Night*, Act V, Scene 1).

45   Techno-capitalism (sometimes called platform capitalism in the relevant literature) refers to the latest form of capitalism grounded on corporate power and technological creativity, especially electronic technologies. For a related discussion, see Nick Srnicek, *Platform Capitalism* (London: Routledge, 2017).

46   Winterson, *Frankisstein*, 154.

47   Debra Satz, *Why Some Things Should Not Be for Sale* (Oxford: Oxford University Press, 2012).

48   David Harvey, *A Brief History of Neoliberalism* (Oxford: Oxford University Press, 2007).

49   Gary Becker, *Human Capital: A Theoretical and Empirical Analysis* (Chicago: University of Chicago Press, [1964] 1994), and *The Economic Approach to Human Behavior* (Chicago: University of Chicago Press, 1978); Daniel Checchi, *The Economics of Education: Human Capital, Family Background and Inequality* (Cambridge: Cambridge University Press, 2008).

50   Michel Foucault, *The Birth of Biopolitics: Lectures at the College de France 1978–1979*, trans. Graham Burchill (London: Palgrave Macmillan, 2004).

51 Zygmunt Bauman, *Liquid Love: On the Frailty of Human Bonds* (Cambridge: Polity Press, 2003), 3.

52 Soohyung Lee and Keunkwan Ryu, 'Plastic Surgery: Investment in Human Capital or Consumption?' *Journal of Human Capital* 6, no. 3 (2012): 224–50.

53 Roy Porter, *Flesh in the Age of Reason* (London: Penguin, 2004): xv.

54 Ibid., 24.

55 Ibid., 271.

56 Rogers Brubaker, 'The Dolezal Affair: Race, Gender, and the Micropolitics of Identity', *Ethnic and Racial Studies* 39, no. 3 (2016): 414–48, 432.

57 Winterson, *Frankisstein*, 310.

58 Merwin Engineer and Linda Welling, 'Human Capital, True Love, and Gender Roles: Is Sex Destiny?' *Journal of Economic Behavior and Organization* 40 (1999): 155–78.

59 B. Joseph Pine and James H. Gilmore, *The Experience Economy: Work Is Theater and Every Business a Stage* (Cambridge, MA: Harvard Business School Press, 1999).

60 Winterson, *Frankisstein*, 160.

61 Shakespeare, *The Two Noble Kinsmen*, Act 5, Scene 1.

Bibliography

Bauman, Zygmunt. *Liquid Love: On the Frailty of Human Bonds.* Cambridge: Polity Press, 2003.

Becker, Gary. *The Economic Approach to Human Behavior.* Chicago: University of Chicago Press, 1978.

Becker, Gary. *Human Capital: A Theoretical and Empirical Analysis.* Chicago: University of Chicago Press, [1964] 1994.

Bostrom, Nick. 'Why I Want To Be a Posthuman When I Grow Up'. In *The Transhumanist Reader*, edited by Max More and Natasha Vita-More, 27–53. Oxford: Wiley-Blackwell, 2013.

Brubaker, Rogers. 'The Dolezal Affair: Race, Gender, and the Micropolitics of Identity'. *Ethnic and Racial Studies* 39, no. 3 (2016): 414–48.

Checchi, Daniel. *The Economics of Education: Human Capital, Family Background and Inequality.* Cambridge: Cambridge University Press, 2008.

Davis, Russell T. *Years and Years.* BBC Productions, 2019.

The Economist. 'Elon Musk's Vision of the Future Takes Another Step Forward'. *The Economist*, 5 September 2020.

Engineer, Merwin and Linda Welling. 'Human Capital, True Love, and Gender Roles: Is Sex Destiny?' *Journal of Economic Behavior and Organization* 40 (1999): 155–78.

Foucault, Michel. *The Birth of Biopolitics: Lectures at the College de France 1978–1979* (trans. Graham Burchill). London: Palgrave Macmillan, 2004.

Geraci, Robert. 'Spiritual Robots: Religion and Our Scientific View of the Natural World'. *Theology and Science* 4, no. 3 (2006): 229–46.

Harvey, David. *A Brief History of Neoliberalism*. Oxford: Oxford University Press, 2007.

Hayles, Katherine. *How We Became Posthuman: Virtual Bodies in Cybernetics, Literature, and Informatics*. Chicago: University of Chicago Press, 1999.

Lee, Soohyung and Keunkwan Ryu. 'Plastic Surgery: Investment in Human Capital or Consumption?' *Journal of Human Capital* 6, no. 3 (2012): 224–50.

Lovelock, James. *Novacene: The Coming Age of Hyperintelligence*. New York: Allen Lane, 2019.

Manzocco, Roberto. *Transhumanism: Engineering the Human Condition*. Chichester: Springer-Praxis, 2019.

More, Max. 'The Philosophy of Transhumanism'. In *The Transhumanist Reader*, edited by Max More and Natasha Vita-More, 3–17. Oxford: Wiley-Blackwell, 2013.

Phillips, Adam. *Monogamy*. New York: Pantheon Books, 1996.

Pine, B. Joseph and Gilmore, James H. *The Experience Economy: Work Is Theater and Every Business a Stage*. Cambridge, MA: Harvard Business School Press, 1999.

Porter, Roy. *Flesh in the Age of Reason*. London: Penguin, 2004.

Rothblatt, Martine. 'Mind Is Deeper Than Matter: Transgenderism, Transhumanism, and the Freedom of Form'. In *The Transhumanist Reader*, edited by Max More and Natasha Vita-More, 317–27. Oxford: Wiley-Blackwell, 2013.

Rothblatt, Martine. 'My Daughter, My Wife, Our Robot, and the Quest for Immortality'. TED, 2015, 21:04. www.ted.com/talks/martine_rothblatt_my_daughter_my_wife_our_robot_and_the_quest_for_immortality?language=en.

Sandberg, Anders. 'Morphological Freedom: Why We Not Just Want It, But Need It'. In *The Transhumanist Reader*, edited by Max More and Natasha Vita-More, 56–64. Oxford: Wiley-Blackwell, 2013.

Satz, Debra. *Why Some Things Should Not Be for Sale*. Oxford: Oxford University Press, 2012.

Srnicek, Nick. *Platform Capitalism*. London: Routledge, 2017.

Szirtes, George. *Metro*. Oxford: Oxford University Press, 1988.

Thaler, Richard H. and Cass R. Sunstein. *Nudge: Improving Decisions about Health, Wealth, and Happiness*. Chicago: Chicago University Press, 2008.

Winterson, Jeanette. '"Different Sex. Same Person": How Woolf's Orlando Became a Trans Triumph'. *The Guardian*, 3 September 2018.

Winterson, Jeanette. *Frankissstein: A Love Story*. New York: Grove Press, 2019.

INDEX

www.ingramcontent.com/pod-product-compliance
Lightning Source LLC
Chambersburg PA
CBHW050417280326
41932CB00013BA/1891